Google Maps JavaScript API Cookbook

Over 50 recipes to help you create web maps and GIS
web applications using the Google Maps JavaScript API

Alper Dincer

Balkan Uraz

BIRMINGHAM - MUMBAI

Google Maps JavaScript API Cookbook

First published: December 2013

Production Reference: 1191213

Published by Packt Publishing Ltd.
Livery Place
35 Livery Street
Birmingham B3 2PB, UK.

ISBN 978-1-84969-882-5

www.packtpub.com

Cover Image by Aniket Sawant (aniket_sawant_photography@hotmail.com)

Credits

About the Authors

Alper Dincer is a civil engineer with an MS degree in Geographical Sciences. He has more than 10 years of experience in developing web and mobile GIS/LBS projects.

Since the beginning of his career, he was always passionate about maps and geo stuff. He started working as a research assistant at a university and then moved to a governmental agency to work with maps. He is also the co-founder of a tech company named Mekansal.

He also has some achievements relating to geo web projects. In 2009, he got the first place in the ESRI Developer Summit Mashup Challenge with his open source project ExtMap. ExtMap was based on the Google Maps JavaScript API v2. He is one of the Google Qualified Developers of the Google Maps JavaScript API program. In 2010, he also worked as a proctor in the same program as a volunteer.

As a developer and entrepreneur, he still likes coding with JavaScript, PHP, and Objective-C on different web and mobile projects. He completely agrees with Steve Jobs' quotes "Love what you do" and "Stay hungry, stay foolish".

First, I would like to dedicate this book to my wife, Begum—the light of my life—for understanding my passion for coding and the digital world. I would like to thank God for having her in my life. Words cannot express my gratitude and love to her.

Second, I wish to acknowledge my loving family, who are always there for me.

Balkan Uraz is a city planner with an MS degree in Geographical Sciences. He has over 15 years of experience in the field of **Geographic Information Systems** (**GIS**).

Throughout his career, he has worked on several projects with one thing in common: GIS. In the early days of his career, he worked on projects involving municipal GIS and city information systems. He has also worked as a research assistant while he was conducting the tedious work on his thesis on routing systems.

He has worked on major LBS projects for mobile operators in Turkey that involve both software development and building the data inventory. He co-founded a tech company that specialized in navigation data collection and navigation products. He has also been a GIS consultant for major companies operating in the areas of field tracking and real estate.

In all his projects, he has worked around the same passion: building up the spatial infrastructure.

I would like to thank Esra for her love, support, and encouragement while writing this book. I would also like to thank my fellow colleagues for their enthusiasm and encouragement that lead to writing this book.

About the Reviewers

Bramus Van Damme is a web enthusiast from Belgium interested in "all Web things" ever since he discovered the Internet back in 1997.

Professionally, after having worked as a web developer for several years at several web agencies, he is now a lecturer of web technologies at a technical university. Next to teaching students basic HTML, CSS, and JavaScript, he also teaches them to write proper SQL statements. In his job, he's also responsible for authoring and maintaining the server-side web scripting (PHP) and web and mobile courses.

In his spare time, he likes to goof around with web-related technologies and keep his blog `bram.us` up-to-date. He can be found attending and speaking at web meetups and conferences. Seeing a nice piece of optimized and secure code can put a smile on his face.

He lives in Vinkt, Belgium, with his girlfriend Eveline, his son Finn, and his daughter Tila. He prefers cats over dogs.

Shreerang Patwardhan completed his bachelor's degree in Computer Engineering and has since been working on various technologies for the last three years. He started off working for a small start-up in Pune, India, on an innovative solar-powered Linux-based hand-held device. He has also worked extensively on the Google Maps API v3 and worked in the GIS domain for more than a year.

He is currently employed with an MNC in Pune, India, as a Sr. Web Developer and works on the frontend development of various web applications. When not working on a project, he blogs about either Google Maps API v3 or the jQuery Mobile framework on his blog "Spatial Unlimited".

When not working or blogging, he loves spending time with his family and friends. If not on the Web, he can be found playing badminton on the weekends. He has been playing badminton for the last 20 years and also takes a keen interest in Ufology.

You can reach him on his blog, LinkedIn, or follow him on Twitter (`@shreerangp`).

Rodolfo Pereira is a web programmer specialized in backend programming. He believes that programming is one of the best things in life, and so makes it one of his main hobbies. After all, having fun while working is not a bad idea, don't you think?

Rick Viscomi is a frontend engineer with a background in web performance. He studied Computer Science at the Binghamton University, where he created and sold a popular course scheduling web application called BingBuilder. He is also an open source developer and has open sourced two projects: *trunk8*, an intelligent text truncation plugin to jQuery, and *Red Dwarf*, a Google Maps heatmap tool for visualizing the GitHub project popularity. Since 2013, he has been a web developer at Google, where he works on improving the speed of YouTube pages and strengthening the frontend infrastructure.

www.PacktPub.com

Support files, eBooks, discount offers, and more

You might want to visit www.PacktPub.com for support files and downloads related to your book.

Did you know that Packt offers eBook versions of every book published, with PDF and ePub files available? You can upgrade to the eBook version at www.PacktPub.com and as a print book customer, you are entitled to a discount on the eBook copy. Get in touch with us at service@packtpub.com for more details.

At www.PacktPub.com, you can also read a collection of free technical articles, sign up for a range of free newsletters and receive exclusive discounts and offers on Packt books and eBooks.

http://PacktLib.PacktPub.com

Do you need instant solutions to your IT questions? PacktLib is Packt's online digital book library. Here, you can access, read and search across Packt's entire library of books.

Why Subscribe?

- ▸ Fully searchable across every book published by Packt
- ▸ Copy and paste, print, and bookmark content
- ▸ On demand and accessible via web browser

Free Access for Packt account holders

If you have an account with Packt at www.PacktPub.com, you can use this to access PacktLib today and view nine entirely free books. Simply use your login credentials for immediate access.

Table of Contents

Preface   1

Chapter 1: Google Maps JavaScript API Basics   5
  Introduction   5
  Creating a simple map in a custom DIV element   6
  Creating a simple fullscreen map   11
  Moving from the Web to mobile devices   13
  Changing map properties programmatically   16
  Changing base maps   21

Chapter 2: Adding Raster Layers   25
  Introduction   25
  Styling of Google base maps   26
  Using different tile sources as base maps   33
  Adding tile overlays to maps   40
  Adding image overlays to maps   44
  Changing the transparency of overlays   48
  Creating a heat map   50
  Adding the traffic layer   56
  Adding the transit layer   58
  Adding the bicycling layer   60
  Adding the weather and cloud layers   62
  Adding the Panoramio layer   65

Chapter 3: Adding Vector Layers   69
  Introduction   69
  Adding markers to maps   70
  Adding popups to markers or maps   74
  Adding lines to maps   77

Adding polygons to maps 80
Adding circles/rectangles to maps 83
Adding animated lines to maps 88
Adding KML/GeoRSS layers 94
Adding GeoJSON to the Google Maps JavaScript API 98
Adding WKT to the Google Maps JavaScript API 104

Chapter 4: Working with Controls 111
Introduction 111
Adding and removing controls 112
Changing the position of controls 117
Creating and adding a geolocation control 120
Creating a table of contents control for layers 124
Adding your own logo as a control 132

Chapter 5: Understanding Google Maps JavaScript API Events 135
Introduction 135
Creating two synced maps side by side 136
Getting the coordinates of a mouse click 141
Creating a context menu on a map 144
Restricting the map extent 151
Creating a control that shows coordinates 155
Creating your own events 158

Chapter 6: Google Maps JavaScript Libraries 163
Introduction 163
Drawing shapes on the map 164
Calculating the length/area of polylines and polygons 175
Encoding coordinates 181
Searching for and showing nearby places 185
Finding places with the autocomplete option 194
Adding drag zoom to the map 200
Creating custom popups/infoboxes 203

Chapter 7: Working with Services 211
Introduction 211
Finding coordinates for an address 212
Finding addresses on a map with a click 219
Getting elevations on a map with a click 224
Creating a distance matrix for the given locations 229
Getting directions for the given locations 238
Adding Street View to your maps 247

Chapter 8: Mastering the Google Maps JavaScript API through Advanced Recipes   253

Introduction	253
Adding WMS layers to maps	254
Adding Fusion Tables layers to maps	261
Adding CartoDB layers to maps	267
Accessing ArcGIS Server with the Google Maps JavaScript API	276
Accessing GeoServer with the Google Maps JavaScript API	286

Index   295

Preface

Currently, there are both open source and proprietary alternatives to the Google Maps JavaScript API, but what makes the API special for developers is that it is a complete solution with base maps, overlays, and technical capabilities.

The API has been especially exciting for developers because it is very easy to build up generic outcomes, and at the same time, it has its own tips and tricks and advanced functionalities within the same box. Therefore, you can swim afloat or dive deep when you are working with the API.

The Google Maps JavaScript API v3 enabled the quick and easy development of mobile scenarios, facilitating location-based solution developers to delve into the subject. Regarding the growth of mobile development, especially location-based applications, the Google Maps JavaScript API v3 has deserved rightful attention.

Last but not least, no mapping API has ever been as successful as the Google Maps API without the support of continuously updated and thoroughly handled vector and satellite data. Google has dedicated immense resources to maintaining the unified structure of the vector data and its cartographic quality, and this effort is paying off in terms of its API usage.

What this book covers

Chapter 1, *Google Maps JavaScript API Basics*, instructs you on how to create a simple Google Maps application centered around a main recipe. The map object and its primary options, including map types, will be introduced by adding details to the recipe.

Chapter 2, *Adding Raster Layers*, presents the addition of external raster data through a series of recipes alongside Google layers such as the Tile, Traffic, Transit, and Weather layers.

Chapter 3, *Adding Vector Layers*, introduces you to drawing vector features together with the display of external vector sources such as KML and GeoRSS.

Chapter 4, *Working with Controls*, explains controls in detail. Creating and customizing a custom user interface for both the Web and mobile will be introduced in this chapter.

Chapter 5, Understanding Google Maps JavaScript API Events, describes events in detail to react to map, layer, or marker's behaviors such as zoom end, layer changed, or marker added. Events will add more interactivity to mapping programming.

Chapter 6, Google Maps JavaScript Libraries, explains the libraries that will extend the capabilities of the Google Maps JavaScript API in detail. These libraries have different abilities to increase the power of the Google Maps JavaScript API.

Chapter 7, Working with Services, elaborates on services that will extend the Google Maps JavaScript API. These services, including Geocoding and Street View, expose the real power of mapping with the Google Maps JavaScript API.

Chapter 8, Mastering the Google Maps JavaScript API through Advanced Recipes, explains the integration of external GIS servers and services with the Google Maps JavaScript API. These includes ArcGIS Server, GeoServer, CartoDB, and Google Fusion Tables with OGC services such as WMS.

What you need for this book

The Google Maps JavaScript API works with HTML, CSS, and JavaScript code. So, a text editor with HTML, JavaScript, and CSS handling capabilities will be a good friend while exploring this book.

For Mac users, there are lots of commercial or free text editors, such as TextWrangler, BBEdit, Sublime Text, or WebStorm. They all handle HTML, JavaScript, and CSS beautifully.

For Windows users, there are different text editors as well, but Notepad++ is the most used and recommended one.

Choosing an editor depends on your computer's habits, so there is no exact solution or recommendation for users to select one editor. Everyone has a different perception that affects these choices.

There is also need for an HTTP server to implement these recipes. There are a bunch of HTTP servers including Apache, IIS, and so on. But the installation process of standalone servers can be a problem for most users. We encourage you to use solutions that bundle HTTP Server, Database Server, and a scripting language together. XAMPP and MAMP are these kinds of solutions for the Windows and Mac OS X platforms respectively.

For better user experience, we have created a main application that allows the desired recipe to run and show its source code. Suppose you have installed and configured a local web server like XAMPP or MAMP, and the bundle code is copied within the HTTP server root content folder in the `googlemaps-cookbook` folder, the user can run the main application by accessing the `http://localhost/googlemaps-cookbook/index.html` URL in the browser.

Who this book is for

This book is great for developers who are interested in adding a simple contact map embedded in their websites as well as for those who wish to develop real-world complex GIS applications. It is also for those who want to create map-based info graphics, such as heat maps, from their geo-related data. It's assumed that you will have some experience in HTML, CSS, and JavaScript already, and also experience in simple concepts related to GIS and prior knowledge of some GIS servers or services.

Conventions

In this book, you will find a number of styles of text that distinguish between different kinds of information. Here are some examples of these styles, and an explanation of their meaning.

Code words in text are shown as follows: "We can include other contexts through the use of the `include` directive."

A block of code is set as follows:

```html
<!DOCTYPE html>
<html>
    <head>
        <!-- Include Google Maps JS API -->
        <script type="text/javascript"
        src="https://maps.googleapis.com/maps/api/js?
          key=INSERT_YOUR_MAP_API_KEY_HERE&sensor=false">
          </script>
```

New terms and **important words** are shown in bold.

 Warnings or important notes appear in a box like this.

 Tips and tricks appear like this.

Reader feedback

Feedback from our readers is always welcome. Let us know what you think about this book—what you liked or may have disliked. Reader feedback is important for us to develop titles that you really get the most out of.

To send us general feedback, simply send an e-mail to `feedback@packtpub.com`, and mention the book title via the subject of your message.

If there is a topic that you have expertise in and you are interested in either writing or contributing to a book, see our author guide on `www.packtpub.com/authors`.

Customer support

Now that you are the proud owner of a Packt book, we have a number of things to help you to get the most from your purchase.

Downloading the example code

You can download the example code files for all Packt books you have purchased from your account at `http://www.packtpub.com`. If you purchased this book elsewhere, you can visit `http://www.packtpub.com/support` and register to have the files e-mailed directly to you.

Errata

Although we have taken every care to ensure the accuracy of our content, mistakes do happen. If you find a mistake in one of our books—maybe a mistake in the text or the code— we would be grateful if you would report this to us. By doing so, you can save other readers from frustration and help us improve subsequent versions of this book. If you find any errata, please report them by visiting `http://www.packtpub.com/submit-errata`, selecting your book, clicking on the **errata submission form** link, and entering the details of your errata. Once your errata are verified, your submission will be accepted and the errata will be uploaded on our website, or added to any list of existing errata, under the Errata section of that title. Any existing errata can be viewed by selecting your title from `http://www.packtpub.com/support`.

Piracy

Piracy of copyright material on the Internet is an ongoing problem across all media. At Packt, we take the protection of our copyright and licenses very seriously. If you come across any illegal copies of our works, in any form, on the Internet, please provide us with the location address or website name immediately so that we can pursue a remedy.

Please contact us at `copyright@packtpub.com` with a link to the suspected pirated material.

We appreciate your help in protecting our authors, and our ability to bring you valuable content.

Questions

You can contact us at `questions@packtpub.com` if you are having a problem with any aspect of the book, and we will do our best to address it.

1
Google Maps JavaScript API Basics

In this chapter, we will cover:

- ▶ Creating a simple map in a custom DIV element
- ▶ Creating a simple fullscreen map
- ▶ Moving from the Web to mobile devices
- ▶ Changing map properties programmatically
- ▶ Changing base maps

Introduction

Location is becoming a very popular topic day by day, and Google is one of the main game changers in this area. Most websites have a contact page with Google Maps showing the location of the business. This is the simplest usage of the Google Maps JavaScript API. There are also other advanced usages of it to show different information on maps. This whole book contains multiple usage recipes on the Google Maps JavaScript API, from beginner to advanced topics. There are different parts that make up the Google Maps JavaScript API such as the raster/vector layers, controls, events, and services, which are all covered in the following chapters.

There are both open source and commercial alternatives to the Google Maps JavaScript API, such as OpenLayers, Leaflet, Bing Maps, MapQuest, and Here Maps (formerly, Nokia Maps), but the Google Maps JavaScript API has great support in base maps, satellite images, and the API itself. For example, the API can be used to show only one location or all the data of a government agency on a map.

The Google Maps JavaScript API is not a free tool to show maps, but its free usage limit is enough for most developers. There is a limit of 25,000 map loads per day per site, which is counted when a map is initialized on a web page.

Creating a simple map in a custom DIV element

When you work with mapping applications, creating a map is the most important task you can do. The map is the main part of the application with which the users interact and where all the visualization occurs. This part may seem trivial, but all of the following chapters rely on this part of the application.

This recipe will guide you through the process of creating a simple map view on a web page.

As described in the preface, we need a web server to host our HTML, JavaScript, and CSS files and a web browser to interpret them on the client side.

Getting ready

As already stated, the Google Maps JavaScript API works with HTML, CSS, and JavaScript code. So a text editor with HTML, JavaScript, and CSS handling capabilities would be a good friend to have on hand while exploring this book.

For Mac users, there are lots of commercial or free text editors such as TextWrangler, BBEdit, Sublime Text, or WebStorm. They all handle HTML, JavaScript, and CSS beautifully.

For Windows users as well, there are different text editors, but **Notepad++** is the most used and recommended one.

Choosing an editor depends on your computer usage habits, so there is no exact solution or recommendation to users to select a particular type of editor. Everyone has different perceptions that affect these choices.

You can find the source code at Chapter 1/ch01_simple_map.html.

Downloading the example code

You can download the example code files for all Packt books you have purchased from your account at http://www.packtpub.com. If you purchased this book elsewhere, you can visit http://www.packtpub.com/support and register to have the files e-mailed directly to you.

How to do it...

Here are the steps we will use to create our first map using the Google Maps JavaScript API.

1. Create a new empty file named `map.html` and insert the following code block into it. This block is required for every app that uses the Google Maps JavaScript API. You must insert your Google Maps JavaScript API key into the URL in the following code.

```
<!DOCTYPE html>
<html>
    <head>
        <!-- Include Google Maps JS API -->
        <script type="text/javascript"
        src="https://maps.googleapis.com/maps/api/js?
          key=INSERT_YOUR_MAP_API_KEY_HERE&sensor=false">
        </script>
```

 Please ensure that you have your Google Maps JavaScript API key from the Google APIs Console (`http://code.google.com/apis/console`) and replace it with `YOUR_API_KEY`. If you do not change that part of the code, your map cannot be seen due to Google's API rules. Also make sure to change the API key before publishing your map's document on another location or production environment.

2. The following part is required in order to place the map where needed. In the `<head>` section, add the HTML styling code to create a map that is 800 px in width and 500 px in height with the `<style>` element as follows:

```
<style type="text/css">
    #mapDiv { width: 800px; height: 500px; }
</style>
```

3. Add the following JavaScript lines to the code to run with the Google Maps JavaScript API. Do not forget to define the `map` object outside the function in order to access it from every part of the code.

```
<!-- Map creation is here -->
<script type="text/javascript">
  //Defining map as a global variable to access from
//other functions
var map;
function initMap() {
  //Enabling new cartography and themes
  google.maps.visualRefresh = true;

  //Setting starting options of map
  var mapOptions = {
    center: new google.maps.LatLng(39.9078, 32.8252),
    zoom: 10,
```

```
        mapTypeId: google.maps.MapTypeId.ROADMAP
    };

    //Getting map DOM element
    var mapElement = document.getElementById('mapDiv');

    //Creating a map with DOM element which is just
    //obtained
    map = new google.maps.Map(mapElement, mapOptions);
}
```

4. Add the following lines to finish the code. This part defines the `<html>` tags where the map will be added and when to initialize the map.

```
        google.maps.event.addDomListener(window, 'load',
            initMap);
    </script>
</head>
<body>
    <b>My First Map </b>
    <div id="mapDiv"></div>
</body>
</html>
```

5. Enter the URL of your local server, where your `map.html` file is stored, in your favorite browser and take a look at the result. You will see a map with navigation controls at the top-left corner and the base map control at the top-right corner.

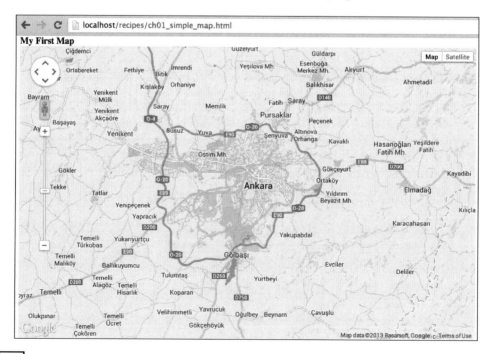

As evident from the preceding screenshot, we have created our simple map with the Google Maps JavaScript API.

How it works...

Let's start examining the code step by step. First, the HTML5 document is defined with the code `<!DOCTYPE html>`. Then the `<html>` and `<head>` tags are added.

Before the `<style>` element, the Google Maps JavaScript API is included as a reference using the `<script>` element as follows:

```
<script type="text/javascript"
         src="https://maps.googleapis.com/maps/api/js?key= INSERT_
YOUR_MAP_API_KEY_HERE&sensor=false">
    </script>
```

Then a new `<script>` tag is added to the code. After the `<head>` section, the `<body>` section starts.

```
        <body>
```

The following line of code listens to the load of the document. This event triggers the `initMap` function when the page is fully loaded. This prevents unpredictable behaviors that would arise from DOM and its related elements.

```
google.maps.event.addDomListener(window, 'load', initMap);
```

Finally, we have the HTML tags to create our page. The `<div>` element with `id="mapDiv"` is the place where our map will be shown. This element gets its style from the CSS tags defined previously, which has a width of 800 px and a height of 500 px.

 The styling of the `mapDiv` element is directly related to CSS rules that can be found on the W3Schools website (`http://www.w3schools.com/css`) in detail.

As stated previously, the main JavaScript code that initializes the map will be explained in detail. First, the `map` object is defined as a global object to access the map from every function that is added later.

```
var map;
```

Then the `initMap` function is defined as follows:

```
function initMap() {

}
```

Before creating a map, the following code is called to change the map's theme to the latest one that was announced at Google IO 2013 in May 2013. This theme is the new look used in the new Google Maps. Both the cartography and styles of components are fresh and up to date; however, using this new feature is optional. If you don't use the following line of code, you'd use the old theme.

```
google.maps.visualRefresh = true;
```

Then, the map options would be defined as follows:

```
var mapOptions = {
    center: new google.maps.LatLng(39.9078, 32.8252),
    zoom: 10,
    mapTypeId: google.maps.MapTypeId.ROADMAP
};
```

There are three important parameters for the map options.

- ▸ `center`: This is the center of the map in latitudes and longitudes. The previously defined parameters are the coordinates of Ankara, Turkey. If you don't know how to get the coordinates of a place, refer to the recipes given in *Chapter 5, Understanding Google Maps JavaScript API Events*.

- ▸ `zoom`: This parameter is an integer that defines the level in which the map is shown. Google Maps have zoom levels from 0 (world level) to 21+ (street level). Users see more details but less area when the zoom level increases.

- ▸ `mapTypeId`: This parameter defines the types of base maps shown on the map. The details of this parameter are given in the later recipes of this chapter.

Before creating the map object, it is necessary to get the `div` element to where the map will be shown. This is done via the classic DOM method, `getElementById`, as follows:

```
var mapElement = document.getElementById('mapDiv');
```

Finally, we have everything in place to create a map object:

```
map = new google.maps.Map(mapElement, mapOptions);
```

This code gets the `mapElement` and `mapOptions` objects to create the map. The first parameter is the `div` element where the map will be placed and the other is the `mapOptions` object that holds the starting parameters of the map. The preceding line of code creates the map with the given options at the given `div` element and returns the map object to interact with the map later.

This recipe is the simplest one in the book but also the most important one to get started with the Google Maps JavaScript API. There are lots of parameters or options of the map, which will be discussed in the later chapters and recipes.

Also remember that in the following recipes, the basic code will not be included in the book in order to provide you with more recipes. Only those lines of code that are changed or required are given in the following chapters and recipes, but you will have access to the complete code with all the omitted lines from the Packt Publishing website (http://www.packtpub.com/support)

Creating a simple fullscreen map

Applications can be mapped in different formats. Some of them show a map after a mouse click or an event, and some of them are shown directly in fullscreen mode.

This recipe will show you how to create a fullscreen map that will be used both in web or mobile applications.

Getting ready

As stated before, some recipes will show only the changed lines in the code in order to make way for more recipes. This recipe is the modified version of the previous recipe, *Creating a simple map in a custom DIV element*.

You can find the source code at Chapter 1/ch01_full_screen_map.html.

How to do it...

You can easily create a simple fullscreen map by following the given steps:

1. Let's start by creating a new empty file named full_screen_map.html. Then, copy all of the code in the previous HTML file (map.html) and paste it into this file.

2. Find the following lines of code in the new file:

```
<style type="text/css">
    #mapDiv { width: 800px; height: 500px; }
</style>
```

3. Add the following lines and change them according to the new values stated. The `width` and `height` values are changed to `100%` in order to make the map full screen in the browser viewport. Also, the margin value of the `body` element is changed to `0` to remove all the spaces around the map.

```
<style type="text/css">
    html { height: 100% }
    body { height: 100%; margin: 0; }
    #mapDiv { width: 100%; height: 100%; }
</style>
```

4. Enter the URL of your local server, where your `full_screen_map.html` file is stored, in your favorite browser and take a look at the result. You will see the map with navigation controls at the top-left corner and the base map control at the top-right corner that fills the entire browser area.

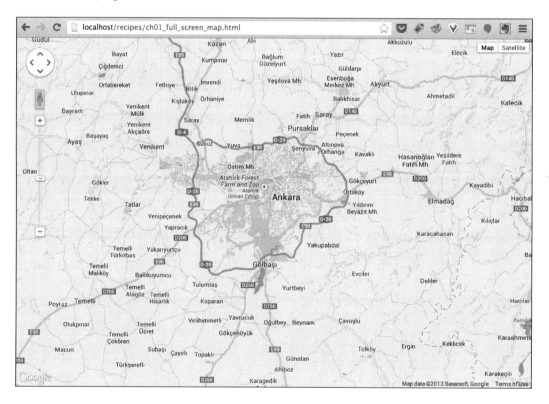

Thus we have successfully created a simple fullscreen map.

How it works...

The Google Maps JavaScript API uses the `div` component of the HTML standard to show the map. The `div` component gets its style and properties from CSS rules, which are defined at the top, in the `<head>` element. The `width` and `height` attributes of `#mapdiv` show that the `div` component will fill the entire browser space. You can easily modify these `width` and `height` properties to change the map dimensions according to your needs.

There's more...

The size of the map is directly related to CSS styles, and there is no direct relation between the map size and the Google Maps JavaScript API. The `DIV` element that holds the Google Maps JavaScript API's base maps and overlays is just a blank container, and as the `DIV` elements get larger, so does your map.

See also

▶ The *Creating a simple map in a custom DIV element* recipe

Moving from the Web to mobile devices

Mobile devices are getting more popular nowadays; all the popular websites are preparing their mobile apps or sites in order for people to access them anywhere. Mapping applications have also become more popular since accessing the location of a device with proper APIs was introduced in HTML5.

In this recipe, we will prepare a mapping application that will run on mobile browsers in full screen, and it will zoom to the location of a device with the help of the W3C Geolocation API. This API is also accessible from desktop browsers to get your location.

Getting ready

This code will be run on a mobile device or simulator, so make sure that your code will be accessible from your mobile device or simulator. In this recipe, I suggest you upload the code to a hosting server or website so that it could be accessed easily from your mobile device or simulator.

You can find the source code at `Chapter 1/ch01_mobile_map.html`.

How to do it...

If you want to create a map that is optimum for mobile devices, you should follow the given steps:

1. Let's start by creating a new empty file named `mobile_map.html`. Then, copy all of the code in the HTML file (`map.html`) that was introduced in the *Creating a simple map in a custom DIV element* recipe, and paste it into the new file.

2. Find the following lines of code in the new file:

```
<!-- Include Google Maps JS API -->
<script type="text/javascript"
    src="https://maps.googleapis.com/maps/api/js?
      key=INSERT_YOUR_MAP_API_KEY_HERE&sensor=false">
</script>
```

3. Insert the following line before the previous code block. This line tells mobile browsers that the current web application is designed for mobile devices:

```
<meta name="viewport" content="initial-scale=1.0,
  user-scalable=no" />
```

4. Add the following CSS styles in order to make the map fullscreen.

```
<style type="text/css">
    html { height: 100% }
    body { height: 100%; margin: 0; }
    #mapDiv { width: 100%; height: 100%; }
</style>
```

5. Then, add the following code block after creating the map object. This code block will check whether your browser supports the Geolocation API and sets the center of the map according to the coordinates of the device.

```
if (navigator.geolocation) {
    navigator.geolocation.getCurrentPosition(
      function(position) {
        var lat = position.coords.latitude;
        var lng = position.coords.longitude;
        //Creating LatLng object with latitude and
        //longitude.
        var devCenter = new google.maps.LatLng(lat, lng);
        map.setCenter(devCenter);
        map.setZoom(15);
    });
}
```

6. Upload your file to a proper hosting site and check this URL on your mobile device or simulator. You will be asked whether to allow the reading of your location or not. If you allow it, you will see the map of your location.

This is how we achieve the goal of creating a simple map for mobile devices.

How it works...

The `<meta>` tags are used by browsers and search engines, and they are not visible to the users. They help browsers know how to behave. In our case, the following `<meta>` tag is used to tell browsers that the current website is optimized for mobile browsers:

```
<meta name="viewport" content="initial-scale=1.0,
    user-scalable=no" />
```

This `<meta>` tag solves zooming problems when the user pinches in or out, because pinching in or out should zoom the map in or out respectively and not the document itself.

In order to get the device location, the W3C Geolocation API implemented by browsers is used. There is a navigator namespace in the HTML5 standard, and the Geolocation subnamespace is checked first if the browser has support for the Geolocation API. If `navigator.geolocation` returns an object, we can get the coordinates with the help of the `getCurrentPosition` function. The callback function gets the latitude and longitude of the device and creates the `google.maps.LatLng` object. Then, the `setCenter` method of the map object is triggered with the `devCenter` object that was created before. This will change the center of the map according to the device location.

The last line of the callback function is used to set the zoom level of the map. This can be changed according to your needs.

There's more...

The HTML5 standard is still in progress, and there can be changes in the W3 Geolocation API. If you want to get more information about geolocation, refer to the W3C documentation site (`http://dev.w3.org/geo/api/spec-source.html`).

See also

▶ The *Creating a simple map in a custom DIV element* recipe

Changing map properties programmatically

Until this recipe, the map has been interactive within itself. Users can zoom in/out, drag the map, change the user interface, or enable/disable mouse interactivity. If you want to play with the map outside of it, you should access the map and change the properties you want, or you can change the properties programmatically in different cases. Changing map properties programmatically is one of the important parts of the Google Maps JavaScript API. In most mapping applications, a user searches for a place, and the application should focus on that point on the map. This is possible with the `map` object's functions. There are lots of map functions, but we will cover only the most used ones.

In this recipe, we will create a mapping application that a user can interact with outside the map. Buttons are used in order to interact with the map.

Getting ready

Before you continue, a map object must be created in order to interact with it. If a map object is not defined, you will get an error. These kinds of problems occur due to JavaScript's asynchronous behavior in most cases.

You can find the source code at `Chapter 1/ch01_interaction_map.html`.

How to do it...

Changing the map properties is quite easy if you follow the given steps:

1. Let's start by creating a new empty file named `interaction_map.html`. Then, copy all of the code in the HTML file (`map.html`) that was introduced in the *Creating a simple map in a custom DIV element* recipe and paste it into the new file.

2. Add the following functions after the `initmap()` function. These functions are called by the buttons defined in HTML, which are used to interact with the map. Functions are explained later in this recipe.

```
function zoomToIstanbul () {
    var istanbul = new google.maps.LatLng(41.0579,29.0340);
    map.setCenter(istanbul);
}

function zoomToStreet () {
    map.setZoom(18);
}

function disableDrag () {
    map.setOptions ({ draggable: false });
}

function setMaxZoom () {
    map.setOptions ({ maxZoom: 12 });
}

function setMinZoom () {
    map.setOptions ({ minZoom: 5 });
}

function changeUI () {
    map.setOptions ({ disableDefaultUI: true });
}

function disableScroll () {
    map.setOptions ({ scrollwheel: false });
}
```

3. Next, add the following function to listen to the click events of the buttons defined in the HTML code in step 5.

```
function startButtonEvents () {
    document.getElementById('btnZoomToIst'
        ).addEventListener('click', function(){
        zoomToIstanbul();
    });
    document.getElementById('btnZoomToStr'
        ).addEventListener('click', function(){
        zoomToStreet();
    });
    document.getElementById('btnDisableDrag'
        ).addEventListener('click', function(){
        disableDrag();
    });
    document.getElementById('btnMaxZoom'
        ).addEventListener('click', function(){
        setMaxZoom();
    });
    document.getElementById('btnMinZoom'
        ).addEventListener('click', function(){
        setMinZoom();
    });
    document.getElementById('btnChangeUI'
        ).addEventListener('click', function(){
        changeUI();
    });
    document.getElementById('btnDisableScroll'
        ).addEventListener('click', function(){
        disableScroll();
    });
}
```

4. The `startButtonEvents` function must be called on initializing the map, so the following line of code is added:

```
startButtonEvents();
```

5. Then, add the following HTML lines of code inside the `<body>` tag. These are the `<button>` tags to be shown on the web page. Each `button` element listens for the click event to fire the related function.

```
<input id="btnZoomToIst" type="button" value="Zoom To
    Istanbul">
```

```
<input id="btnZoomToStr" type="button" value="Zoom To
   Street Level">
<input id="btnDisableDrag" type="button" value="Disable
   Drag">
<input id="btnMaxZoom" type="button" value="Set Max Zoom to
   12">
<input id="btnMinZoom" type="button" value="Set Min Zoom to
   5">
<input id="btnChangeUI" type="button" value="Change UI">
<input id="btnDisableScroll" type="button" value="Disable
   Scroll Zoom">
```

6. Enter the URL of your local server, where your `interaction_map.html` file is stored, in your favorite browser and take a look at the result. You will see the map with buttons at the top. Each button triggers a different function to interact with the map.

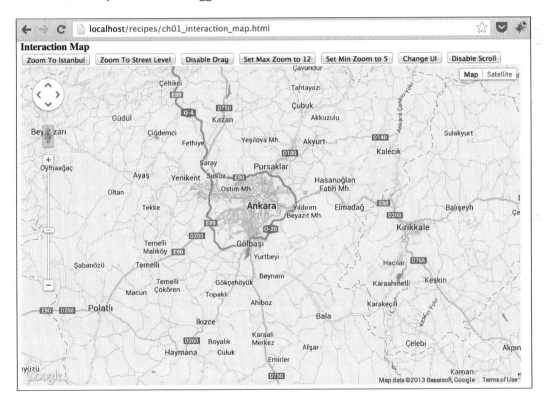

As a result of the recipe, we can change map properties programmatically.

Each JavaScript function defined previously is used to change the different sides of the map. The ones most used are to change the center and zoom level of the map. Most of the time, people just move from one location to another on a map. For example, if you are showing the locations of a coffee chain, the map should focus on each of the locations of the coffee shops. The following code creates a `google.maps.LatLng` object that will be the input of the `setCenter()` function. The `41.0579` and `29.0340` values are the latitude and longitude of Istanbul, Turkey respectively. You will replace these coordinate values with your own coordinate values to change the center of the map. This function will only change the center of the map, not the zoom level.

```
var istanbul = new google.maps.LatLng(41.0579,29.0340);
map.setCenter(istanbul);
```

If you want to zoom in or out of the map in order to cover/show an area, you should also play with the zoom value. For example, your coffee shop location at zoom level 6 cannot provide effective guidance to your customers. It should at least be at level 15 or more to see the street names and the exact location. This can be done with the following code:

```
map.setZoom(18);
```

In some cases, you don't want users to interact with the map, such as fixing the map location, by disabling mouse drags or wheel scrolls. These are some examples of the `google.maps.MapOptions` object's properties. These properties are directly related to the properties of the map. If you want to change one or more properties of the map, you should create a JSON object and call the following map function:

```
map.setOptions ({
    draggable: false,
    maxZoom: 12
});
```

With the `setOptions()` function, you can also enable or disable the default controls, but this will be reviewed in *Chapter 4, Working with Controls*. You can set one or more properties with the `setOptions()` function. You can find short explanations with comments next to the properties:

```
map.setOptions ({
    draggable: false, //Disables the map drag
    maxZoom: 12, //Sets maximum zoom level
    minZoom: 5, //Sets minimum zoom level
    disableDefaultUI: true, //Removes the default controls
    scrollwheel: false //Disables the mouse scroll wheel
});
```

Accessing a map object

Be aware of defining a map object as a global object in order to access it anywhere. This can be a problem in some cases while writing in JavaScript. Please check the following link to get more information on JavaScript and Scopes: `http://coding.smashingmagazine.com/2009/08/01/what-you-need-to-know-about-javascript-scope/`.

See also

▶ The *Creating a simple map in a custom DIV element* recipe

Changing base maps

Base maps are one of the most important parts of the process of mapping the APIs. Base maps show the roads, satellite images, or terrains, which can be used for different situations. For example, a road map can be suitable for showing the location of your coffee shop, but a satellite image cannot. Satellite images can also be suitable for showing parcel information to check whether they are drawn correctly. The Google Maps JavaScript API has four different base maps such as **ROADMAP**, **SATELLITE**, **HYBRID**, and **TERRAIN**. All of these base maps can be seen in the following screenshot wherein they can be compared to each other.

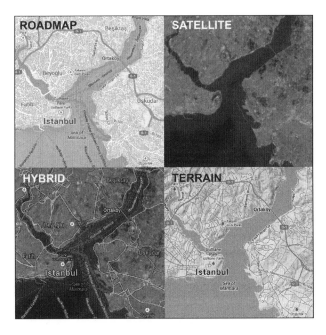

In this recipe, we will go through the Google Maps base maps and learn how to change them programmatically.

Getting ready

In this recipe, we will use the JavaScript arrays in order to make the input parameters of a function readable. I suggest you check Google for the JavaScript arrays if you don't have any experience.

You can find the source code at `Chapter 1/ch01_base_map.html`.

How to do it...

1. If you follow the given steps, you can change the base maps of your map.

2. Let's start by creating a new empty file named `base_map.html`. Then, copy all of the code in the HTML file (`map.html`) that is introduced in the *Creating a simple map in a custom DIV element* recipe and paste it into the new file.

3. Add the following function after the `initMap()` function. It will listen to the click events of the buttons added to the HTML code in step 4. It simply sets the base map according to the IDs of the buttons.

```
function startButtonEvents () {
    document.getElementById('btnRoad'
      ).addEventListener('click', function(){
        map.setMapTypeId(google.maps.MapTypeId.ROADMAP);
    });
    document.getElementById('btnSat'
      ).addEventListener('click', function(){
        map.setMapTypeId(google.maps.MapTypeId.SATELLITE);
    });
    document.getElementById('btnHyb'
      ).addEventListener('click', function(){
        map.setMapTypeId(google.maps.MapTypeId.HYBRID);
    });
    document.getElementById('btnTer'
      ).addEventListener('click', function(){
        map.setMapTypeId(google.maps.MapTypeId.TERRAIN);
    });
}
```

4. The `startButtonEvents` function must be called upon initializing the map, so the following line of code is added after the map is initialized.

```
startButtonEvents();
```

5. Then, add the following HTML lines of code before the map's `div` element. These are the HTML buttons to change the base map:

```
<input id="btnRoad" type="button" value="RoadMap">
<input id="btnSat" type="button" value="Satellite">
<input id="btnHyb" type="button" value="Hybrid">
<input id="btnTer" type="button" value="Terrain">
```

6. Enter the URL of your local server, where your `base_map.html` file is stored, in your favorite browser, and take a look at the result. You will see the map with buttons at the top. Each button changes the base maps according to their names.

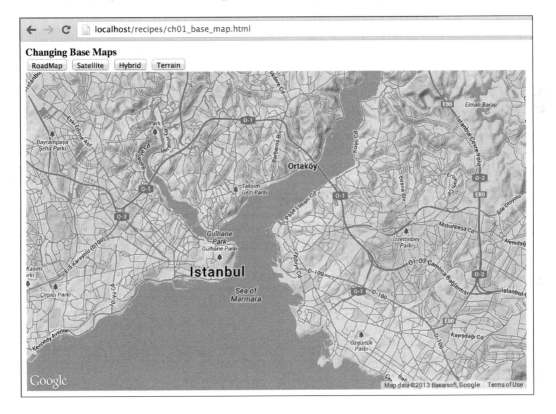

As shown in the preceding screenshot, you can easily change the base maps that are provided by Google.

How it works...

Most of the magic is done by the API itself; you just choose the map type you want to switch to.

These map types are predefined, but there is a possibility to add your own base maps or styled maps to the API and switch to them. Adding your own base maps or styled maps are introduced in *Chapter 2*, *Adding Raster Layers*.

You can also define the starting base map at the `mapOptions` object as follows:

```
var mapOptions = {
    center: new google.maps.LatLng(39.9078, 32.8252),
    zoom: 10,
    mapTypeId: google.maps.MapTypeId.TERRAIN
};
```

After changing the map options, your map will be opened with the `TERRAIN` base map type.

There's more...

Changing base maps may seem to be an easy topic, but the math and tech behind them is not as easy as using them. The base maps and overlays used in the Google Maps JavaScript API are processed in the Web Mercator projection system. In this projection system, the angles are preserved, but the size and shape of large objects change. As a result, the poles seem to be bigger than North America, which is not true at all. This projection is a good way to show the whole world in the same map.

Please check the later chapters for detailed information or check the Wikipedia article at `https://en.wikipedia.org/wiki/Mercator_projection`.

See also

> ▸ The *Creating a simple map in a custom DIV element* recipe

2
Adding Raster Layers

In this chapter, we will cover:

- ▶ Styling of Google base maps
- ▶ Using different tile sources as base maps
- ▶ Adding tile overlays to maps
- ▶ Adding image overlays to maps
- ▶ Changing the transparency of overlays
- ▶ Creating a heat map
- ▶ Adding a traffic layer
- ▶ Adding a transit layer
- ▶ Adding a bicycling layer
- ▶ Adding weather and cloud layers
- ▶ Adding a Panoramio layer

Introduction

This chapter will cover everything about working with raster layers. The collection of recipes is composed of the most common use cases of handling raster layers in the Google Maps JavaScript API.

Raster is one of the prime data types in the **GIS** world. The Google Maps JavaScript API presents an extensive set of tools to integrate external sources of imagery. Also, the API enables application developers to change the styling of its base maps with a palette of practically unlimited array of choices.

This chapter will introduce you to changing the styling of base maps and will then continue by covering how to display raster data, focusing on external **TMS (Tile Map Services)**, where the raster layer is composed of organized tiles in the map display (for example, OpenStreetMap). Lastly, there are a number of raster layers (traffic, transit, weather, bicycle, and Panoramio) that can be presented on the map by integrating them with the Google Maps JavaScript API.

Styling of Google base maps

Google base maps show a variety of details such as water bodies (oceans, seas, rivers, lakes, and so on), roads, parks, and built-up areas (residential, industrial, and so on). As you have observed in the first chapter, all these are shown in predefined cartographic parameters. With the styling capability of base maps, you have a virtually unlimited set of choices in terms of the cartographic representation of base maps.

In your web or mobile applications, it is very beneficial to have a diversity of representations (in all different color schemes with different emphasis) in order to keep your audience more involved; maps blend neatly into your website design.

This recipe will guide you through the process of changing the styling of base maps.

Getting ready

We can continue from the *Creating a simple map in a custom DIV element* recipe from *Chapter 1, Google Maps JavaScript API Basics*, as we do not need to recall the basics of creating the map.

How to do it...

The end product of the recipe will look like bluish Google Maps if you follow the given steps:

1. Create an array of styles as follows:

```
var bluishStyle = [
    {
        stylers: [
            { hue: "#009999" },
            { saturation: -5 },
            { lightness: -40 }
        ]
    }
    {
        featureType: "road",
        elementType: "geometry",
        stylers: [
```

```
                { lightness: 100 },
                { visibility: "simplified" }
            ]
        },
        {
            featureType: "water",
            elementType: "geometry",
            stylers: [
                { hue: "#0000FF" },
                {saturation:-40}
            ]
        },
        {
            featureType: "administrative.neighborhood",
            elementType: "labels.text.stroke",
            stylers: [
                { color: "#E80000" },
                {weight: 1}
            ]
        },
        {
            featureType: "road",
            elementType: "labels.text",
            stylers: [
                { visibility: "off" }
            ]
        },
        {
            featureType: "road.highway",
            elementType: "geometry.fill",
            stylers: [
                { color: "#FF00FF" },
                {weight: 2}
            ]
        }
    ]
```

2. Add your `style` array to the `initMap()` function.

3. Within the `initMap()` function, create a `styledMapType` object with its name and reference it with the `style` array:

```
var bluishStyledMap = new google.maps.StyledMapType(bluishStyle,
    {name: "Bluish Google Base Maps with Pink Highways"});
```

4. Add the `mapTypeControlOptions` object having the `mapTypeIds` property to your original `mapOptions` object:

```
var mapOptions = {
    center: new google.maps.LatLng(39.9078, 32.8252),
    zoom: 10,
    mapTypeControlOptions: {mapTypeIds:
        [google.maps.MapTypeId.ROADMAP, 'new_bluish_style']}
};
```

5. Relate the new `mapTypeId` property to your `styledMapType` object:

```
map.mapTypes.set('new_bluish_style', bluishStyledMap);
```

6. And lastly, set this new `mapTypeId` property to be displayed:

```
map.setMapTypeId('new_bluish_style');
```

7. You can now observe the bluish-styled Google base maps as seen in the following screenshot:

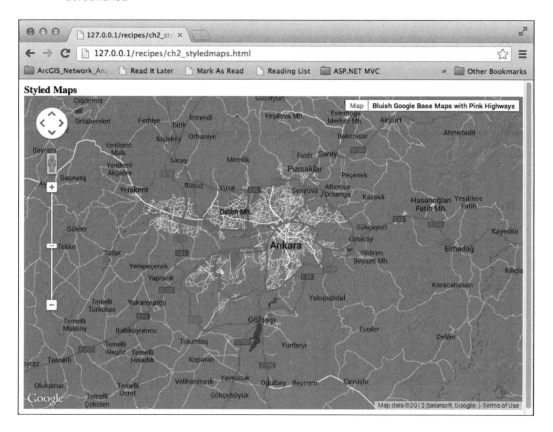

How it works...

Firstly, let's look at the `bluishStyle` array consisting of one or more `google.maps.MapTypeStyle` objects arranged as shown in the following code:

```
var bluishStyle = [
  {
    featureType: '',
    elementType: '',
    stylers: [
      {hue: ''},
      {saturation: ''},
      {lightness: ''},
          ...
    ]
  },
  {
    featureType: '',
        ...
  }
]
```

In this array, you can include several styles for the different map features and their respective elements such as their geometries, labels, and so on (all these are specified in `google.maps.MapTypeStyleElementType`).

Map features embrace the types of geographic representations that are found in the base maps. Administrative areas, landscape features, points of interest, roads, and water bodies are examples of map features.

In addition to these general definitions of map features, the Google Maps JavaScript API enables you to specify the subtypes of these features. For example, you may wish to change the default style on specific `poi` types by giving them the `featureType` property as follows:

```
featureType: 'poi.school'
```

Or, you can be more specific on the landscape map features:

```
featureType: 'landscape.man_made'
```

More about the google.maps.MapTypeStyleFeatureType object

A complete listing of the `MapTypeStyleFeatureType` object specification can be found at `https://developers.google.com/maps/documentation/javascript/reference#MapTypeStyleFeatureType`.

Please note that the first element of our `bluishstyle` array does not include any `featureType` property, making the styler options valid for the entire base map as shown in the following code:

```
{
    stylers: [
        { hue: "#009999" },
        { saturation: -5 },
        { lightness: -40 }
    ]
}
```

In addition to `google.maps.MapTypeStyleFeatureType` and its constants, you can also detail each of its map features such as the geometries, geometry strokes and fills, labels, label texts (also text fill and stroke), and label icons. Taking this opportunity, you can style the geometries of roads in different settings than their related icons.

In our recipe, we have disabled the visibility of all the label texts of the roads, not touching their geometry or label icons as shown in the following code:

```
{
    featureType: "road",
    elementType: "labels.text",
    stylers: [
        { visibility: "off" }
    ]
}
```

> **More about the google.maps.MapTypeStyleElementType object**
>
> A complete listing of the `MapTypeStyleElementType` object specification can be found at `https://developers.google.com/maps/documentation/javascript/reference#MapTypeStyleElementType`.

For every feature type and its element type, you can specify a `google.maps.MapTypeStyler` object that covers the options of hue, `lightness`, `saturation`, gamma, `inverse_lightness`, `visibility`, and `weight` as an array. In our recipe, the styler option that makes the highway road appear in pink is as follows:

```
{
    featureType: "road.highway",
    elementType: "geometry.fill",
    stylers: [
        { color: "#FF00FF" },
        {weight: 2}
    ]
}
```

Here, the `color` option in the `stylers` array is an RGB Hex string of a pink tone, while `weight` defines the weight of the feature in pixels.

More about the google.maps.MapTypeStyler object

A complete listing of the `MapTypeStyler` object specification can be found at `https://developers.google.com/maps/documentation/javascript/reference#MapTypeStyler`.

After defining the `style` array in our `initMap()` function, we created a `StyledMapType` object:

```
var bluishStyledMap = new google.maps.StyledMapType(bluishStyle,
    {name: "Bluish Google Base Maps with Pink Highways"});
```

This object takes two arguments—the first one is the `style` array and the second one is a `google.maps.StyledMapTypeOptions` object. Here, we have included only the `name` property; however, you can additionally include the `maxZoom` and `minZoom` properties between which the `StyledMapType` object will be displayed. In the screenshot of this recipe, you can see that the value we have assigned for the `name` property is displayed in the interface.

After we created the `StyledMapType` object, we added an additional object called `mapTypeControlOptions`, which takes the `mapTypeIds` array in the `mapOptions` object, replacing the `mapTypeId` property:

```
var mapOptions = {
    center: new google.maps.LatLng(39.9078, 32.8252),
    zoom: 10,
    mapTypeControlOptions: {mapTypeIds:
        [google.maps.MapTypeId.ROADMAP, 'new_bluish_style']}
};
```

This enables us to add multiple styles in addition to the standard ROADMAP map type.

Next comes the step of linking the `mapTypeId` (`'new_bluish_style'`) property that we have specified in the `mapTypeIds` array with the `StyledMapType` object (bluishStyledMap):

```
map.mapTypes.set('new_bluish_style', bluishStyledMap);
```

After linking the `mapTypeId` property with the `StyledMapType` object, we can end with the following line of code so that the map interface opens with a base map styled as per our intentions:

```
map.setMapTypeId('new_bluish_style');
```

In our recipe, we have covered how to style the base maps according to our taste. We have made use of the `google.maps.MapTypeStyle` object to select the feature types (`google.maps.MapTypeStyleFeatureType`) and the related elements (`google.maps.MapTypeStyleElementType`) and styled them using the `google.maps.MapTypeStyler` object. Then, we have added our `StyledMapType` object to the map, showing our own styling of the base maps of Google Maps.

There's more...

Using the `StyledMapType` object is only one of the ways of handling the user-defined styled base maps in the Google Maps Javascript API.

Another simpler usage is specifying the `style` array in the `styles` property of the `mapOptions` object:

```
var mapOptions = {
    center: new google.maps.LatLng(39.9078, 32.8252),
    zoom: 10,
    mapTypeId: google.maps.MapTypeId.ROADMAP,
    styles: bluishStyle
};
```

Another alternative is that after defining our `mapOptions` object, we can add the `styles` property later with the following code:

```
map.setOptions({styles: bluishStyle });
```

There is an important difference between using the `StyledMapType` object and the `style` property of the `mapOptions` object. Using the `StyledMapType` object enables us to define a number of (virtually infinite) styles as map types. In addition, these map types can be seen in the map type control of the map interface, so it is very easy for the user to switch back and forth between the map types.

However, if the styles are attached to the map by the `mapOptions` object's `style` property, there is no way for the user to change multiple styles. In fact, in the map type control, there will be an option for you to select new styles, because styles are not attached to a `StyledMapType` object, and therefore cannot be identified as map types.

You can get information on how to use the Styled Maps Wizard at `http://gmaps-samples-v3.googlecode.com/svn/trunk/ styledmaps/wizard/index.html`.

Preparing the `style` arrays is a job with many cartographic details. Finding the correct combination for each feature and the element type in stylers would take too much time, especially if the only way of editing is in a text editor. Google has done a great job by creating the Styled Map Wizard to ease this time-consuming task. It enables you to perform all your styling tasks in an interface, so you can have an overview of what you are changing in real time. After you finish your work, you can export your styles as JSON to be used as a `style` array in your application.

Using different tile sources as base maps

Google base maps display an immense amount of content (local POI information, road hierarchies, driving directions, and so on) and a large styling palette. In addition, it provides tools to change the styling of its base maps in its JavaScript API.

Moreover, you can have your other map tile sources displayed as base maps in the Google Maps interface. This feature enables you to display your tiled maps in the Google Maps interface, utilizing most of the tools of the Google Maps JavaScript API.

In this recipe, we will go through displaying OpenStreetMap tiles as base maps in the Google Maps interface, using the JavaScript API.

Getting ready

We can continue on from the *Creating a simple map in a custom DIV element* recipe from *Chapter 1, Google Maps JavaScript API Basics*, as we do not need to reiterate the basics of getting the map on screen.

How to do it...

With this recipe, you will see the OpenStreetMap tiles on top of Google Maps after completing the given steps:

1. In your `initMap()` function, create an `ImageMapType` object with the following code:

```
var osmMapType = new google.maps.ImageMapType({
    getTileUrl: function(coord, zoom) {
        return "http://tile.openstreetmap.org/" + zoom +
        "/" + coord.x + "/" + coord.y + ".png";
    },
    tileSize: new google.maps.Size(256, 256),
    name: "OpenStreetMap",
```

```
        maxZoom: 18
    });
```

2. Add the `google.maps.mapTypeControlOptions` object having the `mapTypeIds` property to your original `google.maps.MapTypeId` object and the `ImageMapType` object:

```
var mapOptions = {
    center: new google.maps.LatLng(39.9078, 32.8252),
    zoom: 10,
    {mapTypeIds: [google.maps.MapTypeId.ROADMAP,
    'OSM']}
};
```

3. Relate the new `mapTypeId` array to your `ImageMapType` object:

```
map.mapTypes.set('OSM', osmMapType);
```

4. And lastly, set this new `google.maps.mapTypeId` object to be displayed:

```
map.setMapTypeId('OSM');
```

5. You can see the OpenStreetMap tiles on top of the Google base map tiles as shown in the following screenshot:

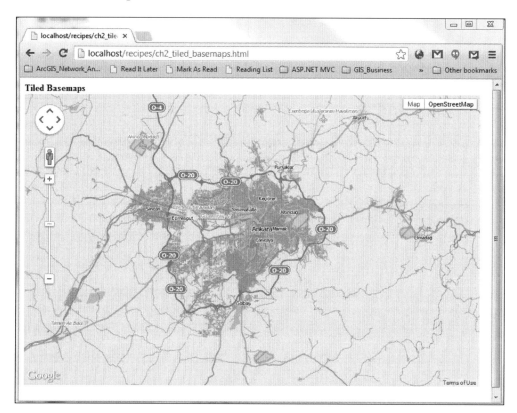

How it works...

You might have observed that there is indeed little difference between the structure of code extracts of the *Styling of the Google base maps* recipe and this recipe. In the former, we have used the `StyledMapType` object to change the styles of the original base maps, while in this recipe, we have used the `ImageMapType` object.

This is because both the `StyledMapType` and `ImageMapType` objects are all special types of the `MapType` object (`google.maps.MapType`), in addition to the original base map types such as Roadmap, Satellite, Hybrid, and Terrain, which were introduced in the previous chapter.

Let's move step by step:

```
var osmMapType = new google.maps.ImageMapType({
    getTileUrl: function(coord, zoom) {
        return "http://tile.openstreetmap.org/" + zoom + "/" +
        coord.x + "/" + coord.y + ".png";
    },
    tileSize: new google.maps.Size(256, 256),
    name: "OpenStreetMap",
    maxZoom: 18
});
```

This part of the recipe creates an `osmMapType` object of `ImageMapType`. To create an `ImageMapType` object, we must supply two required properties: `getTileUrl` and `tileSize`.

Before filling in these two parameters, we must make sure we have a tiled map service of which we can use tiles. OpenStreetMap (`http://www.openstreetmap.org/`) is a kind of a map service, built and existing thanks to the community efforts around the world.

Tiled map services are organized in a manner that the cartographic imagery is broken into parts (tiles) for each predetermined zoom level. These tiles are to be located alongside the x and y axis so that the tile map service consumers (such as the Google Maps API) can recognize their respective locations as seen in the following diagram:

(0, 0)	(1, 0)	(2, 0)
(0, 1)	(1, 1)	(2, 1)
(0, 2)	(1, 2)	(2, 2)

The upper-left tile's coordinate is (0,0), and it is called the origin tile. In Google Maps, the origin is at the upper-left (northwest) corner of the map interface.

Remember that for the `getTileUrl` property, we supply a function that has two parameters: `coord` and `zoom`:

```
getTileUrl: function(coord, zoom) {
    return "http://tile.openstreetmap.org/" + zoom + "/" +
    coord.x + "/" + coord.y + ".png";
}
```

The coord parameter is exactly the coordinate pair that takes the value of the tile coordinates introduced in the preceding screenshot. In other words, in the upper-left corner, coord.x should be 0 and coord.y should be 0.

Assuming that we are at zoom level 0, we can try and get a tile from the Openstreetmap URL supplied for the getTileUrl property:

```
"http://tile.openstreetmap.org/" + zoom + "/" + coord.x + "/" +
coord.y + ".png"
```

This will give the following output:

```
"http://tile.openstreetmap.org/0/0/0.png"
```

If you copy this URL to the address bar of your browser, you will get the output as shown in the following screenshot:

This image is a single tile from Openstreetmap at zoom level 0. It is understood that the single OpenStreetMap tile at zoom level 0 covers the entire world.

Now, let's continue with zoom level 1:

```
http://tile.openstreetmap.org/1/0/0.png
```

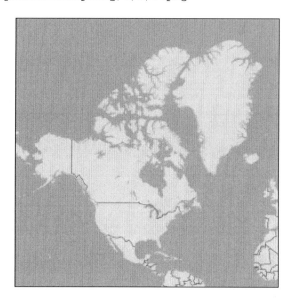

You might have noticed that the level of detail has increased as the zoom level has increased from 0 to 1. Also, the coverage area for each tile has been dramatically reduced (one-fourth in this case).

You can see the complete tile layout at zoom level 1 in the following screenshot:

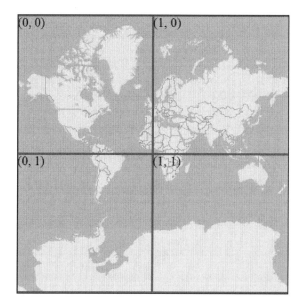

An important property of the tiled map services is that at each zoom level, each tile of the previous zoom level is tiled again to possess the level of detail required for the current zoom level.

Returning to our `osmMapType` creation, the function for the `getTileUrl` property works for placing the tiles of an external source (OpenStreetMap in our recipe). The two arguments named `coord` and `zoom` are handled by the Google Maps API itself. The API detects the bounding box of the map and builds up the tile layout for each zoom level. Therefore, the API recognizes which tile coordinate should be requested at which zoom level. The only thing that is left for you to do is to present the tile URLs of the external tiled map source, which is what you have done in the `getTileUrl` property.

The second property is the `tileSize` property, which accepts a `google.maps.Size` object. As its name implies, this property defines the width and height of each tile in terms of pixel values. The Google Maps tile layout is outlined for 256 px by 256 px tiles; so we supply `google.maps.Size(256,256)`, where the first parameter stands for width and the second parameter stands for height.

The `maxZoom` property sets the maximum zoom level of display for the tiled map service. The external base maps will not be shown at zoom level 19 as `maxZoom` is set at `18` in this recipe.

The `name` property is set for the name of your choice for the tiled map service. It is directly seen in the `mapTypeControl` object at the upper-right corner of the map interface.

The final two lines are the same as the ones in the previous recipe; the first one relates to the `osmMapType` object of `ImageMapType` with `OSM` set for the `mapTypeID` object specified in the `mapTypeControlOptions` property of `mapOptions`:

```
map.mapTypes.set('OSM', osmMapType);
map.setMapTypeId('OSM');
```

See also

Detailed explanations of tile coordinates, pixel coordinates, and world coordinates in conjunction with projection details will be covered in the oncoming chapters.

Furthermore, using tiled map services as overlays to base maps will be covered in the next recipe.

Adding tile overlays to maps

Google Maps has a selection of base maps as street maps and satellite imagery, which we discussed in the previous chapter; we will now discuss how additional base maps can be introduced to the Google Maps interface.

We can also use tiled map services as overlays to the base maps. By overlay, you can think of a separate sheet of map tiles put over the base maps. You can observe the details of the overlaid layer together with the base map. Examples of overlay layers might be of the boundaries of areas of interest, special POIs that are not found in the Google Maps' base maps, statistical results to be presented with aerial or point styling, and so on.

The tile map services that are used as base maps can technically be used as overlays in the Google Maps JavaScript API. However, using these tile map services (such as OpenStreetMaps) as overlays results in blocking the original base maps of Google Maps, as there would be no blank space in the map of overlaid tile map services (originally aimed to be base maps). This is because both the Google Maps base maps and the overlaid tile map services are designed to be base maps. Therefore, it is not recommended to use another tile map service that is meant for base maps as an overlay layer on top of the Google Maps base maps.

In this recipe, we will cover how to show the OpenStreetMap tiles as overlay layers in the Google Maps interface using the JavaScript API.

Getting ready

We can use the previous recipe's code and change it a bit for this recipe in order to eliminate the need of rewriting the `osmMapType` object details.

How to do it...

In this recipe, you will see the OpenStreetMap tiles as an overlay layer if you follow the given steps:

1. In your `initMap()` function, leave the `osmMapType` object as it is:

    ```
    var osmMapType = new google.maps.ImageMapType({
        getTileUrl: function(coord, zoom) {
            return "http://tile.openstreetmap.org/" +
            zoom + "/" + coord.x + "/" + coord.y + ".png";
        },
        tileSize: new google.maps.Size(256, 256),
        name: "OpenStreetMap",
        maxZoom: 18
    });
    ```

2. Change the `google.maps.mapTypeControlOptions` object having `mapTypeIds` of both `google.maps.MapTypeId.ROADMAP` and `google.maps.MapTypeId.SATELLITE` in your `mapOptions` object:

```
var mapOptions = {
    center: new google.maps.LatLng(39.9078, 32.8252),
    zoom: 10,
    mapTypeControlOptions:
        {mapTypeIds: [google.maps.MapTypeId.ROADMAP,
        google.maps.MapTypeId.SATELLITE]}
};
```

3. Delete the following line of code (as no other base maps were specified in the preceding step):

```
map.mapTypes.set('OSM', osmMapType);
```

4. Set the ROADMAP map type to be displayed as the base map:

```
map.setMapTypeId(google.maps.MapTypeId.ROADMAP);
```

5. Overlay the osmMapType map type on top of the base map:

```
map.overlayMapTypes.insertAt(0, osmMapType);
```

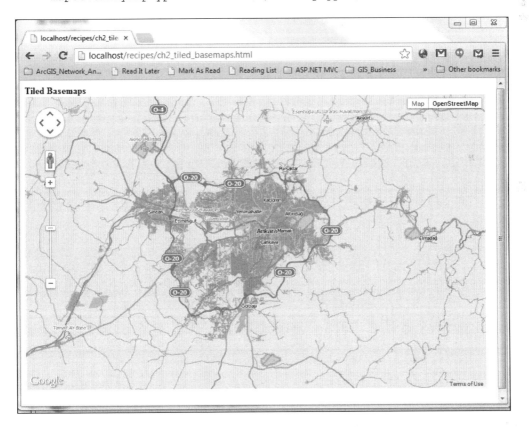

6. You now have the OpenStreetMap tiles as an overlay layer, as shown in the preceding screenshot.

How it works...

There is little difference between the preceding recipe and this recipe as you might have noticed. We have used the same custom osmMapType object of google.maps.imageMapType. We have used another tiled map service, but the structure remains the same.

The modifications have begun with the used mapTypes object in the mapTypeControlOptions property of the mapOptions object:

```
mapTypeControlOptions:
{mapTypeIds: [google.maps.MapTypeId.ROADMAP,
    google.maps.MapTypeId.SATELLITE] }
```

We have included both the ROADMAP and SATELLITE map types to be selected as base maps.

Step 3 is important; we delete the following line:

```
map.mapTypes.set('OSM', osmMapType);
```

We are deleting this because we do not want the osmMapType object to be considered as a base map. We will just use it as an overlay.

In the next step, we are selecting our default base map as ROADMAP. You can change the code line for SATELLITE or you can make the switch from the mapTypeControl object in the map interface.

The final line is the line where our overlay operation happens:

```
map.overlayMapTypes.insertAt(0, osmMapType);
```

Here, the overlayMapTypes property is an array (google.maps.MVCArray). The insertAt method of MVCArray inserts objects at the specified index, and we have inserted our imageMapType object at index 0.

More on google.maps.MVCArray

The google.maps.MVCArray array is a Google implementation of the ordinary JavaScript array. You can construct an MVC Array from an array. More details can be found at https://developers.google.com/maps/documentation/javascript/reference#MVCArray.

You can have multiple overlays over the Google Maps base maps. You must use the overlayMapTypes property to set the associated orders for the overlay maps with the first parameter of the insertAt method as follows:

```
map.overlayMapTypes.insertAt(1, anotherMapType1);
map.overlayMapTypes.insertAt(2, anotherMapType2);
```

There's more...

Overlay layers are placed on top of the base maps, and it is a good practice to turn them on and off to see the base maps. If you need to turn the overlay off, you need to include the following code:

```
map.overlayMapTypes.setAt(0, null);
```

This makes the overlay layer go off the map interface, but remember that the slot in the `overlayMapTypes` array is already allocated by the `insertAt` method. Therefore, if you want to present your user with the opportunity to toggle the overlay layers on and off (by means of a checkbox or so on), you can follow the given steps (copy the code of your current recipe before proceeding):

1. In the `<body>` tag of your HTML code, add a checkbox:

   ```
   <input type="checkbox" id="OSM" class="overlayMaps"
       onclick="toggleOverlayMaps()" />
   <label
       for="OSM">OpenStreetMap Layer</label>
   ```

2. Make `osmMaptype` a global variable outside the `initMap()` function:

   ```
   var osmMapType;
   ```

3. Change the `osmMapType` declaration in your `initMap()` function to assign the new global variable:

   ```
   osmMapType = new google.maps.ImageMapType({
       getTileUrl: function(coord, zoom) {
           return "http://tile.openstreetmap.org/" + zoom +
           "/" + coord.x + "/" + coord.y + ".png";
       },
       tileSize: new google.maps.Size(256, 256),
       name: "OpenStreetMap",
       maxZoom: 18
   });
   ```

4. Replace the `insertAt` method with the `pull(null)` method:

   ```
   map.overlayMapTypes.push(null);
   ```

5. Add an overlay layer toggling function:

   ```
   function toggleOverlayMaps() {
       var OSMLayer = document.getElementById("OSM");
       if (OSMLayer.checked)
       {
           map.overlayMapTypes.setAt(0, osmMapType);
       }
   ```

```
        else
        {
            map.overlayMapTypes.setAt(0, null);
        }
    }
```

6. The main trick of the preceding code extract is to first open a space in the
   `overlayMapTypes` array of the `initMap()` function. After that, you can call the
   `setAt()` method to turn the overlay layer on or off.

Adding image overlays to maps

Overlaying tiled map services is a big capability on hand. It enables a variety of tiled map services that come into the scene using the Google Maps API. The existing stock of tiled map services are, in general, global map services, which means that they cover the whole world or at least some continent/country.

We may be interested, for instance, to overlay a map for a university campus, having its rough plan on hand. Or, we may have found some map of a historical sheet and want to make use of it. Or, we may have an internal building plan of a particular building and we would like to see this building plan on top of Google Maps.

Is it possible to overlay these microscale images on top of Google Maps? Yes, certainly! In fact, technically, there would be no difference between using campus plans or building plans instead of tiled map services as overlays. The important thing to note is that those plan sheets should be aligned as tiles similar to the tiled map services on top of base maps.

In this recipe, we will not go through the details of preparing the tiles, but using them by means of the Google Maps JavaScript API. For convenience, we will use the plan of Google I/O's 2010 venue at Moscone Center, San Francisco.

There are tools to prepare image tiles which can be used as overlays. The most prominent ones are MapTiler (`www.maptiler.org`) and GDAL2Tiles (`http://www.klokan.cz/projects/gdal2tiles/`). With these tools, you can georeference, rectify, and tile your images for the zoom levels of your choice.

Getting ready

We can use the code from the *Using different tile sources as base maps* recipe, as very few modifications are required.

How to do it...

You will have an overlay layer—a building—on top of the Google Maps base maps if you follow the following steps:

1. Insert a `bounds` object:

```
var bounds = {
      17: [[20969, 20970], [50657, 50658]],
      18: [[41939, 41940], [101315, 101317]],
      19: [[83878, 83881], [202631, 202634]],
      20: [[167757, 167763], [405263, 405269]]
};
```

2. Replace the `osmMapType` object with the `buildPlanMapType` object:

```
var buildPlanMapType = new google.maps.ImageMapType({
      getTileUrl: function(coord, zoom) {
          if (zoom < 17 || zoom > 20 ||
              bounds[zoom][0][0] > coord.x ||
              coord.x > bounds[zoom][0][1] ||
              bounds[zoom][1][0] > coord.y ||
              coord.y > bounds[zoom][1][1]) {
                  return null;
          }
          return
            ['http://www.gstatic.com/io2010maps/tiles/5/L2_'
            , zoom, '_', coord.x, '_', coord.y,
            '.png'].join('');
      },
      tileSize: new google.maps.Size(256, 256),
      name: "Google IO Building Plan",
      maxZoom: 20
});
```

3. Change the last line to:

```
map.overlayMapTypes.insertAt(0, buildPlanMapType);
```

4. Center the map on the Moscone Center:

```
map.setCenter(new google.maps.LatLng(37.78320, -
    122.40421));
```

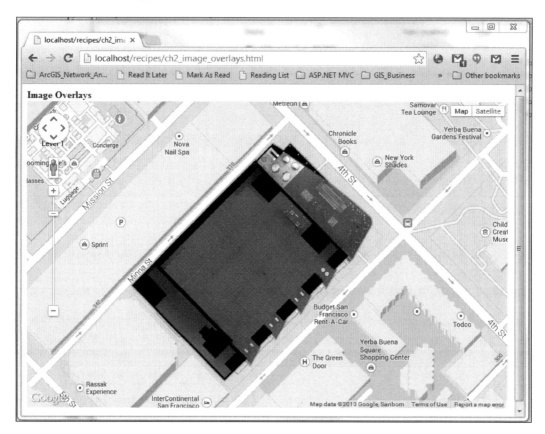

You can see the building floor plan supplied as an image organized in tiles on top of the Google Maps base maps in the preceding screenshot.

How it works...

You may have observed that the main structure stays the same as in the previous recipe. First, you define a `google.maps.ImageMapType` object and then overlay it on top of base maps by using the `overlayMapTypes.insertAt` array of the `map` object.

The only change introduced in this recipe is due to the example building plan's boundaries (bounding box). In the previous recipe, the boundaries of the overlaid tiled map service were of the world, whereas in this recipe, we have limited it to the building, comparably on a much higher scale.

Therefore, we have included the `bounds` object defining the boundaries in terms of tile coordinates for each zoom level. We have limited the zoom level from 17 to 20 as lower zoom levels (<17) would not show the building in a sensible fashion. The building would be just a small rectangle in zoom levels 16 and 15, and it would not show up in zoom levels lower than 14.

For each zoom level property in the `bounds` object, we have an array of x and y tile coordinates, x being the first and y being the second. Inside these arrays, the lower and upper bounds for the tile coordinates are found.

At this point, you may be wondering how these specific numbers are found:

```
var bounds = {
var bounds = {
    17: [[20969, 20970], [50657, 50658]],
    ...
}
```

These numbers are actually the tile coordinates that intersect with the boundaries of the Moscone Center as shown in the following screenshot:

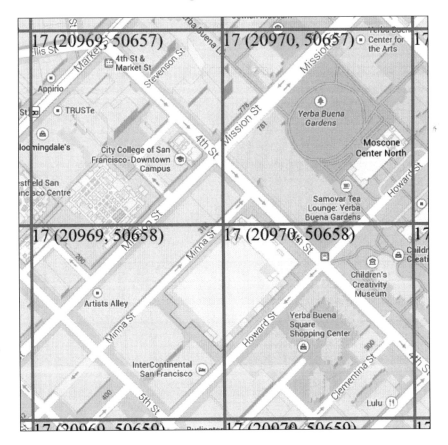

You can observe that in the 17th zoom level, the x coordinate must be between 20969 and 20970, and the y coordinate must be between 50657 and 50658 for our image overlay.

The `bounds` object is used to create constraints for a restricted number of zoom levels to fetch tiles in the definition of the `buildPlanMapType` object's `getTileUrl` function. The function for the `getTileUrl` property checks each tile coordinate against the `bounds` object's items, so that the API does not try to fetch tiles that do not intersect with the boundaries of the building plan.

Changing the transparency of overlays

The Google Maps JavaScript API supports third-party tiled map services or images to be overlaid on top of base maps. However, there is a problem with the overlay layers; they come on top of base maps and make them invisible. Of course, you can turn them on or off according to your choice; however, this is not a solution if you want to see the base maps together with the overlay layers.

In fact, you can just modify the opacity of the overlay layers to see the base maps and the overlay layers.

This recipe is focused on changing the transparency of the overlay layers introduced in the last two recipes.

Getting ready

We can use the code introduced in the *Adding tile overlays to maps* recipe of this chapter and modify it a little to achieve the result. Be sure to copy the code of the recipe first.

How to do it...

You will be able to make your overlay layer transparent after completing the one-step operation presented in the following code:

1. Just change the osmMapType object:

```
var osmMapType = new google.maps.ImageMapType({
    getTileUrl: function(coord, zoom) {
        return "http://tile.openstreetmap.org/" + zoom +
        "/" +coord.x + "/" + coord.y + ".png";},
    tileSize: new google.maps.Size(256, 256),
    name: "OpenStreetMap",
    maxZoom: 18,
    opacity:0.6
});
```

2. You can adjust the transparency of your overlay layers as shown in the following screenshot:

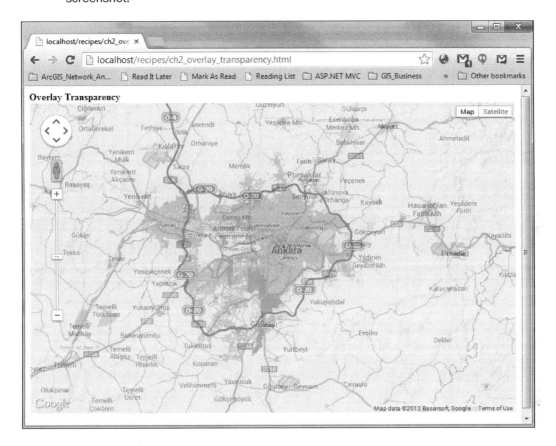

How it works...

Changing the transparency of overlay layers is very simple. Adding the following code to the `imageMapType` object does our work:

```
opacity:0.6
```

The opacity property of the `imageMapType` object makes the incoming tiles transparent according to the values supplied. The value for the opacity property must be between 1 and 0, where 1.0 stands for fully opaque overlays, while 0 stands for fully transparent overlays.

Creating a heat map

The Google Maps API lays the foundation for several map-based analysis, including heat maps. A heat map is a form of visualization that shows the concentration of points through gradient color scales.

Points, in this respect, may be the representation of any geographically represented items such as hospitals, houses, schools, measured values of sea pollution tagged with coordinates, the location of waste collection bins, and so on. The list is practically infinite.

Heat maps are very important inputs for geostatistics. In a map display, you capture the intensity in a moment compared to the sole display of the locations of points:

The preceding screenshot depicts the location of the OpenStreetMap points layer in İstanbul, Turkey, as of July. You might just get an idea of where the concentration of points is from the preceding screenshot, but the following screenshot shows it more clearly. The most intensely concentrated locations are colored in red, whereas lesser concentrated locations are in yellow. And, as you might have guessed, the green-colored locations are the least concentrated ones.

In this recipe, we will create a heat map from a set of points using the Google Maps JavaScript API. It is worth noticing that this feature is not available within the standard Google Maps API; you need to load the visualization library to the API as shown in this recipe.

Getting ready

We can use the first recipe of *Chapter 1, Google Maps JavaScript API Basics,* as a base, because we do not need to reiterate the code for the map display. Please do not forget to copy the code from the original recipe before editing for this recipe.

How to do it...

You will have a heatmap overlay from the set of points you use if you follow the given steps:

1. Reference the `visualization` libraries where you reference the Google Maps API:

```
<script type="text/javascript"
    src="https://maps.googleapis.com/maps/api/js?
    sensor=false&libraries=visualization">
</script>
```

2. Open up a new text file in the same directory that contains our HTML file and name it `ch2_heatMapPoints.js`.

3. Create an array of `google.maps.LatLng` objects (the complete array consists of 217 objects, which you can get from the downloaded code) in the newly created JavaScript file from the previous step:

```
var heatmapPoints = [
new google.maps.LatLng(41.0182827999113,28.973224999734),
new google.maps.LatLng(41.0150707003526,28.9764445996386),
new google.maps.LatLng(41.01140130003,28.9831846001892),
new google.maps.LatLng(41.0148609002104,28.9764469999292),
new google.maps.LatLng(41.0149687001455,28.9764550002981),
new google.maps.LatLng(41.0148247996249,28.9757389996552),
new google.maps.LatLng(41.0020956002318,28.9736237995987),
];
```

4. Reference the `ch2_heatMapPoints.js` file in your HTML code:

```
<script type="text/javascript"
  src="ch2_heatMapPoints.js"></script>
```

5. Create the heatmap layer:

```
var heatmap = new
  google.maps.visualization.HeatmapLayer({
    data: heatmapPoints
});
```

6. Add the heatmap layer to the map:

```
heatmap.setMap(map);
```

7. You should now have your heatmap overlay from your set of points, as shown in the following screenshot:

How it works...

Firstly, creating a heatmap layer in the Google Maps JavaScript API requires the `visualization` library of the API to be added to the section where the Google Maps JavaScript API is referenced:

```
&libraries=visualization
```

With this addition, you can use the `google.maps.visualization.HeatmapLayer` object to create the heatmap layers.

The `google.maps.visualization.HeatmapLayer` object needs a JavaScript array or the `google.maps.MVCArray` object (an array) in which its elements are the `google.maps.LatLng` objects:

```
var heatmap = new google.maps.visualization.HeatmapLayer({
    data: heatmapPoints
});
```

The `google.maps.LatLng` object is constructed with two parameters with a longitude and latitude coordinate pair, to mention a point:

```
new google.maps.LatLng(41.0182827999113,28.973224999734)
```

We have created the array object and its contents with 217 points in another JavaScript file, because it would take too much space in our original HTML file. Also, it is a good practice to have our data and related objects in another file to avoid potential structural problems.

Finally, we can add our heatmap layer to our current map with the following code:

```
heatmap.setMap(map);
```

As you can toggle the overlay layers introduced in the previous recipes, you can also toggle the heatmap layers with the following:

```
heatmap.setMap(null);
```

There's more...

Heat maps are created from a set of points, and these points can be at different places as well as the same places. In other words, multiple `google.maps.LatLng` objects may be placed at the same place. The following code is an example:

```
new google.maps.LatLng(41.0182827999113,28.973224999734),
new google.maps.LatLng(41.0182827999113,28.973224999734),
new google.maps.LatLng(41.0182827999113,28.973224999734)
```

This will increase the intensity of this point; it will be likely to be seen in red in the heat map.

But what if the instances of the `google.maps.LatLng` objects sharing the same coordinate pair increases? One method is to copy the lines as shown in the preceding code. However, there is another smarter way:

```
{location: new
    google.maps.LatLng41.0182827999113,28.973224999734),
    weight: 3
},
```

This object is `google.maps.visualization.WeightedLocation`, and it takes two properties: one is the `google.maps.LatLng` object, and the other one is `weight`. This `weight` parameter takes any numeric value representing the occurrence count of the points.

By default, the `LatLng` object itself has a weight of 1. Therefore, having a `WeightedLocation` object with the `weight` property set to 3 is equivalent to having the same `LatLng` object.

The `WeightedLocation` and `LatLng` objects may be used together in the array supplied for the heatmap layer's `data` property.

The heatmap layer's object possesses a range of options including `gradient`, `radius`, `opacity`, `maxIntensity`, and `dissipating`.

The `gradient` option takes an array of colors:

```
var gradientScheme = [
    'rgba(0, 0, 255, 0)',
    'rgba(0, 60, 200, 1)',
    'rgba(0, 120, 120, 1)',
    'rgba(125, 125, 125, 0)',
    'rgba(125, 120, 60, 0)',
    'rgba(200, 60, 0, 0)',
    'rgba(255, 0, 0, 1)'
];
```

You can set the gradient property by adding a property to the `HeatmapLayer` constructor:

```
var heatmap = new google.maps.visualization.HeatmapLayer({
    data: heatmapPoints,
    gradient: gradientScheme
});
```

Alternatively, you can set the options later:

```
heatmap.setOptions({
    gradient: gradientScheme
});
```

The `dissipating` option is for adjusting the pixels needed to show intensity across zoom levels. Its default value is `false`, and this allows more pixels to be colored per point for intensity when the zoom level is increased.

By using the `maxIntensity` property, you can scroll up or down the heatmap layer:

```
heatmap.setOptions({
    maxIntensity: 2
});
```

The preceding code makes this recipe's output greenish because the intensity is increased. More points at the same location are required to make the heat map look reddish.

You can tweak the `radius` property to adjust the radius of the intensity for each point. The unit is in pixels.

See also

You can create heat maps using Fusion Tables in the cloud, which will be introduced later in the book. There are pros and cons when creating a heat map in either a browser or the cloud; this will be discussed in detail later in the book.

Details on the `LatLng` object and its use to create point vector overlays will be covered in the next chapter.

Adding the traffic layer

In today's world, the condition of traffic is very important information in cities. If there is an accident on the way or a recent construction that blocks an important street, it affects your whole day. How useful would it be to have real-time traffic information directly on your maps?

The Google Maps JavaScript API has a very handy aspect that lets you have traffic information fed on a real-time basis on top of your base maps.

In this recipe, we will cover how to display traffic information on your Google Maps.

Getting ready

We can use the first recipe of *Chapter 1, Google Maps JavaScript API Basics,* as a base for the basic map display. After copying the code of the original recipe, you can proceed forward.

How to do it...

Here are the steps to show the traffic layer:

1. Firstly, change the center of your map to a location where the traffic layer is served (details will be available in the *How it works...* section). For instance, for Barcelona, Spain, use the following values:

   ```
   center: new google.maps.LatLng(41.3854, 2.1822),
   ```

2. Construct the `TrafficLayer` object:

   ```
   var trafficLayer = new google.maps.TrafficLayer();
   ```

3. Add the `TrafficLayer` object to the map:

    ```
    trafficLayer.setMap(map);
    ```

4. You can see the traffic layer colored according to the density of the real-time traffic condition as shown in the following screenshot:

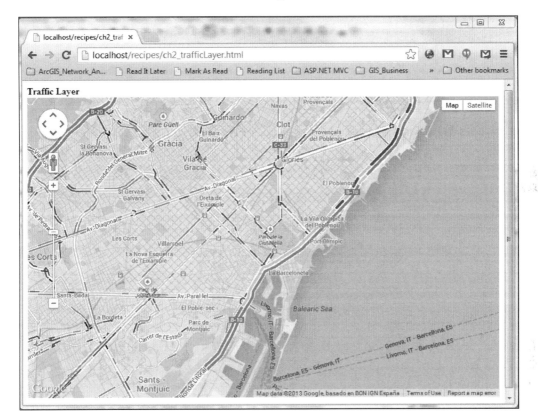

How it works...

In the first step, you might have noticed that we have switched to Barcelona, Spain, because in some countries, the traffic layer is not available. For the list of countries with the availability of traffic layers, you must view the spreadsheet at `http://gmaps-samples.googlecode.com/svn/trunk/mapcoverage_filtered.html`. You can filter the **traffic** column to see all the countries with traffic layers.

The construction of the `TrafficLayer` object and its addition to the map is straightforward. There is no property involved in the construction of the `TrafficLayer` object.

You can toggle the `TrafficLayer` object off with the following code:

```
trafficLayer.setMap(null);
```

Adding the transit layer

Public transit lines have immense importance in cities, especially for tourists and foreigners in the city. Mapping these transit lines (bus, underground, and so on) onto the base maps of several cities is a tedious task, and this is what the Google Maps JavaScript API offers through its special objects.

In this recipe, we will add transit layers to the Google Maps map interface.

Getting ready

Continuing from the previous recipe, *Adding the traffic layer,* will simplify our work, as we will only replace the `TrafficLayer` object with `TransitLayer` classes. Remember to copy the code of the original recipe.

How to do it...

Here are the steps to show public transit lines as an overlay:

1. Delete `TrafficLayer` related lines (the last two lines).

2. Instead of the `TrafficLayer` object, use the `TransitLayer` object:

    ```
    var transitLayer = new google.maps.TransitLayer();
    ```

3. Add the `TransitLayer` object to the map:

    ```
    transitLayer.setMap(map);
    ```

4. You can see the public transit lines as an overlay on Google Maps in your area of preference as shown in the following screenshot:

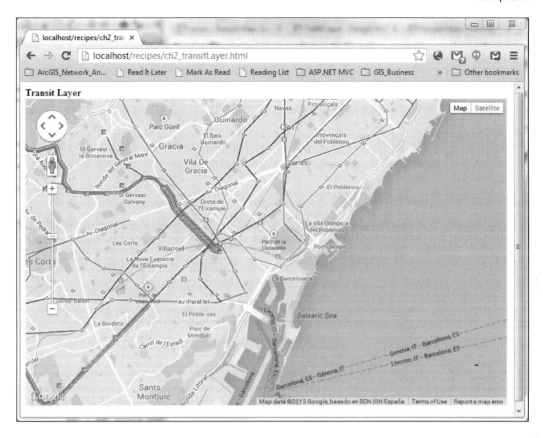

How it works...

The transit layer is offered in certain cities around the world, and you can find the complete listing of these cities at `http://www.google.com/intl/en/landing/transit/`.

The `TransitLayer` object can bring multiple colored public transit lines. The color choices are not random; they are selected based on distinct transit line operators.

The construction and display of the `TransitLayer` object is the same as the `TrafficLayer` object.

Adding the bicycling layer

It is good to have the information about the cycling paths and common routes on top of base maps; Google Maps offers this as an overlay layer.

In this recipe, we will introduce the bicycling layer and its usage as an overlay in the Google Maps JavaScript API.

Getting ready

Continuing from the previous recipe, *Adding the traffic layer*, will simplify our work, as we will only replace the `TransitLayer` object with the `BicyclingLayer` classes. Remember to copy the code of the original recipe.

How to do it...

The steps required for showing the cycling paths and routes are presented as follows:

1. Change the two lines containing `TransitLayer`, supplanting the `BicyclingLayer` object instead of the `TransitLayer` object:

    ```
    var bicyclingLayer = new google.maps.BicyclingLayer ();
    bicyclingLayer.setMap(map);
    ```

2. You can observe the cycling paths and routes on top of the Google Maps base maps as shown in the following screenshot:

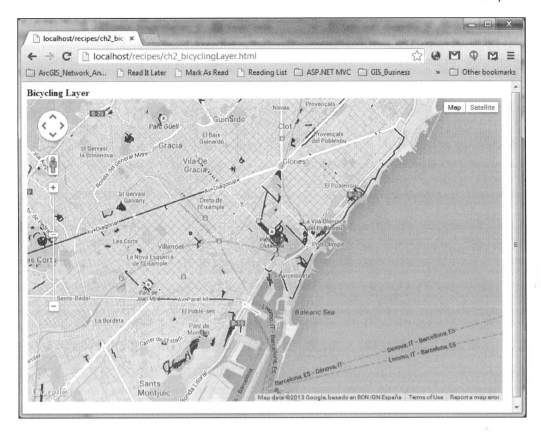

How it works...

The bicycling layer has its own subdivisions reflected in its styles; the dark green routes represent the paths dedicated for cycling, while the light green ones represent streets with bike lanes. Lastly, the dashed routes represent the bicycle paths and streets recommended for use, but are not dedicated.

The steps to display the bicycling layer are totally identical to the transit or traffic layers, so there is no additional detail for the specifics of the bicycling layer.

Adding the weather and cloud layers

Information on the temperature and weather conditions coupled with a map display is very common in weather reports on TVs; Google has put a feature in its API so that we can have this information in our own maps.

In this recipe, we will learn how to display weather-related information on top of base maps as overlays.

Getting ready

We can continue on from the *Creating a simple map in a custom DIV element* recipe from *Chapter 1, Google Maps JavaScript API Basics*, as we do not need to go into detail for the basic map display.

How to do it...

Here are the steps to show the respective temperatures and cloud conditions in your maps:

1. Add the weather library to the end of the reference for the Google Maps JavaScript API:

   ```
   <script type="text/javascript"
    src="https://maps.googleapis.com/maps/api/js?
     sensor=false&libraries=weather">
   </script>
   ```

2. Change the center and zoom of the map in the `mapOptions` object so that we can make use of the related layers:

   ```
   center: new google.maps.LatLng(38.0, 20.4),
   zoom: 5,
   ```

3. Construct an instance of the `google.maps.weatherLayer` object named `weatherLayer`:

   ```
   var weatherLayer = new google.maps.weather.WeatherLayer
   ({
      temperatureUnits:
      google.maps.weather.TemperatureUnit.CELCIUS
   });
   ```

4. Add `weatherLayer` to the map:

   ```
   weatherLayer.setMap(map);
   ```

5. Construct an instance of `google.maps.weather.cloudLayer` named `cloudLayer`:

    ```
    var cloudLayer = new google.maps.weather.CloudLayer();
    ```

6. Add `cloudLayer` to the map:

    ```
    cloudLayer.setMap(map);
    ```

7. You can see the respective temperatures and cloud conditions in your Google Maps application as shown in the following screenshot:

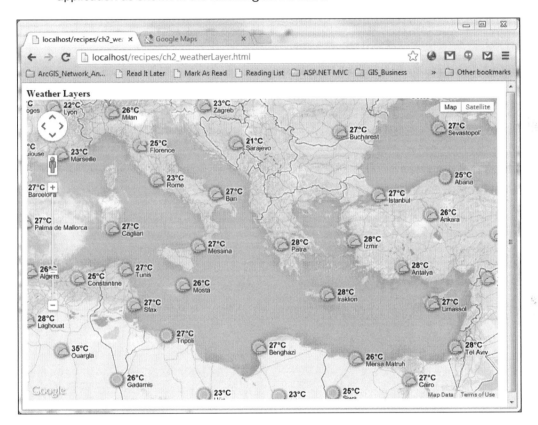

How it works...

In order to see weather-specific layers, we have to reference the `weather` libraries exactly in the same way we have referenced the `visualization` libraries for the heatmap overlays.

We have changed the center and zoom of the map for a purpose. The zoom is set to 5 as cloud layers are only visible between the zoom levels of 0 and 6. Also, we have arranged the center of the map in the Mediterranean to view a couple of countries with the weather information of their big cities.

It is important to note that together with the weather layers, administrative labels such as street and city names are not shown. Also, the weather layer is applicable between the zoom levels of 0 and 12.

In the construction of the `google.maps.weather.weatherLayer` object, you can specify the temperature units through the `temperatureUnits` property. The possible values are defined in `google.maps.weather.TemperatureUnit`:

```
google.maps.weather.TemperatureUnit.CELCIUS
google.maps.weather.TemperatureUnit.FAHRENHEIT
```

You can add the `weatherLayer` and `cloudLayer` layers to the map by calling their respective `setMap()` method and supplying the `map` object as the only argument.

Displaying the weather layer, you view the cities' weather conditions with the temperature information fed by `http://www.weather.com`. The icons displayed on top of the cities will change according to the real-time weather, whether it is the sun, clouds, or rain. Also, clicking on an icon will open a detailed popup showing the weather conditions for the next four days.

There's more...

You can tweak additional properties besides `temperatureUnits` for the `weatherLayer` object. You can suppress the detailed pop-up window or you can set the units for the wind speed and so on.

More about WeatherLayerOptions

The complete listing on `WeatherLayerOptions` can be found at `https://developers.google.com/maps/documentation/javascript/reference#WeatherLayerOptions`.

Adding the Panoramio layer

Panoramio is a geotagged photo-sharing website. This means you can upload your photos provided you geotag (georeference) them. Geotagging involves attaching a coordinate pair to the target object, whether it is a photo, video, or any other resource. You can find detailed information on how to use Panoramio at http://www.panoramio.com/.

You can view Panoramio photos on Google Maps, and this recipe will cover the basics of how to do it.

Getting ready

We can continue on from the *Creating a simple map in a custom DIV element* recipe from *Chapter 1, Google Maps JavaScript API Basics*, as map display basics are already covered here.

As always, please copy the original recipe before proceeding.

How to do it...

You can overlay the variety of Panoramio image stocks on top of Google Maps if you follow the steps presented:

1. Add the Panoramio library to the referenced libraries:

   ```
   <script type="text/javascript"
    src="https://maps.googleapis.com/maps/api/js?
    sensor=false&libraries=panoramio">
   </script>
   ```

2. Construct a new `google.maps.panoramio.PanoramioLayer()` object named `panoramioLayer` after the creation of the map object:

   ```
   var panoramioLayer = new
     google.maps.panoramio.PanoramioLayer();
   ```

3. Add the `panoramioLayer` object to the map:

   ```
   panoramioLayer.setMap(map);
   ```

4. You can now have the Panoramio images overlaid on top of Google Maps as shown in the following screenshot:

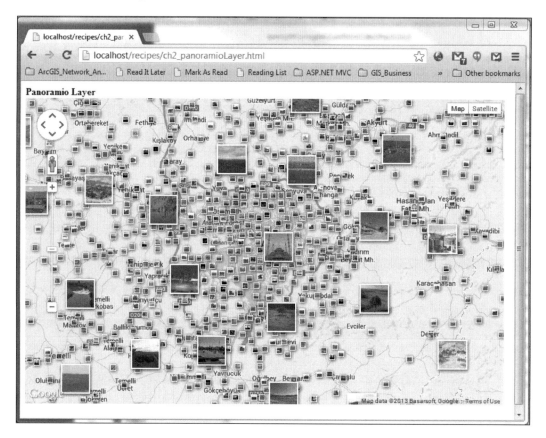

How it works...

Adding the Panoramio layer is technically no different from what we did in the previous recipe. We add the related reference library, construct the layer, and add it to the map in the same pattern.

You can click on the thumbnail photos and a detailed pop-up window will open. In this popup, you can view the photo in a larger size along with its name and the username of the person who uploaded the photo.

There's more...

The Panoramio layer provides extra capability to customize the overlay layer. For instance, you can restrict the photos by filtering tags using the `setTag()` method:

```
panoramioLayer.setTag("Eiffel");
```

This will filter the displayed thumbnails to the ones that include the `Eiffel` keyword in their tags.

Also, you can filter according to the user ID by calling the `setUserId()` method, supplying the `userId` string as an argument.

You can also suppress the detailed pop-up window that opens by using the `suppressInfoWindows` property that the `PanoramioLayer` object takes:

```
var panoramioLayer = new
  google.maps.panoramio.PanoramioLayer({
    suppressInfoWindows:true
});
```

More about PanoramioLayer

The complete listing on `PanoramioLayer` can be found at `https://developers.google.com/maps/documentation/javascript/reference#PanoramioLayerOptions`.

3
Adding Vector Layers

In this chapter, we will cover:

- ▶ Adding markers to maps
- ▶ Adding popups to markers or maps
- ▶ Adding lines to maps
- ▶ Adding polygons to maps
- ▶ Adding circles/rectangles to maps
- ▶ Adding animated lines to maps
- ▶ Adding the KML/GeoRSS layer
- ▶ Adding GeoJSON to the Google Maps JavaScript API
- ▶ Adding WKT to the Google Maps JavaScript API

Introduction

This chapter is about vector layers, which are completely different from raster layers. This chapter gives you the most common and important recipes that you may need while working with the Google Maps JavaScript API.

In the GIS world, both the vector and raster layers are used in different cases. Vectors are used for representing the Earth's features in most cases. For example, **Points of Interest** (**POI**), such as coffee shops or restaurants, are shown with points; rivers or roads are shown with polylines; and parks or buildings are shown with polygons. As it is seen here, there are three different vector types: point, polyline, and polygon. Remember that all vectors consist of points, which are the building blocks of vectors.

In the Google Maps JavaScript API, all types of vectors are called **overlays**. In addition to vectors, popups and symbols are also included in overlays. All the recipes related to them are included in this chapter.

Maps are mostly used for visualization, so static maps are not enough in some cases. Some animations added to polylines make a difference. For example, showing the flow direction with rivers is remarkable for scientists. The Google Maps JavaScript API also supports animated polylines, which is one of the recipes in this chapter.

The Google Maps JavaScript API is a great API with support for KML and GeoRSS, but some of the industry de facto standards are not supported out of the box, such as GeoJSON and WKT. GeoJSON and WKT are the most used vector publishing formats in the industry, especially in open source libraries. These formats will be supported by additional libraries, which are also included in this chapter.

Let's start to explore the recipes.

Adding markers to maps

Maps are used for many cases in websites, but the most used one shows the location of a company or business. The location of a company or business can be called a POI in the LBS or GIS sector and this is a point type of the vector layer. In the Google Maps JavaScript API, POIs or points are shown as **markers**.

This recipe shows how to add markers to maps using the `google.maps.LatLng` and `google.maps.Marker` classes.

Getting ready

In Chapter 1, Google Maps JavaScript API Basics, you learned how to create a map. So, only the additional code lines that will add markers are covered in this recipe.

You can find the source code at `Chapter 3/ch03_adding_markers.html`.

How to do it...

The following are the steps we need to add both standard and icon markers to maps:

1. Let's add the minimum and maximum values of latitudes and longitudes of **bounding box** (**BBOX**) to limit our random markers' area. This bounding box almost defines the area that **Turkey** covers. Also `markerId` is defined to name the random markers. All variables must be defined outside the function:

```
var minLat = 36,
    maxLat = 42,
    minLng = 25,
    maxLng = 44,
    markerId = 1;
```

2. Add the following function after the `initMap()` function. This function starts listening to the click events of the buttons:

```
function startButtonEvents() {
  document.getElementById('addStandardMarker').
    addEventListener('click', function(){
      addStandardMarker();
  });

  document.getElementById('addIconMarker' ).
    addEventListener('click', function(){
      addIconMarker();
  });
}
```

3. Add the following function after the `startButtonEvents()` function. This function creates a random latitude and longitude according to the values given at the beginning of this section and returns the `google.maps.LatLng` object.

```
function createRandomLatLng() {
  var deltaLat = maxLat - minLat;
  var deltaLng = maxLng - minLng;
  var rndNumLat = Math.random();
  var newLat = minLat + rndNumLat * deltaLat;
  var rndNumLng = Math.random();
  var newLng = minLng + rndNumLng * deltaLng;
  return new google.maps.LatLng(newLat, newLng);
}
```

4. Then, the `addStandardMarker()` function is added. This function creates the standard Google Maps red marker. It gets the random `LatLng` object value from the function created in the preceding step. There is a commented line in the code block that will be explained later:

```
function addStandardMarker() {
  var coordinate = createRandomLatLng();
  var marker = new google.maps.Marker({
    position: coordinate,
    map: map,
    title: 'Random Marker - ' + markerId
  });
// If you don't specify a Map during the initialization
//of the Marker you can add it later using the line
//below
//marker.setMap(map);
  markerId++;
}
```

5. There is also another function named `addIconMarker()` described in this step. This is used for adding random markers with random images:

```
function addIconMarker() {
  var markerIcons = ['coffee', 'restaurant_fish',
    'walkingtour', 'postal', 'airport'];
  var rndMarkerId = Math.floor(Math.random() *
    markerIcons.length);
  var coordinate = createRandomLatLng();
  var marker = new google.maps.Marker({
    position: coordinate,
    map: map,
    icon: 'img/' + markerIcons[rndMarkerId] + '.png',
    title: 'Random Marker - ' + markerId
  });
  markerId++;
}
```

6. Finally, we will add HTML tags to finish the code. These links will help to trigger the functions defined in event listeners:

```
<a id="addStandardMarker" href="#">Add Standard Marker</a>
<a id="addIconMarker" href="#">Add Icon Marker</a>
```

7. Go to your local URL where your HTML file is stored in your favorite browser and see the result. Initially, you will see an empty map. Then click on the links on the map to add random markers. The final map can be seen as shown in the following screenshot:

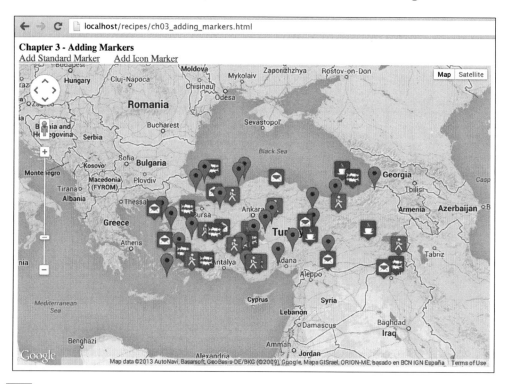

As seen in the preceding screenshot, we created a map with both the standard and icon markers.

How it works...

Google Maps uses the Web Mercator projection system for its tile system, but the coordinates are still in GPS coordinates based on WGS 84 Datum. Coordinates are based on latitudes and longitudes that are between -90 to 90 and -180 to 180 degrees respectively. The combination of a latitude and longitude defines a point on Earth. The Google Maps JavaScript API uses the `google.maps.LatLng` class to create a point. This class is also used in *Chapter 1, Google Maps JavaScript API Basics*, to set the center of a map. The following line defines the coordinates of **Istanbul, Turkey**:

```
var istanbul = new google.maps.LatLng(41.038627, 28.986933);
```

The `google.maps.Marker` class creates the marker with one required parameter, `google.maps.MarkerOptions`. The `MarkerOptions` class also has one required parameter that is named as `position`. This parameter gets the `google.maps.LatLng` object to define the coordinates of the marker. In the code, there are also the `map` and `title` parameters that are not required, but they are needed to show the marker on the map and set the title of the marker respectively. If you want to show the marker immediately after the creation of the marker, you should use the `map` parameter. But in some cases, you want to create markers and show them on the map later. In such a case, you should use the `setMap` method of `marker` with your map reference.

```
var marker = new google.maps.Marker({
    position: new google.maps.LatLng(41.038627, 28.986933)
});
marker.setMap(map);
```

If you want to remove the marker from the map, you must set the map value to null. Do not forget to keep a reference of your markers in order to remove them from the map:

```
marker.setMap(null);
```

Default markers with red icons are not suitable for all cases. The Google Maps JavaScript API lets you customize the icon of a marker. Basically, you should add the `icon` parameter to `google.maps.MarkerOptions` to customize the marker icon. This parameter accepts three different types: `String`, the `google.maps.Icon` object, or the `google.maps.Symbol` object. If you have a simple icon image, you will use the string type with a path to the image. Otherwise, you will create the icon or symbol objects to set a complex visualization for the marker. Showing an icon via a `String` parameter can be done as follows:

```
var marker = new google.maps.Marker({
    position: coordinate,
    icon: 'img/coffeeshop.png',
    title: 'My Coffee Shop'
});
```

There's more...

In this recipe, random coordinates are used to show markers. If you have a data source that includes coordinates, you could easily add them to the map with JavaScript techniques without changing anything while creating the marker. Please be sure about the JavaScript asynchronous behavior while adding markers to the map from external sources because your data will not be available when you need it due to asynchronous behavior.

See also

▸ The *Creating a simple map in a custom DIV element* recipe in *Chapter 1, Google Maps JavaScript API Basics*

Adding popups to markers or maps

Almost every mapping application has an ability to display information related to the features shown on it. Showing all the related information on the map at the same time is an impossible mission for a developer and it is also useless for users. Instead of showing all the information on the map, developers add interaction to points, polylines, or polygons that show the related information with different techniques such as popups or info windows.

Popups or info windows can hold anything that can be written in HTML tags, such as pictures, videos, or standard text.

You will see something like the following screenshot, if you get through to the end of the recipe:

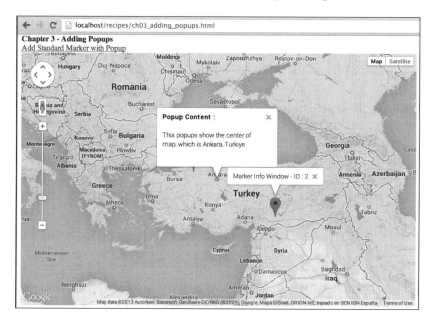

Getting ready

This recipe is the modified version of the previous recipe named *Adding markers to maps*.

You can find the source code at `Chapter 3/ch03_adding_popups.html`.

How to do it...

You can easily add popups to markers or maps by performing the following steps:

1. First, the `initMap()` function is modified by adding the following code lines after creating the `map` object. This will open an info window or popup at the center of the map when the map first initializes:

    ```
    var infowindow = new google.maps.InfoWindow({
      content: '<div style="width:200px; height:100px;
        "><b>Popup Content :</b><br><br>This popups show
        the center of map, which is Ankara, Turkiye</div>',
      position: new google.maps.LatLng(39.9078, 32.8252)
    });

    infowindow.open(map);
    ```

2. Next, add the following function to listen to the click events of the button defined in the HTML:

    ```
    function startButtonEvents() {
      document.getElementById('addStandardMarker').
        addEventListener('click', function(){
          addStandardMarker();
      });
    }
    ```

3. The `startButtonEvents()` function must be called on initializing the map, so the following line is added to the `initMap()` function after `map` is initialized:

    ```
    startButtonEvents();
    ```

4. Then, the `addStandardMarker()` function is modified by adding the following code lines after the creation of the marker:

    ```
    var infowindow = new google.maps.InfoWindow({
      content: 'Marker Info Window - ID : ' + markerId
    });

    google.maps.event.addListener(marker, 'click', function() {
      infowindow.open(map, marker);
    });
    ```

5. Go to your local URL where your HTML file is stored in your favorite browser and take a look at the result. You will see an info window at the beginning of the map. You will also click on the link on the map to add random markers, but these markers are different from the ones before because they will open a popup when the user clicks on them.

How it works...

The Google Maps JavaScript API has a default `InfoWindow` class to create info windows or popups. This class can be initialized in two ways. One way is to give a location at info windows options with the `LatLng` object. By using this, you can open a popup on the map wherever you want. This can be attached to a function or an event. For example, you can attach the `click` event to the map to query something from the server and show the result in the popup. This is common for the Google Maps JavaScript API. The following code creates an info window at the location of 39.9078 (latitude) and 32.8252 (longitude) with the HTML content. Its `open` method with the `map` input shows the info window attached to the given map reference:

```
var infowindow = new google.maps.InfoWindow({
content: '<div style="width:200px; height:100px; "><b>Popup
  Content :</b><br><br>This popups show the center of map,
    which is Ankara, Turkiye</div>',
  position: new google.maps.LatLng(39.9078, 32.8252)
});
infowindow.open(map);
```

Another way to use popups is by binding them to markers. Instead of giving a location, info windows will be anchored to a `marker` object. The `infoWindow` object given in the following code does not have a `position` property, which means it will be anchored to a `marker` object. Remember that `marker` objects are subclasses of the `MVCObject` class in Google Maps JavaScript API. They are a type of anchor parameter of the `open` method of the `InfoWindow` class:

```
var infowindow = new google.maps.InfoWindow({
  content: 'Marker Info Window - ID : ' + markerId
});
google.maps.event.addListener(marker, 'click', function() {
  infowindow.open(map, marker);
});
```

There is an event attached to `marker` in the preceding code, which is the subject of *Chapter 5, Understanding Google Maps JavaScript API Events*. So use the code as it is written; this will be explained in detail later, but basically this code snippet listens to the `marker` object and opens the created `infowindow` object on the `click` event.

As it is seen in this recipe, you can use both simple strings and complex HTML content within the info windows. This means you can even add YouTube videos or Flash content inside info windows.

See also

▶ The *Creating a simple map in a custom DIV element* recipe in *Chapter 1, Google Maps JavaScript API Basics*

▶ The *Adding markers to maps* recipe

Adding lines to maps

Lines or polylines in GIS are an array of points connected to each other to show features on Earth such as roads, paths, or rivers. The properties of polylines on maps are similar to the properties of features represented on Earth. For example, a road is differentiated on Earth by its color and width. The same properties are also defined in the Google Maps JavaScript API to exactly represent the road on the map.

This recipe is focused on showing lines/polylines on a map to show a route from **Istanbul** to **Ankara**.

Getting ready

This recipe uses the same map creation process defined in *Chapter 1, Google Maps JavaScript API Basics*, but there are some minor changes in the zoom level and center coordinates to show the route in detail.

You can find the source code at Chapter 3/ch03_adding_lines.html.

How to do it...

If you want to add line-type geometries to your map, you should perform the following steps:

1. Let's open our first recipe's source code mentioned in *Chapter 1, Google Maps JavaScript API Basics*, and save it as adding_lines.html.

2. Then, add the following lines of code after defining the map object at the beginning of the JavaScript part of the code. The array defined in this step is the route coordinates in latitudes and longitudes from **Istanbul** to **Ankara**:

```
var lineCoordinates = [
    [41.01306,29.14672],[40.8096,29.4818],
    [40.7971,29.9761],[40.7181,30.4980],
    [40.8429,31.0253],[40.7430,31.6241],
    [40.7472,32.1899],[39.9097,32.8216]
];
```

3. Then, create the `addPolyline` function:

```
function addPolyline () {


}
```

4. We need to create a new array composed of `LatLng` objects from the array defined at the beginning in the function:

```
//First we iterate over the coordinates array to create a
// new array which includes objects of LatLng class.
var pointCount = lineCoordinates.length;
var linePath = [];
for (var i=0; i < pointCount; i++) {
  var tempLatLng = new google.maps.LatLng(
    lineCoordinates[i][0] , lineCoordinates[i][1]
  );
  linePath.push(tempLatLng);
}
```

5. Then, we need to create the `polyline` object as follows:

```
//Polyline properties are defined below
var lineOptions = {
  path: linePath,
  strokeWeight: 7,
  strokeColor: '#FF0000',
  strokeOpacity: 0.8
}
var polyline = new google.maps.Polyline(lineOptions);
```

6. Let's add the `polyline` object to `map`:

```
//Polyline is set to current map.
polyline.setMap(map);
```

7. Now, call the `addPolyline()` function at the end of the `initMap()` function as follows:

```
addPolyline();
```

8. Go to your local URL where your HTML file is stored in your favorite browser and see the result. You will see a red route from **Istanbul** to **Ankara** on the map, as shown in the following screenshot:

Thus, we have successfully created a map with a line-type geometry on it, which is the route from one place to another in this case.

How it works...

As stated before, polylines consist of points. Points are defined by the `LatLng` class in the Google Maps JavaScript API, so an array of latitudes and longitudes should be converted to the `LatLng` array. The following code block creates a new array composed of `LatLng` objects. To do this, a classic approach of iterating an array via a loop is used as follows:

```
var pointCount = lineCoordinates.length;
var linePath = [];
for (var i=0; i < pointCount; i++) {
  var tempLatLng = new google.maps.LatLng(lineCoordinates[i][0],
    lineCoordinates[i][1]);
  linePath.push(tempLatLng);
}
```

A route will be created by the `Polyline` class that takes the instance of the `PolylineOptions` class as a parameter. There are many properties of the `PolylineOptions` class, but we only added the most used ones.

The `path` property that defines the route feature contains an array of `LatLng` objects. The `strokeWeight` property is used in order to define the width of the line in pixels. The `strokeColor` property defines the color of the line in the `String` type as a `HEX` format with a leading # symbol.

The `strokeOpacity` property usage can be optional, but it can be useful while showing multiple layers. This parameter gets a value from 0.0 to 1.0. 0.0 means your line is invisible and 1.0 means your line is not transparent. If you have multiple layers, you should define the opacity of your lines to show other features or layers.

This recipe shows the static route defined in the HTML; but in some cases, you can load data from a remote source. In this case, you should change the path array via the method of the `Polyline` class `setPath()`. This method gets the same array defined in the `PolylineOptions` class. For example, you create a new path array named `newRoute`. To change the coordinates to the new route, you should call the following:

```
polyline.setPath(newRoute);
```

If you want to remove `polyline` completely from the map, then you should set the `map` property to null or call the `setMap(null)` method of the `Polyline` class.

See also

▶ The *Creating a simple map in a custom DIV element* recipe in *Chapter 1, Google Maps JavaScript API Basics*

▶ The *Adding polygons to maps* recipe

Adding polygons to maps

Polygons are similar to polylines that are an array of points connected to each other. However, polygons are closed loops to show Earth features such as parks, parcels, or regions. In addition to the properties of polylines, polygons have a fill region inside.

This recipe is focused on showing polygons on a map to show a region around **Ankara**.

Getting ready

This recipe uses the same map-creation process defined in *Chapter 1, Google Maps JavaScript API Basics*, but there are some minor changes in the `zoom` level and center coordinates to show the region in detail.

You can find the source code at `Chapter 3/ch03_adding_polygons.html`.

How to do it...

If you perform the following steps, you can add polygon-type geometries to your map:

1. Let's open our first recipe's source code mentioned in *Chapter 1, Google Maps JavaScript API Basics*, and save it as `adding_polygons.html`.

2. Then, add the following lines of code after defining the map object at the beginning of the JavaScript part. The array defined in this step is the area coordinates of a random region in latitudes and longitudes around **Ankara**:

```
var areaCoordinates = [
    [40.0192,32.6953], [39.9434,32.5854],
    [39.7536,32.6898], [39.8465,32.8106],
    [39.9139,33.0084], [40.0318,32.9260],
    [40.0402,32.7832], [40.0192,32.6953]
];
```

3. Then create the `addPolygon` function:

```
function addPolygon () {


}
```

4. We need to create a new array composed of `LatLng` objects from the array defined at the beginning in the function:

```
//First we iterate over the coordinates array to create a
// new array which includes objects of LatLng class.
var pointCount = areaCoordinates.length;
var areaPath = [];
for (var i=0; i < pointCount; i++) {
  var tempLatLng = new google.maps.LatLng(
    areaCoordinates[i][0] , areaCoordinates[i][1]);
  areaPath.push(tempLatLng);
}
```

5. Then, we need to create the `polygon` object as follows:

```
//Polygon properties are defined below
var polygonOptions = {
  paths: areaPath,
  strokeColor: '#FF0000 ,
  strokeOpacity: 0.9,
  strokeWeight: 3,
  fillColor: '#FFFF00',
  fillOpacity: 0.25
}
var polygon = new google.maps.Polygon(polygonOptions);
```

6. Let's add the `polygon` object to `map`:

```
//Polygon is set to current map.
polygon.setMap(map);
```

7. Now, call the `addPolygon()` function at end of the `initMap()` function as follows:

```
addPolygon();
```

8. Go to your local URL where your HTML file is stored in your favorite browser and see the result. You will see a yellow region surrounded by a red boundary around **Ankara**, as shown in the following screenshot:

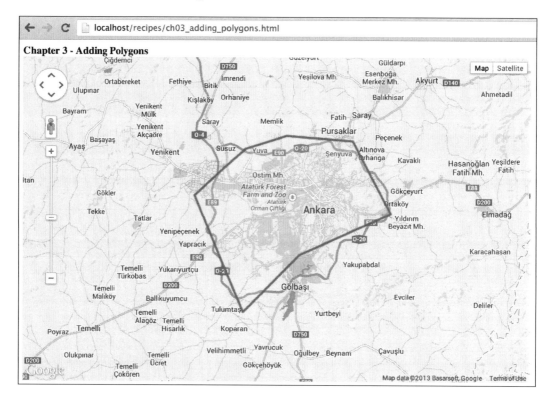

9. This is how we add polygon-type geometry to our map.

How it works...

The `Polygon` class is much like the `Polyline` class in the Google Maps JavaScript API. There are minor differences between the `Polyline` and `Polygon` classes, so we will get into the details of these differences only in this recipe. Please refer to the previous recipe for more details.

As stated in the previous recipe, the `Polygon` class creates objects with the help of the `PolygonOptions` class that includes many parameters for polygons. There are `path`, `strokeWeight`, `strokeColor`, and `strokeOpacity` parameters shared with the `PolylineOptions` class. The usage and purpose of these parameters are the same for both polygons and polylines. The main difference is that polygons fill an area. There must be some new parameters to define the polygon fill.

The `fillColor` property defines the color of the fill area in the `String` type as a HEX format with a leading # symbol. The `fillOpacity` property usage can be optional, but it can also be useful while showing multiple layers at the same time. This parameter gets a value from 0.0 to 1.0. 0.0 means your polygon is invisible and 1.0 means your polygon is not transparent. This parameter is more important in polygons than in polylines because polygons fill areas, which can be an obstacle for some markers or polylines.

Adding or removing the polygons has the same API usage as polylines, so there is no need to talk about it here.

One last thing to mention is that polygons are a closed version of polylines, so we add the same coordinates both at the start and end. This is a good usage but not necessary. Even if you do not add the end coordinates, which are the same as the start coordinates, the Google Maps JavaScript API will close the polygon without any errors.

See also

▶ The *Creating a simple map in a custom DIV element* recipe in *Chapter 1, Google Maps JavaScript API Basics*

▶ The *Adding lines to maps* recipe

Adding circles/rectangles to maps

Circles and rectangles are similar to polygons in that they have stroke and fill colors, weights, and opacities. The main difference between them and polygons is in defining the geometry. As seen in the previous recipes, the `PolygonOptions` class has a `path` parameter that consists of an array of `LatLng` objects. On the other side, the `CircleOptions` class has the `center` and `radius` parameters, and the `RectangleOptions` class has bounds parameters for defining the geometry of the `Circle` and `Rectangle` classes respectively.

In this recipe, we will go through adding circles according to the population of cities and a rectangle to map bounding to **Turkey**. The result map will show the bounding box of **Turkey** and major cities' population in a graph.

Getting ready

In this recipe, we will use the first recipe defined in *Chapter 1, Google Maps JavaScript API Basics*, as a template in order to skip map creation.

You can find the source code at `Chapter 3/ch03_circle_rectangle.html`.

How to do it...

Adding circles or rectangles to your map is quite easy if you perform the following steps:

1. Let's start by creating a new empty file named `circles_rectangles.html`. Then, copy all the code in the HTML file that was introduced in the *Creating a simple map in a custom DIV element* recipe of *Chapter 1, Google Maps JavaScript API Basics*, and paste it into a new file.

2. Add the following lines for defining the global variables used in the functions:

```
// Defining coordinates and populations of major cities in
// Turkey as Ankara, Istanbul and Izmir
var cities = [{
  center: new google.maps.LatLng(39.926588, 32.854614),
  population : 4630000
},
{
  center: new google.maps.LatLng(41.013066, 28.976440),
  population : 13710000
},
{
  center: new google.maps.LatLng(38.427774, 27.130737),
  population : 3401000
}
];

// Defining the corner coordinates for bounding box of
// Turkey
var bboxSouthWest = new google.maps.LatLng(35.817813,
  26.047461);
var bboxNorthEast = new google.maps.LatLng(42.149293,
  44.774902);
```

3. Then, add the `addCircle()` and `addRectangle()` functions before the `initMap()` function:

```
function addCircle() {

}

function addRectangle() {

}
```

4. Now, add the following code block into the `addCircle()` function to initialize the circles:

```
// Iterating over the cities array to add each of them to // map
for (var i=0; i < cities.length; i++) {
  var circleOptions = {
    fillColor: '#FFFF00',
    fillOpacity: 0.55,
    strokeColor: '#FF0000',
    strokeOpacity: 0.7,
    strokeWeight: 1,
    center: cities[i].center,
    radius: cities[i].population / 100
  };
  cityCircle = new google.maps.Circle(circleOptions);
  cityCircle.setMap(map);
}
```

5. Next, add the following lines to the `addRectangle()` function to initialize the rectangle:

```
var bounds = new google.maps.LatLngBounds(bboxSouthWest,
  bboxNorthEast);
var rectOptions = {
  fillColor: '#A19E98',
  fillOpacity: 0.45,
  strokeColor: '#FF0000',
  strokeOpacity: 0.0,
  strokeWeight: 1,
  map: map,
  bounds: bounds
};

var rectangle = new google.maps.Rectangle(rectOptions);
```

6. Then, change the `zoom` level and `center` of the map according to your needs in the `initMap()` function. This example uses the following parameters:

```
var mapOptions = {
  center: new google.maps.LatLng(39.9046, 32.75926),
  zoom: 5,
  mapTypeId: google.maps.MapTypeId.ROADMAP
};
```

7. Finally, add the `addRectangle()` and `addCircle()` functions at the end of the `initMap()` function as follows:

```
addRectangle();
addCircle();
```

8. Go to your local URL where your `circles_rectangles.html` file is stored in your favorite browser and take a look at the result. You will see the map with three circles and a grey rectangle behind them, as shown in the following screenshot:

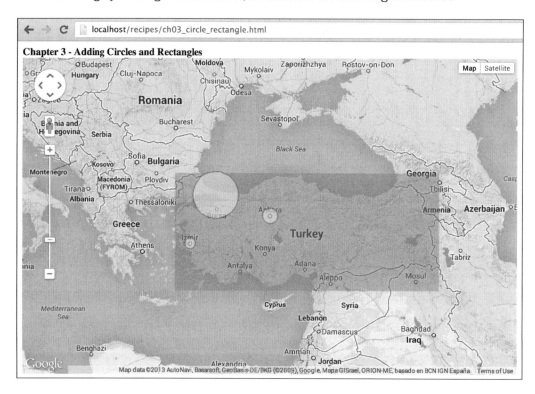

This is the result of the recipe that shows both the circles and rectangles at the same time on the map. This can be a good example to visualize your tabular data on maps.

How it works...

First, let's talk about the circles. Circles are types of polygons, except they are defined by a center in the `LatLng` object with a radius in meters instead of paths. Other parameters are the same as the `PolygonOptions` class.

In this recipe, first three cities of **Ankara**, **Istanbul**, and **Izmir**, are selected. The center and the population of these cities are defined using JSON objects in the array. The centers of cities are defined in `LatLng` objects, so there is no need for extra conversion. The following code block iterates over the cities' array and creates a circle with a `center` parameter defined in the JSON object:

```
var citiesLen = cities.length;
for (var i=0; i < citiesLen; i++) {
```

```
      var circleOptions = {
        fillColor: '#FFFF00',
        fillOpacity: 0.55,
        strokeColor: '#FF0000',
        strokeOpacity: 0.7,
        strokeWeight: 1,
        center: cities[i].center,
        radius: cities[i].population / 100
      };
      cityCircle = new google.maps.Circle(circleOptions);
      cityCircle.setMap(map);
   }
```

The `radius` parameter is defined as a parameter of population, that is, population divided by
`100`; it shows the magnitude of a population. As seen on the map, the higher the population,
the larger the circle. This can be used as a visualization of the population distribution
without knowing the exact numbers. As seen, the other parameters, such as `fillColor`,
`fillOpacity`, `strokeColor`, `strokeOpacity`, and `strokeWeight`, are used in the same
way as in the `PolygonOptions` class. The `setMap()` function is also used as it is used in
the polygon or polyline recipes.

The other element, the rectangle, is also a type of polygon, except that its geometry is defined
by the `LatLngBounds` object. In theory, the `LatLngBounds` object is composed of two
`LatLng` objects that are defined as the southwest and northeast coordinates of a rectangle.
These coordinates can also be defined as the minimum and maximum points of latitudes
and longitudes. In this recipe, the rectangle defined shows the bounding box of **Turkey**. BBOX
can be used for simple geometric calculations such as "point in polygon" or "intersection".
Using BBOX in calculations gives fast results because of the simple geometry, but there is
always an error in this calculation. As seen in the preceding screenshot, some areas are not
on the border of **Turkey**, but they are in the bounding box. If you want to get the geometries
to intersect with **Turkey** using the BBOX method, you can easily get other geometries that are
outside the real geometry object of **Turkey**. As you can see, using the BBOX approach gets
some geometries at the intersection of BBOX that can be outside the real area. The usage of
the `Rectangle` class is as follows:

```
var bounds = new google.maps.LatLngBounds(bboxSouthWest,
   bboxNorthEast);

var rectOptions = {
   fillColor: '#A19E98',
   fillOpacity: 0.45,
   strokeColor: '#FF0000',
   strokeOpacity: 0.0,
   strokeWeight: 1,
   map: map,
   bounds: bounds
};
var rectangle = new google.maps.Rectangle(rectOptions);
```

The Google Maps JavaScript API gives many opportunities to developers that can make their life easier. Circles and rectangles can both be used for geometries or other visualization techniques in your applications.

There's more...

In this recipe, we add circles and rectangles without any order. The most recently added one is shown in the preceding map. In this example, a rectangle is added first in order to show the circles better. If you want to change the display order of markers, info windows, polylines, polygons, circles, or rectangles, you should change the zIndex parameter of the option classes or change them via the setZIndex(3) or setOptions({ zIndex: 3 }) methods.

See also

▸   The *Creating a simple map in a custom DIV element* recipe in *Chapter 1, Google Maps JavaScript API Basics*

▸   The *Adding lines to maps* recipe

▸   The *Adding polygons to maps* recipe

Adding animated lines to maps

Polylines are the representations of Earth's features on the Earth, but sometimes, they are not enough to show the mobility of Earth features. For example, a river can be shown with the help of polylines, but the flow direction of the river can't be demonstrated by the polylines alone. Animating polylines can be a solution to show the mobility of Earth features. The flow direction of a river can be shown with the help of animated polylines.

The Google Maps JavaScript API has a symbol feature that can add vector-based images to a polyline in the form of a symbol. You can create your own symbol with the help of the Symbol class, or you can also use the predefined symbols that are accessed from the SymbolPath class.

In this recipe, we will create an animated polyline from the previous recipe. This animation shows that a car is moving from **Istanbul** to **Ankara**.

Getting ready

In this recipe, we will use the fourth recipe of this chapter as a template.

You can find the source code at Chapter 3/ch03_animating_line.html.

How to do it...

The following are the steps that are needed to add animated line-type geometries to your map:

1. First, start by copying the contents of `ch03_adding_lines.html` to your new HTML file.

2. Then, add the following line after the `map` object to make it global. This is used while animating the line:

```
var polyline;
```

3. Change the function name from `addPolyline()` to `addAnimatedPolyline()` and add the following code block to define your symbol:

```
// Defining arrow symbol
var arrowSymbol = {
  strokeColor: '#000',
  scale: 3,
  path: google.maps.SymbolPath.FORWARD_CLOSED_ARROW
};
```

4. Next, change the polyline options as follows:

```
var lineOptions = {
  path: linePath,
  icons: [{
    icon: arrowSymbol,
    offset: '100%'
  }],
  strokeWeight: 3,
  strokeColor: '#FF0000',
  strokeOpacity: 0.8
}
```

5. Now, add the following function call to start the animation that will be defined right after the following step:

```
// Calling the arrow animation function
animateArrow();
```

6. Add the following function block before the `initMap()` function:

```
function animateArrow() {
  var counter = 0;
  var accessVar = window.setInterval(function() {
    counter = (counter + 1) % 200;
    var arrows = polyline.get('icons');
    arrows[0].offset = (counter / 2) + '%';
    polyline.set('icons', arrows);
  }, 50);
}
```

7. Finally, change the function call from `addPolyline()` to `addAnimatedPolyline()` in the `initMap()` function to add the new animated polyline:

    ```
    addAnimatedPolyline();
    ```

8. Go to your local URL where your HTML file is stored in your favorite browser and take a look at the result. You will see an arrow animating animating the route from **Istanbul** to **Ankara** on the map, as shown in the following screenshot:

As a result of this recipe, we can add the animated line-type geometry to our map, which shows the movement of a vehicle on a route.

How it works...

Animating polylines includes a trick with the JavaScript `setInterval` method and the Google Maps JavaScript API's icons property of the `PolylineOptions` class. As stated, you can create your own symbol or use the predefined ones.

Predefined symbols can be accessible via the `SymbolPath` class, which is shown in the following screenshot, as it is in the Google Maps JavaScript API document:

Name	Description	Example
google.maps.SymbolPath.CIRCLE	A circle.	O
google.maps.SymbolPath.BACKWARD_CLOSED_ARROW	A backward-pointing arrow that is closed on all sides.	∀
google.maps.SymbolPath.FORWARD_CLOSED_ARROW	A forward-pointing arrow that is closed on all sides.	A
google.maps.SymbolPath.BACKWARD_OPEN_ARROW	A backward-pointing arrow that is open on one side.	V
google.maps.SymbolPath.FORWARD_OPEN_ARROW	A forward-pointing arrow that is open on one side.	∧

In this recipe, we will use the `FORWARD_CLOSED_ARROW` type. This symbol is defined as follows:

```
var arrowSymbol = {
    strokeColor: '#000',
    scale: 3,
    path: google.maps.SymbolPath.FORWARD_CLOSED_ARROW
};
```

The `strokeColor` property is used to define the color of the symbol. The `path` property is used for defining the symbol type and the `scale` property is used for the size of the symbol. You can also change the `fillColor` and `fillOpacity` properties of predefined symbols like in polygons.

As seen in the preceding screenshot, the predefined symbols are limited. If you need more types of symbols, you should define them yourself in the `Symbol` class. You need to define custom symbols via the `path` property of the `Symbol` class with the **SVG path notation**.

The SVG path notation is the definition of the shape in SVG commands such as `moveto` (M), `lineto` (L), or `closepath` (Z). For example, the following path notation defines a triangle:

```
var triangle = 'M 100 100 L 300 100 L 200 300 Z';
```

The explanation of the path notation is as follows: move to point (`100,100`), draw a horizontal line from `100,100` to `300, 100`, and draw a second line from (`300,100`) to (`200, 300`). This shape appears as a triangle. Finally, the `Z` command is used to close the path. You can draw any shape with this notation, but you should be aware of the area that will be available for the map use. The Google Maps JavaScript API allows a 22 x 22 px square area to show a defined shape. If the shape is larger than this area, you should use the `scale` parameter to fit the shape into the area. The following code block will change the predefined arrow shape to a yellow triangle moving on the same route:

```
var arrowSymbol = {
    path : 'M 100 100 L 300 100 L 200 300 Z',
    anchor: new google.maps.Point(175,175),
    scale: 0.15,
    fillColor: '#FFFF00',
    fillOpacity: 0.8,
    strokeColor: '#000000',
    strokeWeight: 3
};
```

If you noticed, there is an additional parameter named `anchor`. This parameter is used to define the position of the symbol relative to the polyline. If you do not add this parameter, your symbol will be pinned to the polyline from the (0,0) point as a default. In general, using the center of the symbol as an `anchor` point gives the best result. The `anchor` parameter accepts the `Point` class. It also gets its x and y parameters in pixels.

The trickiest part of this recipe is the animation. In the `animateArrow()` function, we define a trigger that animates the symbol defined before via the `window.setInterval` method at every 50 milliseconds. An anonymous function is defined in this trigger as follows:

```
function() {
  counter = (counter + 1) % 200;
  var arrows = polyline.get('icons');
  arrows[0].offset = (counter / 2) + '%';
  polyline.set('icons', arrows);
}
```

This function gets the first object of the icons array and changes the `offset` parameter of the defined icon with the changing parameter according to the `counter` variable. Running this function every 50 milliseconds moves the symbol over the polyline.

In the anonymous function, you may have noticed that the polyline object has the `get()` and `set()` methods, which are not defined in the documentation. Since the `Polyline` class extends the `MVCObject` class, we can also use the methods of the `MVCObject` class. So, we can use the `get()` and `set()` methods of the parent class.

Using symbols and timers can make different visualizations on the map without the need of an extra library in addition to the Google Maps JavaScript API.

There's more...

SVG is the abbreviation of **Scalable Vector Graphics**. It is an XML-based vector image format for two-dimensional graphics that support interactivity and animation. SVG is supported by all modern browsers. It can be a good solution for mapping platforms in some cases, like this one. SVG is a completely different subject, which is out of the scope of this book.

More about SVG path notation

More details can be found on the W3C site (`http://www.w3.org/TR/SVG/paths.html#PathData`). There is also some editing software to get path notations without learning the language. The following address can be used for creating SVG and getting the path notation: `http://svg-edit.googlecode.com/svn/branches/2.6/editor/svg-editor.html`.

See also

▸ The *Creating a simple map in a custom DIV element* recipe in *Chapter 1, Google Maps JavaScript API Basics*

▸ The *Adding lines to maps* recipe

Adding KML/GeoRSS layers

Keyhole Markup Language (**KML**) has been introduced in Google Earth, which was originally named Keyhole Earth Viewer before Google bought it. KML became an OGC standard in 2008. It is an XML notation for showing features in geo-enabled viewers. **GeoRSS** is also an emerging standard for sharing Earth features to show in geo-enabled viewers mostly used by web feeds or services. Both these standards can be consumable with the Google Maps JavaScript API.

In this recipe, dynamic services will be consumed via the Google Maps JavaScript API. We will use the **U.S. Geological Survey** (**USGS**) web services to show recent earthquakes on maps. These services are updated regularly to reflect recent events.

Getting ready

In this recipe, we will use the simple map recipe introduced in *Chapter 1, Google Maps JavaScript API Basics*, as a template.

The source code of this recipe is at `Chapter 3/ch03_kml_georss.html`.

How to do it...

You can add your KML/GeoRSS files to your map if you perform the following steps:

1. First, start by copying the contents of `ch01_simple_map.html` to our new HTML file.

2. Next, define the following variables as global variables:

   ```
   var georssLayer, kmlLayer;
   ```

3. Add the following function after defining the global variables. This function triggers the adding of the GeoRSS feed to the map:

   ```
   function addGeoRSSLayer() {
     georssLayer = new google.maps.KmlLayer(
       'http://earthquake.usgs.gov/earthquakes/feed/v1.0/
       summary/4.5_month.atom');
     georssLayer.setMap(map);
   }
   ```

4. Then, add the other function after the previous one. This function also triggers adding the KML feed to the map:

   ```
   function addKMLLayer() {
     kmlLayer = new google.maps.KmlLayer('
       http://earthquake.usgs.gov/
       earthquakes/feed/v1.0/summary/2.5_month_depth.kml');
     kmlLayer.setMap(map);
   }
   ```

5. Now, add the following function, `clearMap()`, before the `initMap()` function:

```
function clearMap() {
  if (georssLayer != undefined) {
    georssLayer.setMap(null);
    georssLayer = null;
  }

  if (kmlLayer != undefined) {
    kmlLayer.setMap(null);
    kmlLayer = null;
  }
}
```

6. Next, add the following function to listen to the click events of the buttons defined in the HTML in step 8:

```
function startButtonEvents () {
  document.getElementById('linkGeoRSS'
    ).addEventListener('click', function(){
      addGeoRSSLayer();
  });
  document.getElementById('linkKML'
    ).addEventListener('click', function(){
      addKMLLayer();
  });
  document.getElementById('linkClearMap'
    ).addEventListener('click', function(){
      clearMap();
  });
}
```

7. The `startButtonEvents` function must be called on initializing the map, so the following line is added to the HTML file after the map gets initialized:

```
startButtonEvents();
```

8. Finally, add the following lines to the HTML body tag to trigger functions on clicking the links:

```
<a id="linkGeoRSS" href="#">Add GeoRSS Layer</a>
<a id="linkKML" href="#">Add KML Layer</a>
<a id="linkClearMap" href="#">Clear Map</a>
```

9. Go to your local URL where your HTML file is stored in your favorite browser and take a look at the result. You will see an empty map at the beginning. When you click on the links on the map, you will see two different layers on the map as follows:

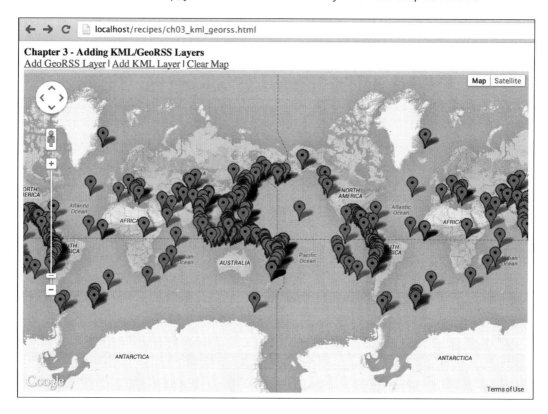

As seen in the preceding screenshot, you can easily add your GeoRSS files or services to the map with the Google Maps JavaScript API.

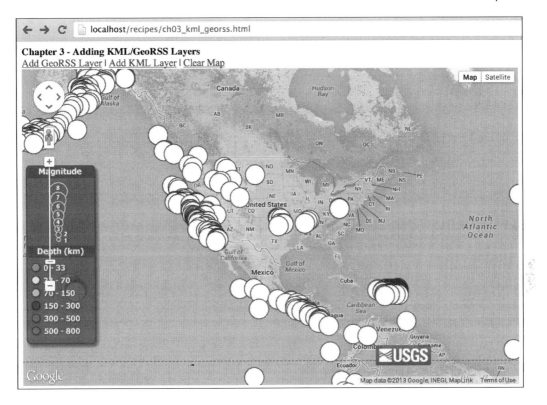

This is the result of adding the KML layer to your map. With Google Maps JavaScript API, you can easily add your KML files or services to the map.

How it works...

Adding the KML/GeoRSS layer is the simplest one. There is only one class for adding both the layers, named `KmlLayer`. This class reads the KML or GeoRSS feed from local or remote locations and decides what to render. The usage of the class is very simple:

```
var vectorLayer = new google.maps.KmlLayer('URL_TO_FEED');
```

After creating the layer, you must set the map with the `setMap(map)` method to show the layer on the map. If you want to remove the layer from the map, you must use the `setMap(null)` method as described earlier in the chapter.

Remember that Google Maps JavaScript API v3 does not have any function to clear all layers or overlays like in v2. All the responsibility to handle the layer states is on your shoulders. In practice, the Google Maps JavaScript API documentation suggests you hold all layers in an array and manage your own add/remove functions via the `setMap()` method. As we did in the `clearMap()` function, we check if a layer is defined. If it is, we remove it; otherwise we do nothing, so that we do not get an error.

See also

▶ The *Creating a simple map in a custom DIV element* recipe in *Chapter 1, Google Maps JavaScript API Basics*

Adding GeoJSON to the Google Maps JavaScript API

XML is the first hero of services in the Web 2.0 zone. With the help of XML, services or machines can easily communicate between them. XML can also be readable by humans. But after browser evolution, JSON has become much more popular due to its native readability for JavaScript and its lightweight compared to XML. GeoJSON is a form of JSON that includes collections of simple features such as points, polylines, or polygons. GeoJSON is not a standard of OGC, but it is a new de facto standard used by most GIS software or services.

The Google Maps JavaScript API does not support GeoJSON natively, but GeoJSON support will be added with a few lines of coding or with some additional libraries. With coding, we will go through the JSON format and read the coordinates one by one. Then, we will show the feature on the map according to its type, which can be point, polyline, or polygon.

In this recipe, we will read GeoJSON from a local file via the jQuery functions and show them on the map. This GeoJSON file is composed of a simplified version of the **Ankara** province border, a sample river, and some POIs.

Getting ready

In this recipe, we will use the simple map recipe introduced in *Chapter 1, Google Maps JavaScript API Basics*, as a template.

You can find the source code at `Chapter 3/ch03_adding_geojson.html`.

How to do it...

If you perform the following steps, you can add your GeoJSON files to your map:

1. First, start by copying the contents of `ch01_simple_map.html` to our new HTML file.

2. Next, we will add a jQuery JavaScript library to make it easy to access local or remote GeoJSON files. In this recipe, we will add the library from Google CDN. This block will be added in the `<head>` section before the Google Maps JavaScript API.

   ```
   <script src="//ajax.googleapis.com/
      ajax/libs/jquery/1.10.2/jquery.min.js"></script>
   ```

3. Then, add the following `drawGeometry()` function after defining the global `map` variable. This function draws each geometry read from the GeoJSON file. We have three types of geometries, so we will switch blocks for each type:

```
function drawGeometry(geom) {


}
```

4. Now, add the following `if` block in the new function. This block will add geometry if its type is `Point`:

```
if (geom.type == 'Point') {
  var coordinate = new
    google.maps.LatLng(geom.coordinates[1],
    geom.coordinates[0]);
  var marker = new google.maps.Marker({
    position: coordinate,
    map: map,
    title: 'Marker'
  });
}
```

5. Next, the `if` block is for `LineString` that shows polylines on the map:

```
else if (geom.type == 'LineString') {
  var pointCount = geom.coordinates.length;
  var linePath = [];
  for (var i=0; i < pointCount; i++) {
    var tempLatLng = new
      google.maps.LatLng(geom.coordinates[i][1],
      geom.coordinates[i][0]);
    linePath.push(tempLatLng);
  }

  var lineOptions = {
    path: linePath,
    strokeWeight: 7,
    strokeColor: '#19A3FF',
    strokeOpacity: 0.8,
    map: map
  };
  var polyline = new google.maps.Polyline(lineOptions);
}
```

6. Finally, the `if` block is used for showing the polygons as follows:

```
else if (geom.type == 'Polygon') {
  var pointCount = geom.coordinates[0].length;
```

```
        var areaPath = [];
        for (var i=0; i < pointCount; i++) {
            var tempLatLng = new google.maps.LatLng(
                geom.coordinates[0][i][1],
                geom.coordinates[0][i][0]);
            areaPath.push(tempLatLng);
        }

        var polygonOptions = {
            paths: areaPath,
            strokeColor: '#FF0000',
            strokeOpacity: 0.9,
            strokeWeight: 3,
            fillColor: '#FFFF00',
            fillOpacity: 0.25,
            map: map
        };

        var polygon = new google.maps.Polygon(polygonOptions);
    }
```

7. Then, add the following function to read the GeoJSON file and iterate over the geometries:

```
function parseGeoJSON() {
    $.getJSON('geojson.js', function(data) {
        $.each(data.features, function(key, val) {
            drawGeometry(val.geometry);
        });
    });
}
```

8. Finally, call the `parseGeoJSON()` function at the end of the `initMap()` function:

```
parseGeoJSON();
```

9. Go to your local URL where your HTML file is stored in your favorite browser and see the result. You will see three different types of geometries on the map with their styles as follows:

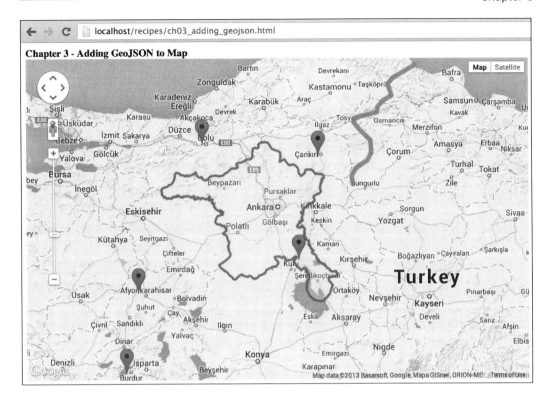

Thus, we have successfully added our GeoJSON files to the map with multiple types of geometries.

How it works...

GeoJSON is a vector format that we described earlier. It is a form of JSON. The GeoJSON format can consist of different types of the same file as follows:

```
{ "type": "FeatureCollection",
  "features": [
    { "type": "Feature",
      "geometry": {"type": "Point", "coordinates": [102.0, 0.5]},
      "properties": {"prop0": "value0"}
    },
    { "type": "Feature",
      "geometry": {
        "type": "LineString",
        "coordinates": [
          [102.0, 0.0], [103.0, 1.0], [104.0, 0.0], [105.0, 1.0]
        ]
```

```
    },
    "properties": {
      "prop0": "value0",
      "prop1": 0.0
    }
  },
  { "type": "Feature",
    "geometry": {
      "type": "Polygon",
      "coordinates": [
        [ [100.0, 0.0], [101.0, 0.0], [101.0, 1.0],
          [100.0, 1.0], [100.0, 0.0] ]
        ]
    },
    "properties": {
      "prop0": "value0",
      "prop1": {"this": "that"}
    }
  }
 ]
}
```

The sample GeoJSON is taken from the `www.geojson.org` site. As seen from the code, it is composed of point, polyline, and polygons in the same file separated by the `feature` keywords. Each `feature` has JavaScript objects named `geometry` and `properties`. The `geometry` part stores the geometry of the object and the `properties` part stores the related information. The `geometry` part is based on the geographic coordinate reference system using WGS84 Datum as default, and the coordinates are in longitudes and latitudes of decimal degrees until it is defined in the `crs` object. The `type` object stores the type of geometry such as `Point`, `Polyline`, or `Polygon`. The `coordinates` array is the actual part that stores the array of point coordinates. The order of coordinates in GeoJSON is different from the Google Maps JavaScript API in terms of its longitudes and latitudes.

More about GeoJSON

More details can be obtained from GeoJSON's unofficial site (`http://www.geojson.org`). There are also some tools to view or edit the GeoJSON without any coding. GitHub (`http://www.github.com`) can easily display your GeoJSON files on the map. The `http://www.geojson.io` site is also a tool from MapBox that displays and edits your GeoJSON files on browsers without the need for any software or coding. Please check these sites to understand GeoJSON in detail.

In this recipe, we will read the local GeoJSON file with the help of the jQuery method, `getJSON()`. jQuery is used in order to focus on coding for the Google Maps JavaScript API. Otherwise, we will have to deal with remote file reading on multiple browser platforms.

This method gets the contents of the `geojson.js` local file and puts them in the `data` variable. Then, we will iterate over the GeoJSON features with the jQuery method, `each()`. Finally, we get each feature's `geometry` part and send it to the `drawGeometry()` function, which will be examined later:

```
$.getJSON('geojson.js', function(data) {
  $.each(data.features, function(key, val) {
    drawGeometry(val.geometry);
  });
});
```

The code written in the `drawGeometry()` function may seem complex, but it is not because we will use all the code written for adding markers, lines, and polygons in this chapter. This function first checks for the type of geometry, then prepares the appropriate options and coordinate(s) for the point, polyline, or polygon.

In polylines or polygons, there is a need to iterate over the `coordinates` array of the `geometry` field to create a path or paths for the `PolylineOptions` or `PolygonOptions` classes.

```
var pointCount = geom.coordinates.length;
var linePath = [];
for (var i=0; i < pointCount; i++) {
  var tempLatLng = new google.maps.LatLng(
    geom.coordinates[i][1], geom.coordinates[i][0]);
  linePath.push(tempLatLng);
}
```

In this recipe, we will process GeoJSON with our functions and these functions can't draw all kinds of GeoJSON geometries. We are only dealing with the simple ones to show you how to deal with GeoJSON on your own. If you need to do a more complex GeoJSON process, there are two ways. One way is to read the full specification of GeoJSON and add it to your functions. The other way, which is also easy, is to use a library that is dedicated to this job. There is a library named **GeoJSON to Google Maps** written by *Jason Sanford* on GitHub (`https://github.com/JasonSanford/geojson-google-maps`). With the help of this library, you do not need to deal with GeoJSON specs. You can just add geometries with your own styles.

See also

- ▶ The *Creating a simple map in a custom DIV element* recipe in *Chapter 1, Google Maps JavaScript API Basics*
- ▶ The *Adding markers to maps* recipe
- ▶ The *Adding lines to maps* recipe
- ▶ The *Adding polygons to maps* recipe
- ▶ The *Adding WKT to the Google Maps JavaScript API* recipe

Adding WKT to the Google Maps JavaScript API

Well-known Text (**WKT**) is a text markup language for representing vector geometry objects on the map according to Wikipedia. This format was originally defined by the **Open Geospatial Consortium** (**OGC**), which is also a standard.

Apart from XML or JSON, WKT is a defined text format that only defines geometries without properties compared to GeoJSON. It was an old and outdated format, but there are still software or services supporting this format. There are 18 distinct geometric objects that represent Earth features, but simple ones are observed in this recipe.

The Google Maps JavaScript API does not support WKT natively, but WKT support will be added with a few lines of coding or with some additional libraries. With coding, we will go through the WKT format, split them into arrays, and read the coordinates one by one. Then, we will show the feature on the map according to its type, which can be point, polyline, or polygon.

In this recipe, we will read a WKT from a local file via jQuery functions and show them on the map. The WKT geometries are within JSON attributes to make iteration easy. This WKT file is composed of a simplified version of the **Ankara** province border, a sample river, and some POIs.

Getting ready

In this recipe, we will use the simple map recipe introduced in *Chapter 1, Google Maps JavaScript API Basics*, as a template.

You can find the source code at `Chapter 3/ch03_adding_wkt.html`.

How to do it...

You can easily add your WKT geometries to the map after performing the following steps:

1. First, start by copying the contents of `ch01_simple_map.html` to our new HTML file.

2. Next, we will add a jQuery JavaScript library to make it easy to access local or remote JSON files with WKT geometries. In this recipe, we will add the library from Google CDN. This block will be added in the `<head>` section before the Google Maps JavaScript API:

    ```
    <script src="//ajax.googleapis.com/ajax/
        libs/jquery/1.10.2/jquery.min.js"></script>
    ```

3. Then, add the following `drawGeometry()` function after defining the global `map` variable. This function draws each WKT geometry read from the JSON file. We have three types of geometries, so we will switch blocks for each type:

```
function drawGeometry(geom) {
  var slices = geom.split('(');
  var geomType = slices[0];
}
```

4. Now, add the following `if` block in the new function. This block will add the geometry if its type is `POINT`:

```
if (geomType == 'POINT') {
  var coords = slices[1].split(')')[0].split(',');
  var finalCoords = coords[0].split(' ');
  var coordinate = new google.maps.LatLng(finalCoords[1],
    finalCoords[0]);
  var marker = new google.maps.Marker({
    position: coordinate,
    map: map,
    title: 'Marker'
  });
}
```

5. Next, add the `if` block for `LINESTRING` that shows polylines on the map:

```
else if (geomType == 'LINESTRING') {
  var coords = slices[1].split(')')[0].split(',');
  var pointCount = coords.length;
  var linePath = [];
  for (var i=0; i < pointCount; i++) {
    if (coords[i].substring(0,1) == ' ') {
      coords[i] = coords[i].substring(1);
    }
    var finalCoords = coords[i].split(' ');
    var tempLatLng = new google.maps.LatLng(finalCoords[1],
      finalCoords[0]);
    linePath.push(tempLatLng);
  }

  var lineOptions = {
    path: linePath,
    strokeWeight: 7,
    strokeColor: '#19A3FF',
    strokeOpacity: 0.8,
    map: map
  }
  var polyline = new google.maps.Polyline(lineOptions);
}
```

6. Finally, the `if` block is used for showing the polygons as follows:

```
else if (geomType == 'POLYGON') {
  var coords = slices[2].split(')')[0].split(',');
  var pointCount = coords.length;
  for (var i=0; i < pointCount; i++) {
    if (coords[i].substring(0,1) == ' ') {
      coords[i] = coords[i].substring(1);
    }
    var finalCoords = coords[i].split(' ');
    var tempLatLng = new google.maps.LatLng(finalCoords[1],
      finalCoords[0]);
    areaPath.push(tempLatLng);
  }

  var polygonOptions = {
    paths: areaPath,
    strokeColor: '#FF0000',
    strokeOpacity: 0.9,
    strokeWeight: 3,
    fillColor: '#FFFF00',
    fillOpacity: 0.25,
    map: map
  }

  var polygon = new google.maps.Polygon(polygonOptions);
}
```

7. Then, add the following function to read the JSON file and iterate over the WKT geometries:

```
function parseWKT() {
  $.getJSON('wkt.js', function(data) {
    $.each(data.objects, function(key, val) {
      drawGeometry(val.geom);
    });
  });
}
```

8. Finally, call the `parseWKT()` function at the end of the `initMap()` function:

```
parseWKT();
```

9. Go to your local URL where your HTML file is stored in your favorite browser and see the result. You will see three different types of geometries on the map with their styles, as shown in the following screenshot:

This is how we add WKT geometries to the map with multiple types of geometries.

How it works...

WKT is a vector format that we defined earlier, which is different from GeoJSON. GeoJSON defines both the geometry and properties of Earth features, but WKT is only used for defining the geometry. Simple types of WKT examples are shown in the following table:

Geometry type	WKT example
POINT	POINT(31.541742 40.730608)
POLYLINE	LINESTRING(35.24414 41.742627, 34.859619 41.586688, 34.7717285 41.508577, 34.832153 41.364441)
POLYGON	POLYGON((33.759299 38.779907, 33.73552 38.758208, 33.73187 38.748987, 33.703537 38.723535, 33.677514 33.800384 38.876017, 33.783532 38.842548, 33.759299 38.779907))

WKT geometries are exactly the same as used in the *Adding GeoJSON to Google Maps JavaScript API* recipe, but they are formatted in WKT geometries. WKT geometries are not alone due to their text format. So we put them in a JSON file with the `geom` attribute. This is used for easy parsing. If you have different types of formats that include WKT geometries, you should parse them with JavaScript.

First, we will read the JSON file to get the WKT geometries. We will read the local JSON file with the help of the jQuery method, `getJSON()`. jQuery is used for focusing on the Google Maps JavaScript API instead of writing and fixing JavaScript code for each browser. Otherwise, we will have to deal with a remote file reading on multiple browser platforms. This method gets the contents of the `wkt.js` local file and puts them in the `data` variable. Then, we will iterate over the JSON objects with a jQuery method, `each()`. Finally, we get each object's `geom` part and send it to the `drawGeometry()` function, which will be examined later:

```
$.getJSON('wkt.js', function(data) {
  $.each(data.objects, function(key, val) {
    drawGeometry(val.geom);
  });
});
```

Parsing of WKT is much harder than GeoJSON because we need to deal with text parsing. With the `drawGeometry()` function, we will split the WKT text into smaller arrays and make them significant. Before parsing each type, we need to get the type of their geometry. Since they have no separate attribute for defining the type, we need to extract the type from the WKT text. As seen from the examples, the type is separated with the (character from the coordinates. If we slice string from the (character, the first array element is the type of geometry. This is done as follows:

```
var slices = geom.split('(');
var geomType = slices[0];
```

The contents of `geomType` can be POINT, LINESTRING, or POLYGON. Then, we will check each type of geometry in different blocks. Let's go through each geometry type starting with point.

Point is the simplest WKT geometry to parse with JavaScript. First, we get the second element of the `slice` array and slice it from the) character to only get the coordinates separated by a comma. Then, we will split the result text by a comma into an array. This array has only one element, so we will easily access the coordinates. To access the coordinates, we must slice the final text with the space character. This final array contains the latitude and longitude. The Google Maps JavaScript API uses latitude and longitude in order to define a point, but WKT uses longitude and latitude order to define a point. As described in the *Adding GeoJSON to Google Maps JavaScript API* recipe, the order of coordinates is also the same for WKT, which is in the reverse order of the Google Maps JavaScript API as longitudes and latitudes:

```
var coords = slices[1].split(')')[0].split(',');
var finalCoords = coords[0].split(' ');
```

```
var coordinate = new google.maps.LatLng(finalCoords[1],
  finalCoords[0]);
```

The second type is the polyline that is defined as LINESTRING in WKT. Parsing polylines is much more complex than points. First, we get the arrays of coordinates by splitting) and comma as described earlier. Then, we will iterate in this array to get each coordinate. Before splitting the text with a space, we must check if there is a space at the beginning of the text. If there is a space, we will get the rest of the text to get only numbers for valid latitudes and longitudes.

```
var coords = slices[1].split(')')[0].split(',');
var pointCount = coords.length;
var linePath = [];
for (var i=0; i < pointCount; i++) {
  if (coords[i].substring(0,1) == ' ') {
    coords[i] = coords[i].substring(1);
  }
  var finalCoords = coords[i].split(' ');
  var tempLatLng = new google.maps.LatLng(finalCoords[1],
    finalCoords[0]);
  linePath.push(tempLatLng);
}
```

The last, simple type is polygon that is also defined as POLYGON in WKT. Parsing polygon is very similar to parsing polylines, except that the polygon definition has two parentheses, which is one more than polylines. We will get the third element of the array instead of the second, because WKT can contain multiple polygon geometries so in this case we have only one. If you have multiple geometries then you should iterate over the geometries. The only difference is written as follows:

```
var coords = slices[2].split(')')[0].split(',');
```

The code blocks written in the drawGeometry() function may seem complex, but they are not because we will use all the codes written for adding markers, lines, and polygons in this chapter. The result of this recipe is exactly the same as the *Adding GeoJSON to* the *Google Maps JavaScript API* recipe, which is the expected result. We do not imagine we will get different outputs on changing the vector formats.

In this recipe, we will process WKT with our own functions, and these functions can't draw all kinds of WKT geometries defined in its standard. We are only dealing with the simple ones to show you how to deal with WKT on your own. If you need to do more complex WKT geometries, then there are two ways. One way is to read the full specification of WKT and add them to your functions. The other, easier way is to use a library that is dedicated for this job. There is a library named **Wicket** written by *K. Arthur Endsley* on GitHub (https://github.com/arthur-e/Wicket). With the help of this library, you do not need to deal with WKT specs. You can just add geometries with your own styles.

See also

- ▸ The *Creating a simple map in a custom DIV element* recipe in *Chapter 1, Google Maps JavaScript API Basics*
- ▸ The *Adding markers to maps* recipe
- ▸ The *Adding lines to maps* recipe
- ▸ The *Adding polygons to maps* recipe
- ▸ The *Adding GeoJSON to the Google Maps JavaScript API* recipe

4
Working with Controls

In this chapter, we will cover:

- ▶ Adding and removing controls
- ▶ Changing the position of controls
- ▶ Creating and adding a geolocation control
- ▶ Creating a table of contents control for layers
- ▶ Adding your own logo as a control

Introduction

This chapter covers the controls that are found in the Google Maps JavaScript API. Generally speaking, controls are UI elements that interact with the user. At a very basic level, they comprise of simple HTML elements or a combination of them.

Controls enable the user to pan the map, zoom in or out, measure distances or areas, and so on. Complex controls involve the administration of multiple overlay layers (introduced in *Chapter 2, Adding Raster Layers*) in the form of a **table of contents** (**ToC**) control, or an editing toolbar for drawing vector features.

The Google Maps JavaScript API presents developers with the opportunity to use and customize built-in controls as well as build custom controls from the ground up.

This chapter will first focus on dealing with built-in controls and their configurations in detail, including the customization of the UI. Then, creating custom controls from very basic to complex ones (such as ToCs) will be covered.

Adding and removing controls

The Google Maps default UI has several controls that are displayed by default or if certain conditions are met. These include:

- ▶ Zoom control
- ▶ Pan control
- ▶ MapType control
- ▶ Scale control
- ▶ Street View control
- ▶ Rotate control
- ▶ Overview Map control

The Google Maps JavaScript API presents the opportunity for developers to opt in or out of these controls or customize them in terms of functionality or look.

In this recipe, we will cover ways to alter the UI by adding or removing built-in controls and how to change their properties through presented options.

Getting ready

The first recipe of *Chapter 1, Google Maps JavaScript API Basics*, will do our work. We will alter it for this recipe.

How to do it...

You will opt for the appearance of the built-in controls if you perform the following step:

1. Alter the `mapOptions` object as follows:

```
var mapOptions = {
  center: new google.maps.LatLng(43.771094,11.25033),
  zoom: 13,
  mapTypeId: google.maps.MapTypeId.ROADMAP,
  panControl: true,
  scaleControl: false,
```

```
    zoomControl: true,
    zoomControlOptions: {
        style: google.maps.ZoomControlStyle.SMALL
    },
    overviewMapControl: true,
    overviewMapControlOptions: {
        opened: true
    },
    mapTypeControl: false
}
```

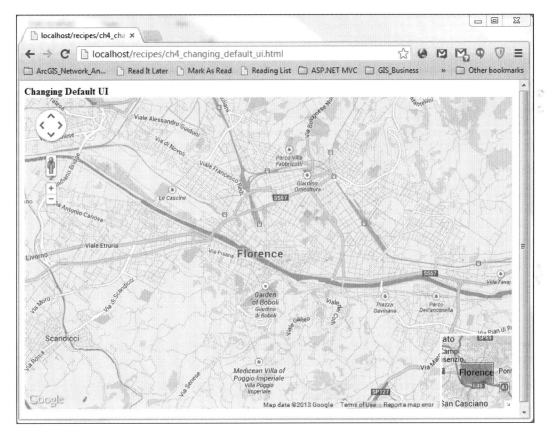

You can have your built-in controls On or Off according to your taste as displayed in the preceding screenshot.

How it works...

You might have observed that we have added a lot to the `mapOptions` object. This is because you can make the controls visible or invisible in the `google.maps.mapOptions` object:

```
panControl: true,
scaleControl: false,
zoomControl: true,
mapTypeControl: false,
overviewMapControl: true
```

By assigning Boolean (true/false) values, you can display `panControl`, `zoomControl`, and `overviewMapControl`, while `scaleControl` and `mapTypeControl` are hidden.

Some controls appear by default. For instance, we have not mentioned `streetViewControl` in our `mapOptions` object; however, it is displayed in the interface because it is there by default. The built-in controls and their default presence in the UI are as follows:

Control name	Default presence
Zoom control	Yes
Pan control	Yes
Scale control	No
MapType control	Yes
Street View control	Yes
Rotate control	Yes (for oblique imagery)
Overview Map control	No

Although `rotateControl` is displayed by default, you might have noticed that it is not found in the interface because it appears only when oblique imagery is shown. Tweaking the `mapOptions` object as follows, we can view the control:

1. Enable `mapTypeControl` so that you can select satellite imagery in the UI, as shown in the screenshot following the code:

    ```
    mapTypeControl: true
    ```

You can see `mapTypeControl` in the preceding screenshot.

Oblique imagery (45 degree imagery) is served in certain locations, and wherever present, `mapTypeControl` updates itself to include a submenu toggle for displaying oblique imagery.

The `RotateControl` control is displayed between the Pan and Zoom controls. It allows users to rotate the oblique imagery at 90 degree intervals. Also, the Pan control is altered to have a ring, letting us change the heading of the oblique imagery when it is displayed:

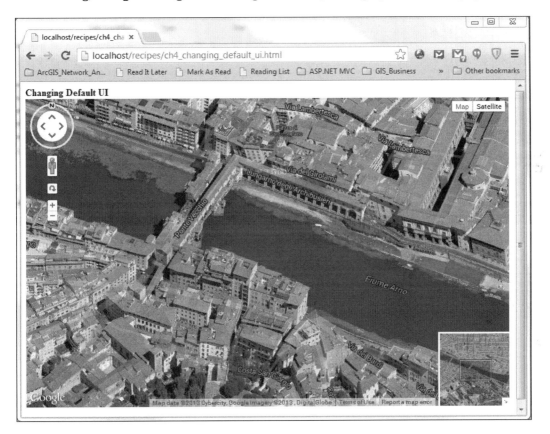

There's more...

The Google Maps JavaScript API allows us to not only toggle the built-in controls between On and Off, but also customize their properties and styles. For instance:

```
overviewMapControlOptions: {
  opened: true
}
```

This sets the Overview Map control in the `opened` state. Please remember that the Overview Map control's default state is collapsed, and this setting sets the control to `opened` at the start of your application. You can collapse or open the control whenever you want by pressing the small arrow in the lower-right corner of the control.

For the Zoom control, the options presented in the recipe are as follows:

```
zoomControlOptions: {
    style: google.maps.ZoomControlStyle.SMALL
}
```

This option sets the Zoom control to be styled as small, comprising of two small buttons, one for zoom in and the other for zoom out. Other options for the `style` property for `zoomControlOptions` are:

```
google.maps.ZoomControlStyle.LARGE
google.maps.ZoomControlStyle.DEFAULT
```

The `LARGE` option sets the Zoom control to be seen as a long stick where you can traverse between zoom levels. The `DEFAULT` option decides whether to display either the large Zoom controls or the small Zoom controls according to the screen size.

You might have noted that options for controls are handled by objects with the `Options` suffix. In the same manner, there are options for `mapTypeControl` as well within the `MapTypeControlOptions` object. Adding the following lines to the code will make some alterations:

```
mapTypeControl: true,
mapTypeControlOptions: {
    mapTypeIds: [google.maps.MapTypeId.ROADMAP,
      google.maps.MapTypeId.HYBRID],
    style: google.maps.MapTypeControlStyle.DROPDOWN_MENU
}
```

The settings in the `mapTypeControlOptions` property make `mapTypeControl` offer only the `ROADMAP` and `HYBRID` map types, so you will not be able to select the `SATELLITE` and `TERRAIN` map types. As you would recall from *Chapter 2, Adding Raster Layers*, the `mapTypeIds` property not only accepts built-in map types, but also styled map types through a `StyledMapType` object and any tiled image source—either as a base map or overlay map—through the `ImageMapType` object.

The second property, `style`, sets `mapTypeControl` to be displayed as a drop-down menu instead of a standard horizontal bar. The other options for the `style` property of `mapTypeControlOptions` are:

```
google.maps.MapTypeControlStyle.HORIZONTAL_BAR
google.maps.MapTypeControlStyle.DEFAULT
```

The `DEFAULT` option is for dynamically picking the Zoom control as either a horizontal bar or a drop-down menu according to the screen estate.

Complete options list for controls

The complete options list for controls can be found at the Google Maps JavaScript API Reference documentation URL `https://developers.google.com/maps/documentation/javascript/reference`.

Changing the position of controls

Google Maps controls have their default positions, and the Google Maps JavaScript API offers a level of flexibility over changing these default positions. You can also position your custom controls according to the places in the UI that are offered as in the following screenshot:

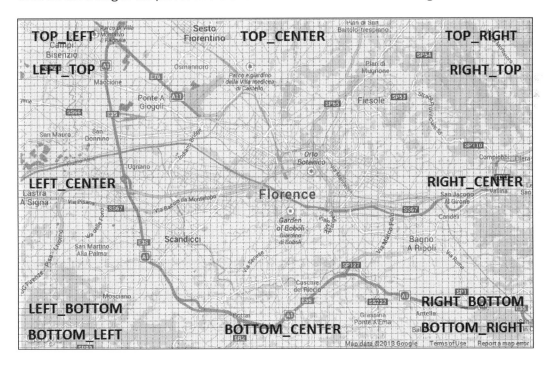

The preceding screenshot depicts the possible locations where you can place your controls. It is noteworthy that **TOP_LEFT** is not equal to **LEFT_TOP**, with **TOP_LEFT** the first one on the top.

In this recipe, we will describe how to specify the corresponding positions of controls in the Google Maps UI.

Getting ready

This recipe is based on the previous recipe's code; therefore, having that will do most of our work.

How to do it...

You can flush the positioning of the controls with the following step:

2. Completely renew the `mapOptions` object as follows:

```
var mapOptions = {
  center: new google.maps.LatLng(43.771094,11.25033),
  zoom: 13,
  mapTypeId: google.maps.MapTypeId.ROADMAP,
  panControl: true,
  panControlOptions: {
    position:google.maps.ControlPosition.TOP_RIGHT
  },
  zoomControl: true,
  zoomControlOptions: {
    style: google.maps.ZoomControlStyle.SMALL,
    position: google.maps.ControlPosition.BOTTOM_CENTER
  },
  mapTypeControl: true,
  mapTypeControlOptions: {
    position: google.maps.ControlPosition.LEFT_TOP
  },
  streetViewControlOptions: {
    position: google.maps.ControlPosition.LEFT_CENTER
  }
};
```

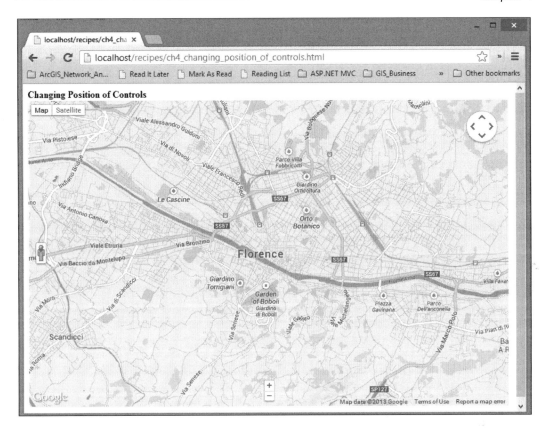

You can change your controls' positions in the map UI as per your taste as you can observe in the preceding screenshot.

How it works...

In the `mapOptions` object, we have specified each control's position by its `position` property in its own options as you can see in the following code snippet:

```
mapTypeControlOptions: {
  position: google.maps.ControlPosition.LEFT_TOP
}
```

The following code directs `mapTypeControl` to be placed in the left-top corner of the map's `div` element, while `panControl` is placed in the top-right corner:

```
panControlOptions:{
  position: google.maps.ControlPosition.TOP_RIGHT
},
```

Complete listing for control positions

The complete listing for control positions can be found at the Google Maps JavaScript API Reference documentation URL (`https://developers.google.com/maps/documentation/javascript/reference#ControlPosition`).

Creating and adding a geolocation control

The Google Maps UI has many built-in controls introduced in previous recipes. These controls serve numerous needs, such as panning, zooming, and changing the map type. However, the user needs are infinite, and the user might be very creative. It is impossible to present a built-in control for every need.

Instead, the Google Maps JavaScript API has presented a path for creating custom controls for every specific need. Custom controls are basically simple HTML elements wrapped in a single element, mostly the `<div>` element.

In this recipe, we will go over the basics of creating a custom control, placing it on the Google Maps UI, and using it through event-handling routines.

Getting ready

This recipe will be based on the *Moving from Web to mobile devices* recipe introduced in *Chapter 1, Google Maps JavaScript API Basics*. Our recipe will utilize the geolocation code extract from this recipe; therefore, it will be helpful to revisit this recipe.

How to do it...

You will have a brand new custom geolocation control if you perform the following steps:

1. First, create a JavaScript object that will be our custom control at the end (the constructor will take two parameters that will be explained in the later steps):

```
function GeoLocationControl(geoLocControlDiv, map){
}
```

2. Inside the `GeoLocationControl` class, set the `class` property to contain the `div` element referenced as the first argument in the constructor:

```
geoLocControlDiv.className = 'controlContainer';
```

3. Inside the `GeoLocationControl` class, set the internal HTML `div` element details, including its `class` attribute, so that this element looks like a button:

```
var controlButton = document.createElement('div');
controlButton.className = 'controlButton';
controlButton.innerHTML = 'Geolocate';
```

4. Add this internal `div` element (`controlButton`) to the container `div` element as follows:

```
geoLocControlDiv.appendChild(controlButton);
```

5. Add the `click` event listener for `controlButton` inside the `GeoLocationControl` class:

```
google.maps.event.addDomListener(controlButton, 'click',
  function() {
    if (navigator.geolocation) {
      navigator.geolocation.
        getCurrentPosition(function(position) {
          var lat = position.coords.latitude;
          var lng = position.coords.longitude;
          var devCenter = new google.maps.LatLng(lat, lng);
          map.setCenter(devCenter);
          map.setZoom(15);

          var marker = new google.maps.Marker({
            position: devCenter,
            map: map,
          });

        });
    }
  });
```

6. Now, in the ordinary `initMap()` function that we have used over all the recipes, add the container HTML `div` element in addition to the standard definition of the `map` and `mapOptions` objects:

```
var geoLocationControlDiv = document.createElement('div');
```

7. Instantiate the custom control class, the `GeoLocationControl` class inside `initMap()`, supplying two arguments: the container `div` element created in the previous step and the `map` object itself:

    ```
    var geoLocationControl = new
      GeoLocationControl(geoLocationControlDiv, map);
    ```

8. Place the custom control among other controls in the map UI:

    ```
    map.controls[google.maps.ControlPosition.RIGHT_CENTER].push
      (geoLocationControlDiv);
    ```

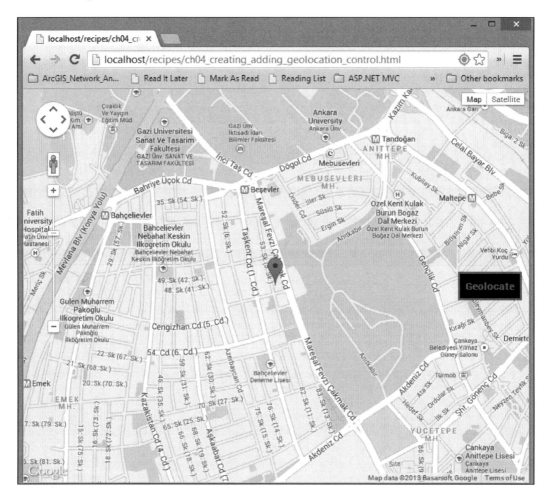

You should have a custom control functioning as a geolocation control as seen in the preceding screenshot.

How it works...

This recipe might seem confusing compared to the preceding recipes, but in essence, there is just one important point to create custom controls in the Google Maps JavaScript API; you can utilize any HTML element to be used as a custom control. In fact, the following simple code extract is sufficient to have a custom control:

```
var controlDiv = document.createElement('div');
map.controls[google.maps.ControlPosition.RIGHT_CENTER].push
  (controlDiv);
```

This code creates an HTML `div` element and then adds it to the controls array of the `map` object. The controls array is a two-dimensional array, the first dimension being the available positions defined in the `google.maps.ControlPosition` class and the second dimension being the controls. This transparent control with no label inside will do anything as there is no event-handling code for the `div` element; however, this reality does not change the fact that this is a custom control.

Other details, such as CSS styling, filling in attributes, and event handling, are necessary for a professional custom control to be used for map UI users.

In our recipe, we have chosen to create a JavaScript class to wrap all these details in order to be structural:

```
function GeoLocationControl(geoLocControlDiv, map)
{
}
```

Our class constructor makes use of two elements: the container `div` element and the `map` object. It needs the reference for the container `div` element to add the child element `controlButton` to it:

```
geoLocControlDiv.appendChild(controlButton);
```

The `controlButton` object (an HTML `div` element) has to respond to some user-originated events for the custom control to be useful and meaningful:

```
google.maps.event.addDomListener(controlButton, 'click',
function() {

});
```

The `google.maps.event.addDomListener` method acts as an event handler registration, and it works in the same way on every browser. These method- and event-related subjects will be covered in *Chapter 5, Understanding Google Maps JavaScript API Events*. For now, it is alright to be aware of the `click` event, which will be listened to by the `controlButton` object.

The geolocation code extract from *Chapter 1, Google Maps JavaScript API Basics,* resides inside the `addDomListener` method, making use of the Geolocation API of the browser. If there is support for the Geolocation API and if the location is retrieved, a marker is added to the map for this location:

```
var marker = new google.maps.Marker({
    position: devCenter,
    map: map,
});
```

This whole creation of child elements and event-handling logic is enveloped in one JavaScript class constructor, which is called by the following:

```
var geoLocationControl = new
    GeoLocationControl(geoLocationControlDiv, map);
```

The following is the only other code snippet required to accomplish this task:

```
map.controls[google.maps.ControlPosition.RIGHT_CENTER].
    push(geoLocationControlDiv);
```

It is worth noting that the `controls` array takes the container `div` element as the custom control. Also, bear in mind that `controls[google.maps.ControlPosition.RIGHT_CENTER]` might already have other controls in other scenarios. We are using `push` so that the existing controls are not replaced.

Creating a table of contents control for layers

Table of Contents (ToC) controls such as UI elements are very common in desktop GIS software, such as ArcGIS Desktop, Mapinfo, and Geomedia. Also, their web counterparts make use of ToCs intensively in their UI, including ArcGIS and .Net web components.

The main use of ToCs is to turn On and Off the various raster or vector layers so as to overlay and view multiple strata of data. For vector layers, the options might be enriched by allowing the users to change the symbology of the vector layer with respect to ToCs.

The Google Maps UI does not have a built-in ToC control; however, with the flexibility of building up a custom control, there are virtually infinite possibilities.

The Google Maps JavaScript API allows developers to utilize the third-party base maps such as OpenStreetMaps or display the overlay raster layers on top of base maps (discussed in detail in *Chapter 2, Adding Raster Layers*). Also, in *Chapter 3, Adding Vector Layers*, various kinds of vector data has been overlaid in the respective recipes.

In this recipe, we will only take base maps to be shown on our ToC in order to have an understanding of the structure, including keeping the state of the control and having multiple event handlers for multiple HTML elements wrapped in one control. This structure might be, of course, enriched with the addition of overlay and vector layers.

Getting ready

This recipe will make use of the *Using different tile sources as base maps* recipe in *Chapter 2, Adding Raster Layers*. It would be extremely helpful to review this recipe before beginning our current recipe. Also, to understand how a simple custom control is created, the previous recipe will be key.

How to do it...

The following are the steps to create a working ToC control inside the Google Maps UI:

1. Create a JavaScript class that will contain all our child controls and event handlers (up to step 12, all code will be embedded in this class constructor):

   ```
   function TableOfContentsControl(tocControlDiv, map){
   }
   ```

2. Have `this` as a variable as it will be out of scope in the event handlers:

   ```
   var tocControl = this;
   ```

3. Set the CSS properties of the container `div` element inside the class constructor:

   ```
   tocControlDiv.className ='tocControl';
   ```

4. Set the title of the ToC:

   ```
   var tocLabel = document.createElement('label');
   tocLabel.appendChild(document.createTextNode('Base
     Layers'));
   tocControlDiv.appendChild(tocLabel);
   ```

5. Create a radio button for the **OpenStreetMap Base Map**:

   ```
   var osmStuffDiv = document.createElement('div');

   var osmRadioButton = document.createElement('input');
   osmRadioButton.type = 'radio';
   osmRadioButton.name = 'BaseMaps';
   osmRadioButton.id = 'OSM';
   osmRadioButton.checked = false;
   ```

```
var osmLabel = document.createElement('label');
osmLabel.htmlFor = osmRadioButton.id;
osmLabel.appendChild(document.createTextNode('OpenStreetMap
  Base Map'));

osmStuffDiv.appendChild(osmRadioButton);
osmStuffDiv.appendChild(osmLabel);
```

6. Create a radio button for the **Google Roadmap** base map:

```
var roadmapStuffDiv = document.createElement('div');

var roadmapRadioButton = document.createElement('input');
roadmapRadioButton.type = 'radio';
roadmapRadioButton.name = 'BaseMaps';
roadmapRadioButton.id = 'Roadmap';
roadmapRadioButton.checked = true;

var roadmapLabel = document.createElement('label');
roadmapLabel.htmlFor = roadmapRadioButton.id;
roadmapLabel.appendChild(document.createTextNode('Google
  Roadmap'));

roadmapStuffDiv.appendChild(roadmapRadioButton);
roadmapStuffDiv.appendChild(roadmapLabel);
```

7. Create a radio button for the **Google Satellite** base map:

```
var satelliteStuffDiv = document.createElement('div');

var satelliteRadioButton = document.createElement('input');
satelliteRadioButton.type = 'radio';
satelliteRadioButton.name = 'BaseMaps';
satelliteRadioButton.id = 'Satellite';
satelliteRadioButton.checked = false;

var satelliteLabel = document.createElement('label');
satelliteLabel.htmlFor = roadmapRadioButton.id;
satelliteLabel.appendChild(document.createTextNode('Google
  Satellite'));

satelliteStuffDiv.appendChild(satelliteRadioButton);
satelliteStuffDiv.appendChild(satelliteLabel);
```

8. Put all the radio buttons and their labels in the parent `div` element:

```
tocControlDiv.appendChild(osmStuffDiv);
tocControlDiv.appendChild(roadmapStuffDiv);
tocControlDiv.appendChild(satelliteStuffDiv);
```

9. Create the `click` event handler for `osmRadioButton` (the `setActiveBasemap` and `getActiveBasemap` methods will be clarified in the following code):

```
google.maps.event.addDomListener(osmRadioButton, 'click',
function() {
    if (osmRadioButton.checked) {
        tocControl.setActiveBasemap('OSM');
        map.setMapTypeId(tocControl.getActiveBasemap());
    }
});
```

10. Create the `click` event handler for `roadmapRadioButton` as follows:

```
google.maps.event.addDomListener(roadmapRadioButton,
'click', function() {
    if (roadmapRadioButton.checked){
        tocControl.setActiveBasemap
(google.maps.MapTypeId.ROADMAP);
        map.setMapTypeId(tocControl.getActiveBasemap());
    }
});
```

11. Create the `click` event handler for `satelliteRadioButton`:

```
google.maps.event.addDomListener(satelliteRadioButton,
'click', function() {
    if (satelliteRadioButton.checked) {
        tocControl.setActiveBasemap
(google.maps.MapTypeId.SATELLITE);
        map.setMapTypeId(tocControl.getActiveBasemap());
    }
});
```

12. Outside the `TableOfContentsControl` class constructor, define a property for keeping the active base map:

```
TableOfContentsControl.prototype._activeBasemap = null;
```

13. Define the getter and setter methods for the `_activeBasemap` property:

```
TableOfContentsControl.prototype.getActiveBasemap =
function() {
  return this._activeBasemap;
};


TableOfContentsControl.prototype.setActiveBasemap =
function(basemap) {
  this._activeBasemap = basemap;
};
```

14. In the `initMap()` function, define the `mapOptions` object as follows:

```
var mapOptions = {
  center: new google.maps.LatLng(39.9078, 32.8252),
  zoom: 10,
  mapTypeControlOptions: {
    mapTypeIds: [google.maps.MapTypeId.ROADMAP,
      google.maps.MapTypeId.SATELLITE, 'OSM']
  },
  mapTypeControl: false
};
```

15. Define the `osmMapType` object as `ImageMapType`:

```
var osmMapType = new google.maps.ImageMapType({
  getTileUrl: function(coord, zoom) {
    return 'http://tile.openstreetmap.org/' + zoom + '/' +
      coord.x + '/' + coord.y + '.png';
  },
  tileSize: new google.maps.Size(256, 256),
  name: 'OpenStreetMap',
  maxZoom: 18
});
```

16. Relate the `'OSM'` `mapTypeId` object to the `osmMapType` object:

```
map.mapTypes.set('OSM', osmMapType);
```

17. Set `mapTypeId` for startup:

```
map.setMapTypeId(google.maps.MapTypeId.ROADMAP);
```

18. Create the container `div` element, instantiate the `TableOfContentsControl` class, and position the container `div` element as a custom control:

```
var tableOfContentsControlDiv =
  document.createElement('div');

var tableOfContentsControl = new
  TableOfContentsControl(tableOfContentsControlDiv, map);

map.controls[google.maps.ControlPosition.TOP_RIGHT].push
  (tableOfContentsControlDiv);
```

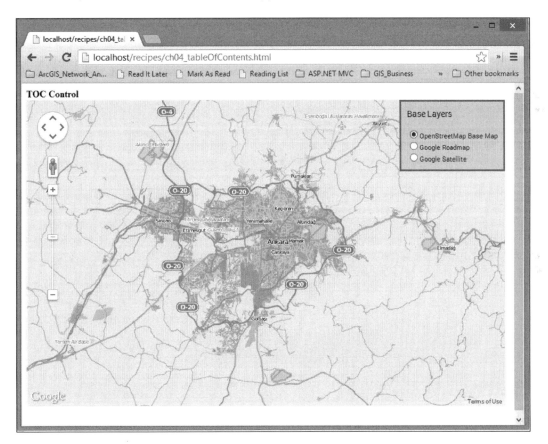

You should have your own ToC control as a custom control in your map's UI as observed in the preceding screenshot.

How it works...

This recipe actually carries the same structure as the previous recipe; however, there are HTML elements in the custom control that make it seem more complex. We will take a look at the details bit by bit so that things will become clearer. As in the previous recipe, we have started by creating a JavaScript class constructor that embeds all the details, including the necessary radio buttons and their event handlers:

```
function TableOfContentsControl(tocControlDiv, map){
}
```

The radio button section for `osmRadioButton` embedded in `TableOfContentsControl` is as follows:

```
var osmRadioButton = document.createElement('input');
osmRadioButton.type = 'radio';
osmRadioButton.name = 'BaseMaps';
osmRadioButton.id = 'OSM';
osmRadioButton.checked = false;

var osmLabel = document.createElement('label');
osmLabel.htmlFor = osmRadioButton.id;
osmLabel.appendChild(document.createTextNode('OpenStreetMap Base
  Map'));

tocControlDiv.appendChild(osmRadioButton);
tocControlDiv.appendChild(osmLabel);


google.maps.event.addDomListener(osmRadioButton, 'click',
function() {
    if (osmRadioButton.checked) {
        tocControl.setActiveBasemap('OSM');
        map.setMapTypeId(tocControl.getActiveBasemap());
    }
});
```

The preceding code extract for `osmRadioButton` is the same for `roadmapRadioButton` and `satelliteRadioButton`. The code creates the radio button and its associated label, adds it to the container `div` element (that is referenced as the first argument of the constructor), and then registers the `click` event for the radio button.

The `click` event checks whether the radio button is checked or not, then—if checked—it sets the active base map as an OSM base map. Then, it uses the active base map information to set `mapTypeId` for the map; this is referenced as the second argument of the constructor.

To set and get the active base map information, two methods are used:

```
setActiveBasemap('OSM')
getActiveBasemap()
```

These methods are defined outside the constructor as:

```
TableOfContentsControl.prototype.getActiveBasemap = function() {
  return this._activeBasemap;
};

TableOfContentsControl.prototype.setActiveBasemap =
function(basemap) {
    this._activeBasemap = basemap;
};
```

Here, the `_activeBasemap` local variable is defined as:

```
TableOfContentsControl.prototype._activeBasemap = null;
```

There is just one tiny but important detail here. For the `click` event handler to see getter and setter methods of the `TableOfContentsControl` object, we have added a single line:

```
var tocControl = this;
```

Here, `this` would be out of scope inside the event handler.

The OpenStreetMap base map section is located in the `initMap()` function. The details of how to display external base maps are covered in *Chapter 2, Adding Raster Layers*, so there is no need to go over specific bits and pieces on this.

The final piece of work is actually running the control in the UI. As we do not call the constructor of `TableOfContentsControl`, nothing will be shown as a custom ToC control. But, before having the ToC control, we have to reserve some estate in the `mapOptions` object:

```
mapTypeControlOptions: {
  mapTypeIds: [google.maps.MapTypeId.ROADMAP,
    google.maps.MapTypeId.SATELLITE, 'OSM']
},
mapTypeControl:false
```

In `mapTypeControlOptions`, we list the possible map type IDs for the map in the `mapTypeIds` property.

However, we do not need `maptypeControl` anymore as we would have a ToC control instead; therefore, we set the `mapTypeControl` property to `false`.

Then the last phase comes: placing the custom ToC control:

```
var tableOfContentsControlDiv = document.createElement('div');

var tableOfContentsControl = new
    TableOfContentsControl(tableOfContentsControlDiv, map);

map.controls[google.maps.ControlPosition.TOP_RIGHT].push
    (tableOfContentsControlDiv);
```

First, we create an arbitrary `div` that will act as a container `div` element for our custom control. Then, we call the constructor of the `TableOfContentsControl` class supplying the container `div` element and the `map` object as arguments. After that, the curtain closes with adding the container `div` element to the two-dimensional controls array that controls the `map` object in its default place in `mapTypeControl`; that is, `google.maps.ControlPosition.TOP_RIGHT`.

Adding your own logo as a control

The Google Maps JavaScript API has designed the addition of custom controls in a very flexible manner so that you can have a variable type of HTML elements in one HTML `div` element.

Adding your own logo of choice, such as adding your company's logo on top of the map UI in your own application, is a good sign for customization and shows off your work.

In this recipe, we will show a logo as a control in the map UI using the Google Maps JavaScript API.

Getting ready

This recipe will make use of the very first recipe of *Chapter 1, Google Maps JavaScript API Basics*, as we only need the basics to develop this recipe.

How to do it...

The following are the steps to display a logo as a custom control in the Google Maps UI:

1. After creating the `map` object in the `initMap()` function, create the container `div` element:

   ```
   var logoDiv = document.createElement("div");
   ```

2. Then, create the HTML `img` element that contains your logo of preference:

   ```
   var logoPic = document.createElement("img");
   logoPic.src = "ch04_logo.PNG";
   logoPic.id = "CompanyLogo";
   ```

3. Insert the `img` element into the container `div` element:

```
logoDiv.appendChild(logoPic);
```

4. Add the container `div` element to the `controls` array of the `map` object:

```
map.controls[google.maps.ControlPosition.LEFT_BOTTOM].
   push(logoDiv);
```

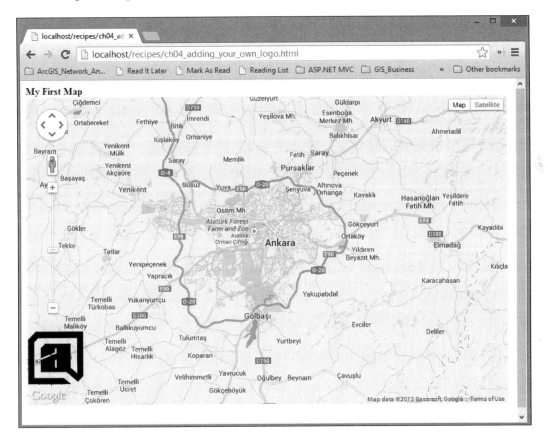

You can have the logo of your taste as a custom control in your map's UI as seen in the preceding screenshot.

How it works...

The code of this recipe is actually the simplest form of custom controls in the Google Maps JavaScript API. There is no event handler for the control, and there is no state information in conjunction with the control. The only thing that exists is the control itself, which is the container div `logoDiv` element.

The `logoPic` element and the `img` element keep a reference to the logo file and are embedded in `logoDiv`:

```
var logoPic = document.createElement("img");
logoPic.src = "ch04_logo.PNG";
logoDiv.appendChild(logoPic);
```

Lastly, `logoDiv` is added to the `controls` array in the **LEFT_BOTTOM** position. When you open your application, you can see your logo in your map UI in its designated position.

5
Understanding Google Maps JavaScript API Events

In this chapter, we will cover:

- ▶ Creating two synced maps side by side
- ▶ Getting the coordinates of a mouse click
- ▶ Creating a context menu on a map
- ▶ Restricting the map extent
- ▶ Creating a control that shows coordinates
- ▶ Creating your own events

Introduction

If you have ever worked on JavaScript programming, you should know the importance of events. Events are the core of JavaScript. There are events behind interactions in web pages. There can be user interactions or browser actions that can be handled with the help of events.

For example, in every code from the beginning of this book, we have wrote something like the following line of code:

```
google.maps.event.addDomListener(window, 'load', initMap);
```

This line is a simple form of event definition. This line tells the browser to call the `initMap()` function when all the contents are loaded. This event is required to start mapping functions after loading all DOM elements.

This chapter is about using events in the Google Maps JavaScript API to interact with maps in different ways. The Google Maps JavaScript API has the `google.maps.event` namespace to work with events. This namespace has static methods to listen to events defined in the API. You should check the supported event types of objects in the API via the Google Maps API reference documentation.

Creating two synced maps side by side

Maps are useful to human beings. With the help of maps, people explore or compare their surrounding area. Sometimes they need to compare two maps side by side to see the difference in real time. For example, you might want to check a satellite imagery side by side with terrain maps to see where the mountains are.

This recipe shows you how to add two maps in the same page and sync them together to show the same area and compare them with the help of Google Maps JavaScript API events.

Getting ready

You already know how to create a map from the previous chapters. So, only additional code lines are written.

You can find the source code at `Chapter 5/ch05_sync_maps.html`.

How to do it...

If you want to create two maps that are synced together, you should perform the following steps:

1. First, add the CSS styles of the `div` objects in the header to show them side by side:

   ```
   .mapClass { width: 500px; height: 500px; display:
     inline-block; }
   ```

2. Then define two global map variables to access them within event callbacks:

   ```
   var map1, map2;
   ```

3. Next create the function that initializes the left map:

   ```
   function initMapOne() {
     //Setting starting options of map
     var mapOptions = {
       center: new google.maps.LatLng(39.9078, 32.8252),
   ```

```
    zoom: 10,
    maxZoom: 15,
    mapTypeId: google.maps.MapTypeId.ROADMAP
  };

  //Getting map DOM element
  var mapElement = document.getElementById('mapDiv');

  //Creating a map with DOM element which is just obtained
  map1 = new google.maps.Map(mapElement, mapOptions);

  //Listening center_changed event of map 1 to
  //change center of map 2
  google.maps.event.addListener(map1, 'center_changed',
    function() {
      map2.setCenter(map1.getCenter());
  });

  //Listening zoom_changed event of map 1 to change
  //zoom level of map 2
  google.maps.event.addListener(map1, 'zoom_changed',
    function() {
      map2.setZoom(map1.getZoom());
  });
}
```

4. Now, add the second function that initializes the right map. The contents of the functions created before are almost the same, except for variable names, the div ID, the map type, and timers in event handlers:

```
function initMapTwo() {
  //Setting starting options of map
  var mapOptions2 = {
    center: new google.maps.LatLng(39.9078, 32.8252),
    zoom: 10,
    maxZoom: 15,
    mapTypeId: google.maps.MapTypeId.TERRAIN
  };

  //Getting map DOM element
  var mapElement2 = document.getElementById('mapDiv2');

  //Creating a map with DOM element which is just
  //obtained
  map2 = new google.maps.Map(mapElement2, mapOptions2);
```

```
//Listening center_changed event of map 2 to
//change center of map 1
google.maps.event.addListener(map2, 'center_changed',
    function() {
        setTimeout(function() {
            map1.setCenter(map2.getCenter());
        }, 10);
    });

//Listening zoom_changed event of map 2 to change
//zoom level of map 1
google.maps.event.addListener(map2, 'zoom_changed',
    function() {
        setTimeout(function() {
            map1.setZoom(map2.getZoom());
        }, 10);
    });
}
```

5. We now have two maps, and we must initialize both of them at the start, so we need a single function to call the previous functions:

```
//Starting two maps
function initMaps() {
    initMapOne();
    initMapTwo();
}
```

6. Call the `initMaps()` function when everything has been loaded on the `load` event of the `window` element:

```
google.maps.event.addDomListener(window, 'load', initMaps);
```

7. Do not forget to add the two `div` objects in HTML tags:

```
<div id="mapDiv" class="mapClass"></div>
<div id="mapDiv2" class="mapClass"></div>
```

8. Go to your local URL where your HTML file is stored in your favorite browser and see the result. You will see two maps side by side. When you drag or zoom in on one map, then the other map is also changed based on the changed one. The final map will look like the following screenshot:

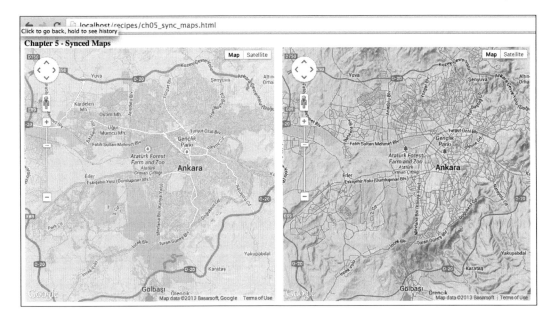

As a result of the recipe, we can create two maps that are synced together to show the same area of different map types.

How it works...

The important point in this recipe is to keep two maps in synchronization at the same position and zoom level. To achieve this goal, we need to know when the map has moved and when the zoom level has changed.

The `map` object has different events to trigger. The `center_changed` and `zoom_changed` events are two of those events. The `center_changed` event is triggered every time the map center is changed. There are also `bounds_changed`, `drag`, `dragstart`, and `dragend` events that can be used to achieve our goal, but `center_changed` is the simplest one to handle. The `zoom_changed` event is triggered when there is a change in the zoom level.

To listen for the events, we need to register these events with the `google.maps.event` namespace as follows:

```
google.maps.event.addListener(map1, 'center_changed', function() {
  map2.setCenter(map1.getCenter());
});
```

The `addListener()` method gets three parameters; an object to listen, an event type, and an event handler. The event handler can be a function that has been defined earlier or an anonymous function used only here. In this example, we listen for the left map object— map1—for the `center_changed` event and set the center of the right map to the center of the left map. The zoom part also works in the same way. When the zoom level of the left map changes, the event handler of `zoom_changed` sets the zoom level of the right map to the zoom level of the left map.

This should be the same for the right map, but the code used for event handling in the right map is a bit different from that of the left one because of an infinite event loop. If we use the same code for event handling, we create an infinite loop between the two maps. This loop will cause your browser to crash in most cases. To avoid this infinite loop, we create a small break (10 milliseconds) between events. This break will solve all the problems and users will not recognize the difference. This break is created with the `setTimeout()` function of JavaScript. There is also a better version to use instead of using timeouts, which is explained in the *There's more...* section of this recipe. The recipe covers the ways to use map events in these cases:

```
google.maps.event.addListener(map2, 'zoom_changed', function() {
  setTimeout(function() {
    map1.setZoom(map2.getZoom());
  }, 10);
});
```

There's more...

In this recipe, our events are being listened for continuously, which is as expected. But what if you need to listen for an event for a limited time? There are two options. One option is that of storing the returning `google.maps.MapEventListener` object of the `addListener()` function and removing it when needed as follows:

```
var eventObj = google.maps.event.addListener(map1,
  'center_changed',function() {
    map2.setCenter(map1.getCenter());
});
function removeListener() {
    google.maps.event.removeListener(eventObj);
}
```

Another option to remove event listeners is to use the `clearInstanceListeners()` or `clearListeners()` functions of the `google.maps.event` namespace, which are used for removing all listeners for all events for the given instance or removing all listeners for the given event for the given instance, respectively. You can look at the following code for example usages:

```
var eventObj = google.maps.event.addListener(map1,
  'center_changed',function() {
    map2.setCenter(map1.getCenter());
});
//This one removes all the listeners of map1 object
google.maps.event.clearInstanceListeners(map1);
//This one removes all center_changed listeners of map1 object
google.maps.event.clearListeners(map1, 'center_changed');
```

The Google Maps JavaScript API also provides other methods to listen for DOM events, named `addDomListener()` under the `google.maps.event` namespace. There is also the `addListenerOnce()` method to listen for events once.

There is also an alternate method to sync maps. The following code block just syncs two maps' events:

```
map2.bindTo('center', map1, 'center');
map2.bindTo('zoom', map1, 'zoom');
```

See also

▶   The *Creating a simple map in a custom DIV element* recipe of *Chapter 1, Google Maps JavaScript API Basics*

Getting the coordinates of a mouse click

The mouse has been the most effective input device for computers for a long time. Nowadays, there is an attempt to change it with touchscreens, but nothing can be compared to the ease of use that a mouse provides.

The mouse has different interactions on maps, such as click, double-click, right-click, move, and drag. These events can be handled in different ways to interact with users.

In this recipe, we will get the coordinates of a mouse click on any point on the map. Users will see an info window upon a mouse click, which can be seen in the following screenshot:

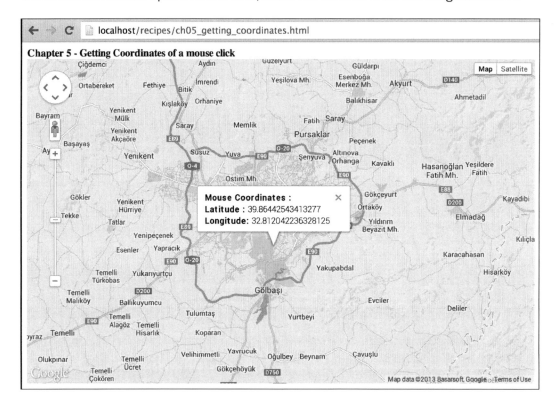

This is how we achieve the creation of a map that is listening for each mouse click to get coordinates.

Getting ready

We assume that you already know how to create a simple map. We will only cover the code that is needed for showing an info window upon mouse clicks.

You can find the source code at `Chapter 5/ch05_getting_coordinates.html`.

How to do it...

If you perform the following steps, you can get the coordinates of each mouse click on the map:

1. First, we must add an `infowindow` variable at the beginning of the JavaScript code to use as a global object:

```
var infowindow = null;
```

2. Then, add the following lines to the `initMap()` function after the initialization of the `map` object:

```
google.maps.event.addListener(map, 'click', function(e) {
  if (infowindow != null)
    infowindow.close();

  infowindow = new google.maps.InfoWindow({
    content: '<b>Mouse Coordinates : </b>
      <br><b>Latitude : </b>' + e.latLng.lat() + '
      <br><b>Longitude: </b>' + e.latLng.lng(),
    position: e.latLng
  });
  infowindow.open(map);
});
```

3. Go to your local URL where your HTML is stored in your favorite browser and click on the map to see the result. Each mouse click opens an info window with the coordinate information.

How it works...

After initializing the map, we create an event listener to handle mouse clicks on the map:

```
google.maps.event.addListener(map, 'click', function(e) {

});
```

The `click` event type has a different handler than other events. The handler has an input parameter that is an object derived from the `google.maps.MouseEvent` class. This object has a property named `LatLng`, which is an instance of the `google.maps.latLng` class. This property gives us the coordinates of the mouse click.

We want to show an info window upon each mouse click, and we want to see only one info window. To achieve this, we create `infowindow` as a global variable at the beginning of the JavaScript code and check whether it is still defined or not. If there is an `infowindow` object from previous clicks, then we will close it as follows:

```
if (infowindow != null)
   infowindow.close();
```

Upon each mouse click, we will create a new `infowindow` object with new contents, coordinates, and position from the `e.latLng` object. After creating `infowindow`, we will just open it on the map defined previously:

```
infowindow = new google.maps.InfoWindow({
   content: '<b>Mouse Coordinates : </b><br><b>Latitude :
     </b>' + e.latLng.lat() + '<br>
     <b>Longitude: </b>' + e.latLng.lng(),
   position: e.latLng
});
infowindow.open(map);
```

There's more...

As already mentioned, some event types have different event handlers that can get a parameter. This parameter is an object derived from the `google.maps.MouseEvent` class. The `google.maps.Map` class has the following events that return `MouseEvent` objects to the handlers: `click`, `dblclick`, `mousemove`, `mouseout`, `mouseover`, and `rightclick`.

See also

> ▸ The *Creating a simple map in a custom DIV element* recipe of *Chapter 1, Google Maps JavaScript API Basics*

Creating a context menu on a map

Using menus in a user interface is a way to communicate with users. Users select a menu item to interact with web applications. Some of the menu types can be accessible from a visible place, but some of them can be accessible with some extra actions, such as **context menus**. Context menus usually appear on applications with a right-click of the mouse.

In this recipe, we will create a context menu on the map that opens when we right-click on the map. This menu includes zoom in, zoom out, and add marker functions. You will also get the position of the right-click to use it in some geo methods such as adding a marker in this example.

Getting ready

This recipe is also like the other recipes in that we assume you already know how to create a simple map. So, we will only show extra lines of code to add the context menu.

You can find the source code at `Chapter 5/ch05_context_menu.html`.

How to do it...

The following are the steps we need to create a map with a context menu to show extra commands:

1. Let's start by adding CSS styles of the context menu to the header of HTML:

    ```css
    .contextmenu{
      visibility: hidden;
      background: #ffffff;
      border: 1px solid #8888FF;
      z-index: 10;
      position: relative;
      width: 100px;
      height: 50px;
      padding: 5px;
    }
    ```

2. The next step is to define the global variables for the context menu and coordinates:

    ```javascript
    var contextMenu, lastCoordinate;
    ```

3. Then, we will add lines that define the context menu class. The details will be explained later:

    ```javascript
    //Defining the context menu class.
    function ContextMenuClass(map) {
      this.setMap(map);
      this.map = map;
      this.mapDiv = map.getDiv();
      this.menuDiv = null;
    };

    ContextMenuClass.prototype = new google.maps.OverlayView();
    ContextMenuClass.prototype.draw = function() {};
    ContextMenuClass.prototype.onAdd = function() {
      var that = this;
      this.menuDiv = document.createElement('div');
      this.menuDiv.className = 'contextmenu';
    ```

```
      this.menuDiv.innerHTML = '<a
        href="javascript:createMarker()">Create Marker
        Here</a><br><a href="javascript:zoomIn()">Zoom
        In</a><br><a href="javascript:zoomOut()">Zoom
        Out</a><br>';
      this.getPanes().floatPane.appendChild(this.menuDiv);

      //This event listener below will close the context menu
      //on map click
      google.maps.event.addListener(this.map, 'click',
        function(mouseEvent) {
          that.hide();
      });
    };

    ContextMenuClass.prototype.onRemove = function() {
      this.menuDiv.parentNode.removeChild(this.menuDiv);
    };

    ContextMenuClass.prototype.show = function(coord) {
      var proj = this.getProjection();
      var mouseCoords = proj.fromLatLngToDivPixel(coord);
      var left = Math.floor(mouseCoords.x);
      var top =  Math.floor(mouseCoords.y);
      this.menuDiv.style.display = 'block';
      this.menuDiv.style.left = left + 'px';
      this.menuDiv.style.top = top + 'px';
      this.menuDiv.style.visibility = 'visible';
    };

    ContextMenuClass.prototype.hide = function(x,y) {
      this.menuDiv.style.visibility= 'hidden';
    }
```

4. Now, add the functions to be used in the context menu:

```
    //Defining context menu functions
    function zoomIn() {
      map.setZoom(map.getZoom() + 1);
    }

    function zoomOut() {
      map.setZoom(map.getZoom() - 1);
    }

    function createMarker() {
      var marker = new google.maps.Marker({
        position: lastCoordinate,
```

```
    map: map,
    title: 'Random Marker'
  });
}
```

5. Add the following code block after initializing the `map` object. This block will create an object from the `ContextMenuClass` class and start listening in the `map` object for the right-click to show the `contextMenu` object created:

```
//Creating a context menu to use it in event handler
contextMenu = new ContextMenuClass(map);

//Listening the map object for mouse right click.
google.maps.event.addListener(map, 'rightclick',
  function(e) {
    lastCoordinate = e.latLng;
    contextMenu.show(e.latLng);
  });
```

6. Go to your local URL where your HTML is stored in your favorite browser and right-click to see the context menu.

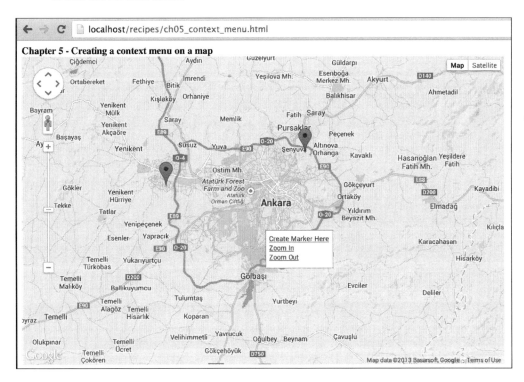

As it can be seen in the preceding screenshot, we created our simple map with the context menu.

How it works...

JavaScript is a prototype-based scripting language that supports object-oriented programming in a different way compared to classical server-side programming languages. There isn't any classic class definition, but you have prototypes to create classes or inherit other classes. This book is not a JavaScript book. If you have any questions about these concepts of JavaScript, you should google it to learn the details.

The Google Maps JavaScript API has a `google.maps.OverlayView` class to create your own custom types of overlay objects on the map. We will inherit this class to create our own context menu class. First, we will define the `ContextMenu` class with its constructor as follows:

```
function ContextMenuClass (map) {
  this.setMap(map);
  this.map = map;
  this.mapDiv = map.getDiv();
  this.menuDiv = null;
};
```

Then, we will set a prototype of the `ContextMenu` class to an object created from the `google.maps.OverlayView` class:

```
ContextMenuClass.prototype = new google.maps.OverlayView();
```

The `google.maps.OverlayView` class has three methods to be implemented in our newly created class: `onAdd()`, `draw()`, and `onRemove()`. In addition to these methods, we add two methods to show or hide the context menu. Each method's mission is explained as follows:

> ▶ `onAdd()`: The creation of DOM objects and appending them as children of the panes is done in this method. We will create a `div` object with the CSS class defined at the top of the HTML. Menu items are also added to this `div` object with the `innerHTML` property. We will also create an event listener of map clicks to remove the context menu from other actions:

```
ContextMenuClass.prototype.onAdd = function () {
  var that = this;
  this.menuDiv = document.createElement('div');
  this.menuDiv.className = 'contextmenu';
  this.menuDiv.innerHTML = '<a href=
    "javascript:createMarker()">Create Marker Here</a><br>
    <a href="javascript:zoomIn()">Zoom In</a><br>
    <a href="javascript:zoomOut()">Zoom Out</a><br>';
  this.getPanes().floatPane.appendChild(this.menuDiv);
```

```
    //This event listener below will close the context menu
    // on map click
    google.maps.event.addListener(this.map, 'click',
      function(mouseEvent){
        that.hide();
    });
};
```

- ▶ `draw()`: The positioning of created elements is done via this method, but we skip steps to fill this method. We create `show()` and `hide()` methods instead of adding or removing the context menu each time:

```
ContextMenuClass.prototype.draw = function() {};
```

- ▶ `onRemove()`: Removing the created elements is done in this method:

```
ContextMenuClass.prototype.onRemove = function() {
  this.menuDiv.parentNode.removeChild(this.menuDiv);
};
```

- ▶ `show(coord)`: Showing the context menu when we right-click on the mouse is done in this method. The input parameter is a `latLng` object, so we have to convert it to pixel coordinates in the `div` element. To achieve this, we need extra objects created from the `google.maps.MapCanvasProjection` class. This class has a method named `fromLatLngToDivPixel` to convert the `latLng` object to simple `google.maps.Point` objects. This object is used to set the `x` and `y` coordinates of the context menu from the top-left corner of the map. We also change the visibility style of `div` to show on the map:

```
ContextMenuClass.prototype.show = function(coord) {
  var proj = this.getProjection();
  var mouseCoords = proj.fromLatLngToDivPixel(coord);
  var left = Math.floor(mouseCoords.x);
  var top =  Math.floor(mouseCoords.y);
  this.menuDiv.style.display = 'block';
  this.menuDiv.style.left = left + 'px';
  this.menuDiv.style.top = top + 'px';
  this.menuDiv.style.visibility = 'visible';
};
```

- ▶ `hide()`: Hiding the context menu is done in this method. We just change the visibility property of the context menu `div` to `hidden` to hide it:

```
ContextMenuClass.prototype.hide = function(x,y) {
  this.menuDiv.style.visibility = 'hidden';
}
```

The `ContextMenuClass` class has been defined earlier, but there isn't any object created from this class. We created a `contextMenu` object from our new class as follows:

```
contextMenu = new ContextMenuClass(map);
```

In order to use this `contextMenu` object, we should listen for the `map` object's `rightclick` event and show the context menu in its handler. We will also update the global variable `lastCoordinate` to keep the last right-click coordinate to use it in the `createMarker()` function:

```
google.maps.event.addListener(map, 'rightclick', function(e) {
    lastCoordinate = e.latLng;
    contextMenu.show(e.latLng);
});
```

Context menu functions are covered in previous chapters, so they are not explained here. You can also create other types of overlays like in this recipe with the help of the `google.maps.OverlayView` class.

More on JavaScript prototype-based inheritance

If you are interested in the details of JavaScript prototype-based inheritance, please get more details from the following page: `http://javascript.crockford.com/prototypal.html`.

This article is written by *Douglas Crockford*, who is the guru of JavaScript and the father of the JSON format. I suggest you read his popular JavaScript book *JavaScript: The Good Parts* to delve deeper into JavaScript.

See also

- The *Creating a simple map in a custom DIV element* recipe of *Chapter 1, Google Maps JavaScript API Basics*

- The *Changing map properties programmatically* recipe of *Chapter 1, Google Maps JavaScript API Basics*

- The *Adding markers to maps* recipe of *Chapter 3, Adding Vector Layers*

Restricting the map extent

Google Maps has a worldwide extent that shows almost every street on the earth. You can use the Google Maps JavaScript API for the whole earth, but sometimes you need to show only the related area in the mapping application. You can zoom to a fixed location, but this doesn't stop users from moving to another place that is not in the extent of your application.

In this recipe, we will listen for map events to check if we are in an allowed extent. If we are not in the allowed extent, then we move the map to the allowed center within the extent. We used Turkey's geographic extent in this recipe.

Getting ready

This recipe is still using the same map creation process defined in *Chapter 1, Google Maps JavaScript API Basics*, but there are some additional code blocks to listen for map events and to check for the restricted extent.

You can find the source code at `Chapter 5/ch05_restrict_extent.html`.

How to do it...

Restricting the map extent is quite easy if you perform the following steps:

1. First, we must add the `allowedMapBounds` and `allowedZoomLevel` variables as global variables after defining the `map` variable. This is the geographic boundary of Turkey:

```
var allowedMapBounds = new google.maps.LatLngBounds(
  new google.maps.LatLng(35.817813, 26.147461),
  new google.maps.LatLng(42.049293, 44.274902)
);
var allowedZoomLevel = 6;
```

2. The next step is to listen for the `drag` and `zoom_changed` events of the map after initializing the map:

```
google.maps.event.addListener(map, 'drag', checkBounds);
google.maps.event.addListener(map, 'zoom_changed',
  checkBounds);
```

3. Then, we create a `checkBounds()` function to handle events when they are fired. The first part of the function is to check for zoom levels. We choose 6 to minimize the zoom level of the map for this recipe:

```
function checkBounds() {
  if (map.getZoom() < allowedZoomLevel)
    map.setZoom(allowedZoomLevel);
}
```

4. The following lines of code will add to the `checkBounds()` function to get the allowed bounds, recent bounds, and recent center of the map:

```
if (allowedMapBounds) {
  var allowedNELng = allowedMapBounds.getNorthEast().lng();
  var allowedNELat = allowedMapBounds.getNorthEast().lat();
  var allowedSWLng = allowedMapBounds.getSouthWest().lng();
  var allowedSWLat = allowedMapBounds.getSouthWest().lat();

  var recentBounds = map.getBounds();
  var recentNELng = recentBounds.getNorthEast().lng();
  var recentNELat = recentBounds.getNorthEast().lat();
  var recentSWLng = recentBounds.getSouthWest().lng();
  var recentSWLat = recentBounds.getSouthWest().lat();

  var recentCenter = map.getCenter();
  var centerX = recentCenter.lng();
  var centerY = recentCenter.lat();

  var nCenterX = centerX;
  var nCenterY = centerY;
}
```

5. The important part of the `checkBounds()` function is the comparing of allowed bounds with recent bounds. If there is a difference between `centerX` and `centerY` with the `nCenterX` and `nCenterY` variables, then we move the map to the center that is within the allowed bounds:

```
if (recentNELng > allowedNELng) centerX = centerX-
  (recentNELng - allowedNELng);
if (recentNELat > allowedNELat) centerY = centerY-
  (recentNELat - allowedNELat);
if (recentSWLng < allowedSWLng) centerX = centerX+
  (allowedSWLng - recentSWLng);
if (recentSWLat < allowedSWLat) centerY = centerY+
  (allowedSWLat - recentSWLat);

if (nCenterX != centerX || nCenterY != centerY) {
  map.panTo(new google.maps.LatLng(centerY,centerX));
}
else {
  return;
}
```

6. Go to your local URL where your HTML is stored in your favorite browser and try to move the map of other countries near Turkey. You will see that the map moves back to its previous position that is allowed within the boundaries defined at the top.

As it can be seen in the preceding screenshot, you can easily restrict the map extent by events provided by the Google Maps JavaScript API.

How it works...

As it is stated in previous event recipes, the Google Maps JavaScript API gives the developer many events that are related to mapping activities. The `drag` and `zoom_changed` events are the ones we are using in this recipe to listen for. This time, we do not create anonymous event handlers because we use the same event handler for two event listeners, named `checkBounds()`:

```
google.maps.event.addListener(map, 'drag', checkBounds);
google.maps.event.addListener(map, 'zoom_changed', checkBounds);
```

The Google Maps JavaScript API has the `google.maps.LatLngBounds` class for defining geographical bounds. This class' constructor gets two objects as parameters created from the `google.maps.LatLng` class. The parameters are the geographical coordinates of the south-west and north-east corners respectively. This creates a geographical boundary for our application. South-west has the minimum latitude and longitude while on the other side, north-east has the maximum latitude and longitude:

```
var allowedMapBounds = new google.maps.LatLngBounds(
  new google.maps.LatLng(35.817813, 26.147461),
  new google.maps.LatLng(42.049293, 44.274902)
);
```

The main trick in this recipe is in the `checkBounds()` function. First, we get the minimum and maximum latitudes and longitudes of the allowed bounds and recent bounds. The `NE` label is the maximum value and the `SW` label is the minimum value of latitudes and longitudes:

```
var allowedNELng = allowedMapBounds.getNorthEast().lng();
var allowedNELat = allowedMapBounds.getNorthEast().lat();
var allowedSWLng = allowedMapBounds.getSouthWest().lng();
var allowedSWLat = allowedMapBounds.getSouthWest().lat();

var recentBounds = map.getBounds();
var recentNELng = recentBounds.getNorthEast().lng();
var recentNELat = recentBounds.getNorthEast().lat();
var recentSWLng = recentBounds.getSouthWest().lng();
var recentSWLat = recentBounds.getSouthWest().lat();
```

The center of the map is used for both checking the difference and centering the map according to this value. The `nCenterX` and `nCenterY` values are used for checking if there is a change in the `centerX` and `centerY` values. The `if` statement checks for the recent values and allowed values. If the map is going out of the allowed bounds, it will change the `centerX` or `centerY` values:

```
var recentCenter = map.getCenter();
var centerX = recentCenter.lng();
var centerY = recentCenter.lat();

var nCenterX = centerX;
var nCenterY = centerY;

if (recentNELng > allowedNELng) centerX = centerX -
  (recentNELng - allowedNELng);
if (recentNELat > allowedNELat) centerY = centerY -
  (recentNELat - allowedNELat);
if (recentSWLng < allowedSWLng) centerX = centerX +
  (allowedSWLng - recentSWLng);
if (recentSWLat < allowedSWLat) centerY = centerY +
  (allowedSWLat - recentSWLat);
```

If there is a change in the `centerX` or `centerY` values, then we must keep the map in the bounds with the help of the `panTo()` method; otherwise, do nothing using `return`:

```
if (nCenterX != centerX || nCenterY != centerY) {
  map.panTo(new google.maps.LatLng(centerY,centerX));
}
else {
  return;
}
```

There may be different ways to check the allowed bounds, such as only checking the center of the map, but this method will not limit the exact bounds you want.

See also

- ▶ The *Creating a simple map in a custom DIV element* recipe of *Chapter 1, Google Maps JavaScript API Basics*
- ▶ The *Changing map properties programmatically* recipe of *Chapter 1, Google Maps JavaScript API Basics*

Creating a control that shows coordinates

Geographical coordinates are very important for showing where you are on the earth. Latitudes and longitudes come together to create a two-dimensional grid that simulates the earth's surface. Showing the latitude and longitude in a control on the map while you are moving the mouse can be a good usage of controls and events together.

In *Chapter 4, Working with Controls*, we have seen recipes such as *Adding your own logo as a control*, and we have also seen how to use map events in this chapter. In this recipe, we will create a control with the help of the `mousemove` event of the map that shows the coordinates in real time.

Getting ready

In this recipe, we will use the first recipe defined in *Chapter 1, Google Maps JavaScript API Basics* as a template in order to skip the map creation.

You can find the source code at `Chapter 5/ch05_coordinate_control.html`.

How to do it...

You can easily create a simple control to show the coordinates on mouse moves by performing the following steps:

1. First, we will add a CSS class at the style part of the head section. This will decorate the coordinate control:

```css
.mapControl {
  width: 165px;
  height: 16px;
  background-color: #FFFFFF;
  border-style: solid;
  border-width: 1px;
  padding: 2px 5px;
}
```

2. After initializing the map, we will define the control parameters:

```javascript
//Defining control parameters
var controlDiv = document.createElement('div');
controlDiv.className = 'mapControl';
controlDiv.id = 'mapCoordinates';
controlDiv.innerHTML = 'Lat/Lng: 0.00 / 0.00';
```

3. Then, add a control to the map with the following line:

```javascript
//Creating a control and adding it to the map.
map.controls[google.maps.ControlPosition.LEFT_BOTTOM].
  push(controlDiv);
```

4. Now, we add an event listener to the map to handle the `mousemove` event and update the coordinates on each `mousemove` event:

```javascript
//Listening the map for mousemove event to show it in control.
google.maps.event.addListener(map, 'mousemove', function(e) {
  var coordinateText = 'Lat/Lng: ' +
    e.latLng.lat().toFixed(6) + ' / ' +
    e.latLng.lng().toFixed(6);
  controlDiv.innerHTML = coordinateText;
});
```

5. Go to your local URL where your HTML is stored in your favorite browser and try to move the mouse. You will see the coordinate control changes in the left-bottom corner of the map.

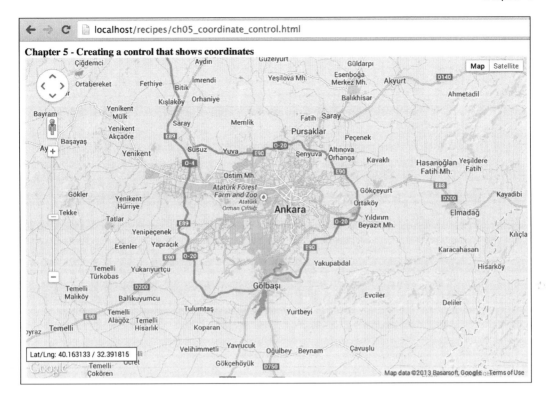

We have successfully created a simple control that shows coordinates on mouse moves.

How it works...

This recipe is a combination of two chapters: *Chapter 4, Working with Controls*, and this chapter. More detailed information about controls can be gathered from *Chapter 4, Working with Controls*.

As it has been stated earlier, the Google Maps JavaScript API gives us different events to listen for, for different purposes. In this recipe, we will use the `mousemove` event of the map to get the coordinates of the mouse. The `mousemove` event handler has an input parameter to get coordinates. We will get the latitude and longitude from the `e.latLng` object with the help of the `lat()` and `lng()` functions, respectively. Then, we will fix their decimals to 6 digits in order to make an ordered view in the coordinate control with the Math function `toFixed()`:

```
//Listening the map for mousemove event to show it in control.
google.maps.event.addListener(map, 'mousemove', function(e) {
  var coordinateText = 'Lat/Lng: ' + e.latLng.lat().
    toFixed(6) + ' / ' + e.latLng.lng().toFixed(6);
  controlDiv.innerHTML = coordinateText;
});
```

The remaining part of the code is related to simple map creation and creating a custom control, which is not the scope of this chapter.

See also

▶ The *Creating a simple map in a custom DIV element* recipe of *Chapter 1, Google Maps JavaScript API Basics*

▶ The *Adding your own logo as a control* recipe of *Chapter 4, Working with Controls*

Creating your own events

Events are very important for JavaScript programming, and all JavaScript frameworks and APIs give developers access to some predefined event types related to their classes. The Google Maps JavaScript API is doing the same, and it gives us the most used event types with their classes. But what if you need a custom event type?

The Google Maps JavaScript API has a base class named `google.maps.MVCObject` that is the top class that most of the classes inherit. The class is ready for using in custom events with the `google.maps.event` namespace.

In this recipe, we will create a custom object with the `google.maps.MVCObject` class and bind it to a custom event to create your own events. The usage of the custom event cannot be a real-world case, but it will give you an idea about listening and firing your own events.

Getting ready

This recipe is still using the same map creation process defined in *Chapter 1, Google Maps JavaScript API Basics*, but there are some additional code blocks to create a table of contents (ToC) control and the custom event.

You can find the source code at `Chapter 5/ch05_custom_events.html`.

How to do it...

If you perform the following steps, you can add and create your own types of events:

1. First, we add the CSS class of our custom control:

```css
.mapControl {
  width: 165px;
  height: 55px;
  background-color: #FFFFFF;
  border-style: solid;
  border-width: 1px;
  padding: 2px 5px;
}
```

2. Now, we create a `customObject` variable as a global variable after the `map` variable:

```
var customObject;
```

3. Then, we create `createTOCControl()` to create our table of contents control as follows:

```
function createTOCControl () {
  var controlDiv = document.createElement('div');
  controlDiv.className = 'mapControl';
  controlDiv.id = 'layerTable';
  map.controls[google.maps.ControlPosition.RIGHT_TOP].push
    (controlDiv);
  var html = '<b>Map Layers</b><br/>';
  html = html + '<input type="checkbox"
    onclick="checkLayers(this)" value="geojson">
    GeoJSON Layer<br/>';
  html = html + '<input type="checkbox"
    onclick="checkLayers(this)" value="marker">
    MarkerLayer';
  controlDiv.innerHTML = html;
}
```

4. The next step is adding another function, named `checkLayers()`, that is the function calling from the `onclick` event of the checkboxes:

```
function checkLayers(cb) {
  //Firing customEvent with trigger function.
  google.maps.event.trigger(customObject, 'customEvent',
    {layerName: cb.value, isChecked: cb.checked});
}
```

5. All the functions are ready to be added to the `initMap()` function. Add the following lines after initialization of the map:

```
//Creating Table of Contents Control.
createTOCControl();

//Creating custom object from Google Maps JS Base Class
customObject = new google.maps.MVCObject();

//Start listening custom object's custom event
google.maps.event.addListener(customObject,
  'customEvent', function (e) {
    var txt = '';
    if(e.isChecked) {
      txt = e.layerName + ' layer is added to the map';
    }
```

```
    else {
      txt = e.layerName + ' layer is removed from the map';
    }
    alert(txt);
  });
```

6. Go to your local URL where your HTML is stored in your favorite browser and see the map. When you click on one of the checkboxes in the table of contents control, you will see an alert box with the name of the layer and its status as to whether it has been added or removed.

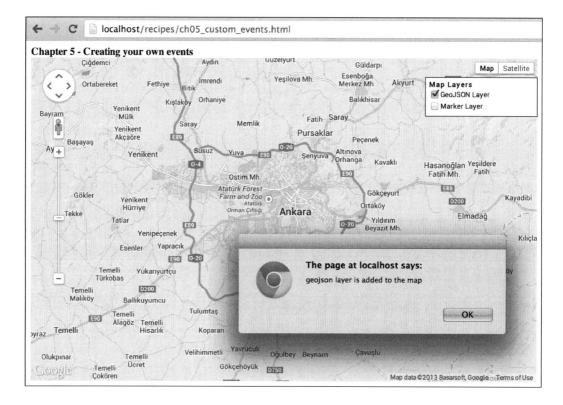

This is the result of the recipe that shows both triggering and listening for the custom events defined by yourself.

How it works...

JavaScript has an inheritance that is one of the core concepts of object-oriented programming. This makes your life easier in order not to write the same methods again and again.

The Google Maps JavaScript API uses the inheritance of JavaScript both for itself and API developers. There are core classes that are the bases for other classes. The Google Maps JavaScript API has a base class named `google.maps.MVCObject` that all other classes are produced from.

If you want to create a custom class as in previous recipes, you should create a class from the `google.maps.MVCObject` class. In this recipe, we just create an object from the `MVCObject` class instead of creating a new class. Then, we will listen for `customEvent` of this created object just like other events:

```
//Creating custom object from Google Maps JS Base Class
customObject = new google.maps.MVCObject();

//Start listening custom object's custom event
google.maps.event.addListener(customObject, 'customEvent',
   function (e) {
     var txt = '';
     if(e.isChecked) {
       txt = e.layerName + ' layer is added to the map';
     }
     else {
       txt = e.layerName + ' layer is removed from the map';
     }
     alert(txt);
});
```

Firing the custom event is much easier than listening for it. We use the `google.maps.event.trigger()` function to fire the event with additional parameters. Parameters should be in the JSON object format to send it to the event handler:

```
//Firing customEvent with trigger function.
google.maps.event.trigger(customObject, 'customEvent',
   {layerName: cb.value, isChecked: cb.checked});
```

Creating a custom event in this recipe cannot be directly used in real-life cases, but this should give you an idea about how to use them. Events should be used carefully in order to use memory efficiently.

See also

- ▶ The *Creating a simple map in a custom DIV element* recipe of *Chapter 1, Google Maps JavaScript API Basics*
- ▶ The *Adding your own logo as a control* recipe of *Chapter 4, Working with Controls*

6
Google Maps JavaScript Libraries

In this chapter, we will cover:

- ▶ Drawing shapes on the map
- ▶ Calculating the length/area of polylines and polygons
- ▶ Encoding coordinates
- ▶ Searching for and showing nearby places
- ▶ Finding places with the autocomplete option
- ▶ Adding drag zoom to the map
- ▶ Creating custom popups / infoboxes

Introduction

This chapter delves into the additional JavaScript libraries that are part of the Google Maps JavaScript API. These libraries are not added to your application by default when you reference the Google Maps API; however, these can be added manually.

These libraries are classified into the following six categories:

- ▶ `drawing`
- ▶ `geometry`
- ▶ `places`
- ▶ `panoramio`
- ▶ `visualization`
- ▶ `weather`

The last three libraries in the preceding list—panoramio, visualization, and weather—have been discussed thoroughly in *Chapter 2, Adding Raster Layers*, with respect to their related topics and usages. In this chapter, we will learn in detail about Drawing and Geometry libraries. We will also use two external libraries.

The intention of these libraries, as extensions to the core API, is to ensure that the Google Maps JavaScript API is self-sufficient in order to provide all of the tasks that it offers to accomplish. That means, without these extra libraries, you can develop using the API without any problem.

In addition, these libraries are somehow autonomous. They have very well-defined and designed objectives and boundaries, so adding them will provide additional functionality, but removing them will not take away any functionality from the core API.

This optionality of the extra libraries definitely accounts for faster loads of the API. Unless you request these libraries explicitly, they are not loaded. This componental structure lets you have the option of including the cost of loading these libraries or not.

This chapter will first deal with the drawing library, which will enable you to draw vector overlays on top of your base maps. Then, it will deal with the geometry library and get the properties of the vector overlays, such as the length and areas. Finally, the places library will explain in detail how to search for places and show the details of these places in the Google Maps JavaScript API.

Drawing shapes on the map

You have probably explored vector overlays in *Chapter 3, Adding Vector Layers*. Without getting into details, you can add markers, lines, and polygons programmatically using the Google Maps JavaScript API. But if you wanted to draw these vector overlays—not programmatically, but with mouse clicks or touch gestures, like in AutoCAD or ArcGIS for Desktop—what would you do?

The drawing library handles this job, enables you to draw vector shapes as per your preference, and shows them on top of your base maps.

In this recipe, we will go over the details of how to draw shapes, deal with their extensive set of options, and how to handle their specific events.

Getting ready

The first recipe of *Chapter 1, Google Maps JavaScript API Basics*, will do our work. We will alter the Google Maps API bootstrap URL to have this recipe.

How to do it...

The following steps show how you can have the drawing control and draw some shapes using that control:

1. Alter the Google Maps API bootstrap URL adding the `libraries` parameter:

    ```
    <script type="text/javascript"
        src="https://maps.googleapis.com/maps/api/js? libraries=drawin
        g&sensor=false">
    </script>
    ```

2. Create the `drawingManager` object:

    ```
    var drawingManager = new google.maps.drawing.DrawingManager();
    ```

3. Enable the drawing functionality:

    ```
    drawingManager.setMap(map);
    ```

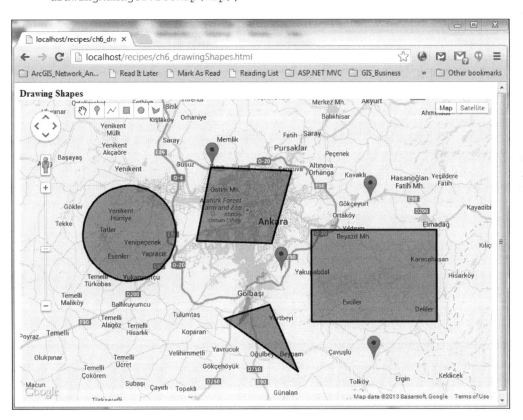

In the previous screenshot, you can see the varieties of shapes you can draw by clicking on the buttons in the top-left corner.

How it works...

Adding the drawing functionality to your application using the Google Maps JavaScript API is easy. First, you have to include the `libraries` parameter to your Google Maps JavaScript API URL with the `drawing` value inside to include the `drawing` library into your application:

```
&libraries=drawing
```

Next, you can use the `drawing` library's supported functions and objects in addition to the standard Google Maps JavaScript API.

To draw your vector shapes, it is necessary to have a `DrawingManager` object:

```
var drawingManager = new google.maps.drawing.DrawingManager();
```

Having a `DrawingManager` object, you have all your drawing functionalities, but you have to attach it to the current map instance in order to make use of it:

```
drawingManager.setMap(map);
```

After this, you will see a drawing control containing the marker, polyline, rectangle, circle, and polygon drawing buttons. By using these buttons, you can draw any vector overlay you want. In the toolset, you can also see a pan tool to go out of the drawing mode to use the pan and zoom controls. If you want to draw a vector shape again, press the related button (marker, polyline, and so on) and draw on the map.

There's more...

Until this point, having the drawing functionality is so simple that you can implement it by adding two lines of code. However, there is an extensive set of options you can make use of, which are related to the `DrawingManager` object and vector shapes you draw. It's worth going over them, because they enrich your drawing experience in your application.

The settings of `DrawingManager` can be modified either in its initialization or through its `setOptions` method. All the settings that pertain to the `DrawingManager` class are properties of the `DrawingManagerOptions` class.

Let's alter our recipe to include the `DrawingManager` options:

```
var drawingManager = new google.maps.drawing.DrawingManager({
    drawingControl: true,
});
```

The `drawingControl` property enables or disables the drawing control seen in the map UI:

Setting the `drawingControl` property to `false` will hide the drawing control. Its default is `true`; therefore, although it is not included in our original recipe code, it is shown in the map.

It is important to note that the drawing functionality comes with attaching the `DrawingManager` class to the map.

```
drawingManager.setMap(map);
```

Therefore, hiding the drawing control is not related to the drawing functionality. In fact, you can create your own user controls to use `DrawingManager` instead of the standard drawing controls.

The drawing control has its own options embedded in the `drawingControlOptions` property. Remember from *Chapter 4, Working with Controls*, that you can position your controls at the predefined places in the Google Maps UI whether they be the default controls or the controls you actually develop.

The `drawingControl` property is no exception. You can position `drawingControl` by using the following code snippet:

```
var drawingManager = new google.maps.drawing.DrawingManager({
    drawingControl: true,
    drawingControlOptions: {
        position: google.maps.ControlPosition.BOTTOM_CENTER
    }
});
```

The preceding code is reflected in the map UI in the following manner:

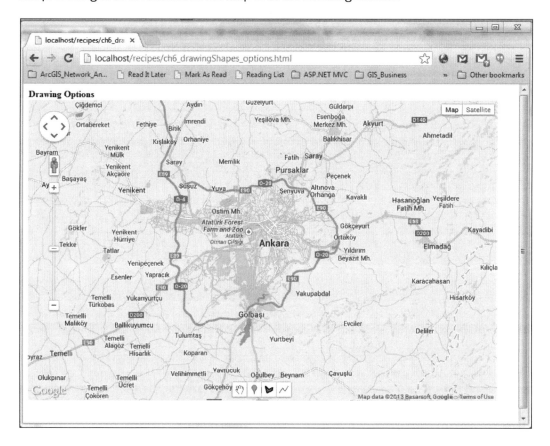

Notice that the `drawingControl` property is placed at the bottom center, as we have mentioned in the `position` property of the `drawingControlOptions` property.

Complete listing for google.maps.ControlPosition

The complete listing for control positions can be found in the Google Maps JavaScript API reference documentation at the following link:

`https://developers.google.com/maps/documentation/javascript/reference`

Apart from the `position` property, you can also select which type of shape you would like to draw, in other words, which buttons you would like to include in `drawingControl`:

```
var drawingManager = new google.maps.drawing.DrawingManager({
    drawingControl: true,
    drawingControlOptions: {
        position: google.maps.ControlPosition.BOTTOM_CENTER,
        drawingModes: [
            google.maps.drawing.OverlayType.MARKER,
            google.maps.drawing.OverlayType.POLYGON,
            google.maps.drawing.OverlayType.POLYLINE
        ]
    }
});
```

We have apparently selected three drawing shape types listed in an array in the `drawingModes` property:

- Marker
- Polygon
- Polyline

These are reflected in the `drawingControl` property:

By default, all vector shape buttons are available in `drawingControl`. This means that, in addition to the three types listed in our example, the following shapes are also available:

- Rectangle
- Circle

If you have followed the recipe up to this point, you may have realized that at the start of your application you can zoom and pan your map as usual. Then, you have to click a vector overlay button in the `drawingControl` property to start drawing your shape.

However, you can change this programmatically through a setting. For instance:

```
var drawingManager = new google.maps.drawing.DrawingManager({
    drawingMode: google.maps.drawing.OverlayType.POLYGON,
    ...
});
```

The `drawingMode` property takes the vector shape type `google.maps.drawing.OverlayType`, as the API implies, as its data type and sets that vector shape type so that it can be drawn. In our example, when the user clicks on the map, they immediately start drawing the `POLYGON` vector overlays.

But what happens if it becomes necessary to change the `drawingMode` programmatically in the program flow? Luckily, there is a solution to this:

```
drawingManager.setDrawingMode(null);
```

Setting the property to `null` makes the `drawingMode` property turn to its default value, allowing the end user to use the Google Maps JavaScript UI as usual. This means that clicking on the map does not draw any vector shape overlay.

You can also use the `setOptions` method of `drawingManager` for the same purpose:

```
drawingManager.setOptions({
    drawingMode: google.maps.drawing.OverlayType.POLYGON,
});
```

Until now, we have dealt with the `drawingManager` and `drawingControl` property options. But what about the shapes and their styles that we will draw? As you may have expected, you can set the properties of the vector shapes you draw in `google.maps.drawing.DrawingManagerOptions`:

```
var drawingManager = new google.maps.drawing.DrawingManager({
    ...
    polylineOptions: {
        strokeColor: 'red',
        strokeWeight: 3
    },
    polygonOptions: {
        strokeColor: 'blue',
        strokeWeight: 3,
        fillColor: 'yellow',
        fillOpacity: 0.2
    }
    ...
});
```

We can now draw our shapes as shown in the following screenshot:

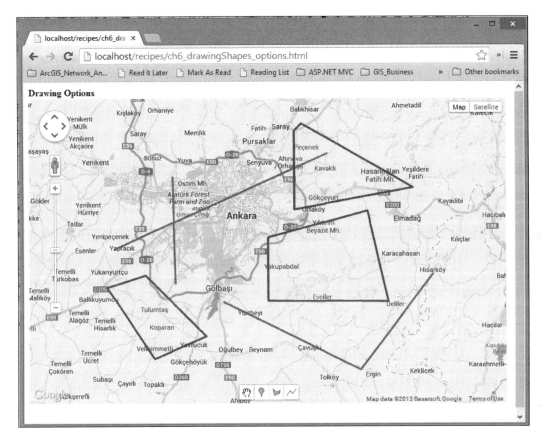

You may have observed that the styles of the polyline and polygon shapes have changed completely. The polylines have become red in color, because their `strokeColor` property is set as `red`, whereas the `strokeColor` property for polygons is set as `blue`, their `fillColor` as `yellow`, and their `opacity` being near transparent—`0.2`—so that you can see the base map through them.

For each vector overlay type, there is an `options` property for `drawingManager`:

- `markerOptions`
- `polylineOptions`
- `polygonOptions`
- `circleOptions`
- `rectangleOptions`

There is a bunch of interesting properties for vector overlays, most of them being common for all overlay types. We have already touched on the stroke and fill properties for customizing the styles according to your taste.

For instance, you can try the `editable` and `draggable` properties, which are worth commenting on:

```
polygonOptions: {
            strokeColor: 'blue',
            strokeWeight: 3,
            fillColor: 'yellow',
            fillOpacity: 0.2,
            editable: true,
            draggable: true
    }
```

The preceding code snippet makes the polygons drawn on Google Maps UI editable, as shown in the following screenshot (you have to go out of polyline drawing mode by clicking the pan button in the drawing control):

Observe the white dots that represent the nodes (`LatLng` objects) comprising the entire polygon. You can change the location of these dots by clicking and dragging the dots; this will allow you to change the shape of the polygon, as shown in the following screenshot:

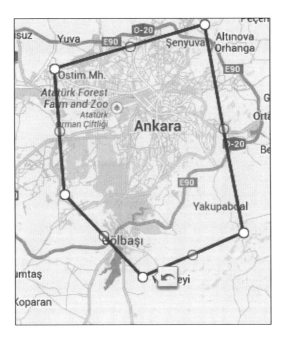

You may have spotted that the white dot located in the middle of the south edge has been dragged downwards, and thus, the shape of the polygon has changed.

In addition to changing the original shape, you can also drag the shape, as shown in the following screenshots:

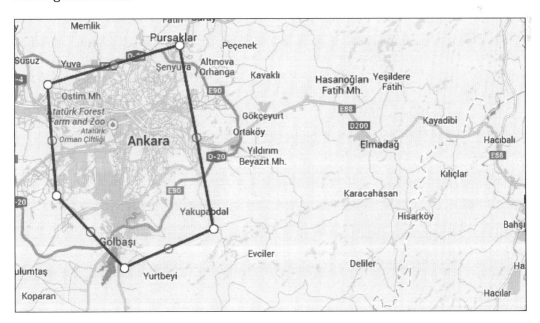

As you can see, the shape has moved to the east in the second screenshot.

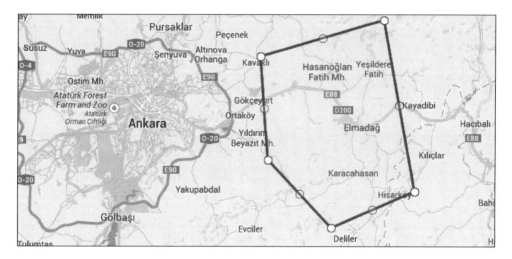

When the `draggable` property is set to `true` and your mouse is on the shape, you can drag your shape wherever you want on the map.

Complete listing for google.maps.drawing.DrawingManager properties

The complete listing for the `DrawingManager` properties and related options can be found in the Google Maps JavaScript API reference documentation at the following link:

`https://developers.google.com/maps/documentation/javascript/reference#DrawingManager`

`DrawingManager` is not limited to its properties and options; it also has some events associated with it. These events are fired when you finish drawing a shape:

```
google.maps.event.addListener(drawingManager, '    polygoncomplete',
function(polygon) {
    polygon.setEditable(true);
    polygon.setDraggable(true);
});
```

You may notice that the type of the event is `polygoncomplete`, and there is a callback function taking the polygon, which has been completed, as an argument.

There is an event for every type of shape:

▶ `markercomplete`
▶ `linestringcomplete`

- ▸ polygoncomplete

- ▸ rectanglecomplete

- ▸ circlecomplete

There is one additional event type that covers all of these shape types:

```
google.maps.event.addListener(drawingManager, 'overlaycomplete',
    function(event) {
        if (event.type == google.maps.drawing.OverlayType.POLYGON) {
            event.overlay.setEditable(true);
            event.overlay.setDraggable(true);
        }
});
```

The preceding event behaves in the same way as the previous example. Instead of the `shapecomplete` pattern there is an `overlaycomplete` argument for the event. This event is particularly useful for all the shape events, regardless of their type. However, being a generic event for all shapes, you can also get the shape type from `event.type`, and you can get the reference for the shape drawn from `event.overlay`. Utilizing these, you can have conditional statements for different shape types in one event handler.

Calculating the length/area of polylines and polygons

As described in the first recipe of this chapter—*Drawing shapes on the map*—you can draw your shapes as per your taste. But how about getting some information about these shapes, for instance, information about their length and area?

The Google Maps JavaScript API places the opportunity to gather this information in the `geometry` library. From this library, you can access the static utility functions that give information on the length/area calculations and so on.

This recipe will show us how to get the length and area information of the arbitrary shapes drawn.

Getting ready

Having a sneak preview at the *Drawing shapes on the map* recipe will ease your work, as much detail on drawing shapes and their background is needed.

How to do it...

You can view the area and length information of your shapes by carrying out the following steps:

1. Add the `drawing` and `geometry` libraries to the bootstrap URL:

```
<script type="text/javascript"
    src="https://maps.googleapis.com/maps/api/js?
    libraries=drawing,geometry&sensor=false">
</script>
```

2. Create a `drawingManager` object with the following settings:

```
var drawingManager = new google.maps.drawing.DrawingManager({
    drawingMode: null,
    drawingControl: true,
    drawingControlOptions: {
        position:
            google.maps.ControlPosition.BOTTOM_CENTER,
        drawingModes: [
        google.maps.drawing.OverlayType.POLYGON,
        google.maps.drawing.OverlayType.POLYLINE
        ]
    },
    polylineOptions: {
        strokeColor: 'red',
        strokeWeight: 3
    },
    polygonOptions: {
        strokeColor: 'blue',
        strokeWeight: 3,
        fillColor: 'yellow',
        fillOpacity: 0.2
    }
});
```

3. Enable the drawing functionality:

```
drawingManager.setMap(map);
```

4. Add an event listener for the completion of your polygons:

```
google.maps.event.addListener(drawingManager,
'polygoncomplete', function(polygon) {
    var path = polygon.getPath();
    var area =
        google.maps.geometry.spherical.computeArea(path);
    var length =
        google.maps.geometry.spherical.computeLength(path);
    console.log('Polygon Area: ' + area/1000000 + ' km
        sqs');
```

```
console.log('Polygon Length: ' +  length/1000 + '
    kms');
});
```

5. Add an event listener for the completion of your polylines:

```
google.maps.event.addListener(drawingManager,
'polylinecomplete', function(polyline) {
    var path = polyline.getPath();
    var length =
        google.maps.geometry.spherical.computeLength(path);
    console.log('Polyline Length: ' +  length/1000 + '
        kms');
});
```

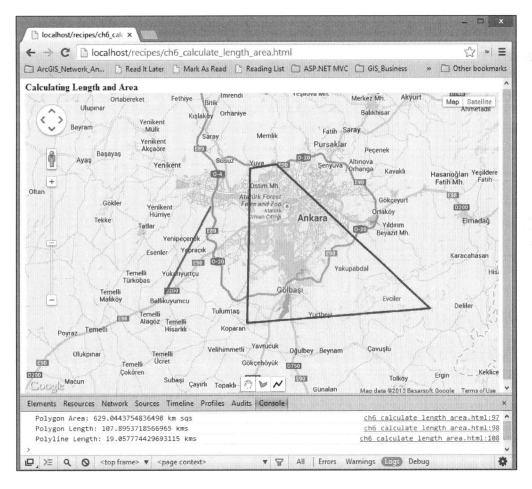

As shown in the preceding screenshot, you can view the area and length information in the console window.

How it works...

To use the `drawing` and `geometry` utilities in the Google Maps JavaScript API, we have added two libraries—`drawing` and `geometry`—to the Google Maps JavaScript API bootstrap URL at the top of the code:

```
libraries=drawing,geometry
```

It is important to note that you can add multiple libraries with a comma separating each list, as in this case.

We have added the `drawingManager` object, after the usual mapping details, in the `initMap()` function itself. In this `drawingManager` object, we set the properties so that we can only draw polylines and polygons:

```
drawingModes:
[
    google.maps.drawing.OverlayType.POLYGON,
    google.maps.drawing.OverlayType.POLYLINE
]
```

We do not need any marker drawing as there will be no length and area information related to markers.

At the start of the application, we implied that the users can use standard mapping controls (zoom, pan, and so on) instead of drawing shapes:

```
drawingMode:null,
```

This control on the user input is particularly useful in professional applications, because even if the application is the sole drawing application, users may need to specify their drawing areas by using the pan and zoom controls first hand.

We have placed the `drawingControl` object at the bottom center of the map UI:

```
position: google.maps.ControlPosition.BOTTOM_CENTER,
```

It is up to you where to place `drawingControl`; we just selected BOTTOM_CENTER as an example.

We have finally attached the `drawingManager` object to the map instance to enable the functionality:

```
drawingManager.setMap(map);
```

After all this setting up, users can open their application and draw polylines and polygons as per their wish. But, how do we get the length and area info of their shapes?

We have to add event handlers to be aware that they have finished drawing shapes. The calculation of the length and area must be performed for every polygon and polyline. Therefore, we have used the `polygoncomplete` and `polylinecomplete` events. First, let's perform the calculations for the polygons:

```
google.maps.event.addListener(drawingManager, 'polygoncomplete',
function(polygon) {
    var path = polygon.getPath();
    var area = google.maps.geometry.spherical.computeArea(path);
    var length =
        google.maps.geometry.spherical.computeLength(path);
    console.log('Polygon Area: ' + area/1000000 + ' km sqs');
    console.log('Polygon Length: ' + length/1000 + ' kms');
});
```

In the `polygoncomplete` event handler that gets fired when the users finish drawing each of their polygons, we first get the path of the polygon they draw:

```
var path = polygon.getPath();
```

The `getPath()` method returns an `MVCArray` of the object of type `LatLng` being latitude and longitude pairs comprising the polygon itself. For instance, for an imaginary polygon that we have drawn, calling `polygon.getPath().getArray().toString();` gives the following result:

```
"(39.92132255884663,
32.7337646484375),(39.75048953595117,
32.754364013671875),(39.78110197709871,
33.061981201171875),(39.98132938627213, 33.0084228515625)"
```

It is now clear that the imaginary polygon that is drawn comprises four latitude and longitude pairs.

Why did we need the path of the polygons? We needed it because the `computeArea()` function that we use does not take the polygon, but its path as an argument:

```
var area =
google.maps.geometry.spherical.computeArea(path);
```

What does this `spherical` namespace stand for?

As you have observed, maps are 2D surfaces. However, the Earth's surface is not. To reflect the Earth's surface on a 2D canvas, projections are used. However, this reflection is not as smooth as it first seems. It comes with a cost; distortion of the Earth's shapes and properties occurs. To handle these side effects, spherical geometry calculations are needed, and `google.maps.geometry.spherical` exists exactly for this purpose.

When you call the `computeArea()` or `computeLength()` method, the area calculations are performed as if the shapes are warped to the Earth's surface, taking the earth curvature into account.

The unit of the return values of the two methods is meters. We have converted them to square kilometers and kilometers respectively in order to have more meaningful values while printing them in the console window:

```
console.log('Polygon Area: ' +  area/1000000 + ' km sqs');
console.log('Polygon Length: ' +  length/1000 + ' kms');
```

The event handlers for the `polygoncomplete` and `polylinecomplete` events are identical, except in `polylinecomplete`, where there is no area calculation.

There's more...

There's a strong possibility that having the length and area information attached to the shapes would be nice. You can extend the `Polygon` and `Polyline` JavaScript classes to have them. But bear in mind that extending JavaScript objects may lead to unexpected errors; you may clobber a different library's object extension. Therefore, think twice before extending the JavaScript classes:

```
google.maps.Polygon.prototype.getArea = function()
{
    return
    google.maps.geometry.spherical.computeArea(this.getPath());
};

google.maps.Polygon.prototype.getLength = function(){
    return
    google.maps.geometry.spherical.computeLength(this.getPath());
};

google.maps.Polyline.prototype.getLength=function(){
    return
    google.maps.geometry.spherical.computeLength(this.getPath());
};
```

Having extended the `Polygon` and `Polyline` classes, you can call the `getArea()` and `getLength()` methods directly from their objects:

```
polygon.getArea();
polyline.getLength();
```

See also

▸   The *Drawing shapes on the map* recipe in this chapter

Encoding coordinates

The polylines and polygons that you draw using the Google Maps JavaScript API consist of arrays of `LatLng` objects in latitude and longitude pairs.

The length of these arrays increases substantially, especially when you have shapes with too many nodes, in the case of long polylines or polygons that have too much detail.

Dealing with these arrays (that can be retrieved by the `getPath()` methods of polylines and polygons) is a major problem, especially when you have to save the shape to a DB. Serializing and deserializing lengthy arrays is frequently hulky.

However, you can compress the paths of the shapes with Google's **polyline encoding algorithm**.

Detailed information on Google's polyline encoding algorithm

You can find detailed information about the polyline encoding algorithm at the following link:

`https://developers.google.com/maps/documentation/`
`utilities/polylinealgorithm`

By using the `geometry` library, you can encode and decode the paths of polylines and polygons.

This recipe will show you how to encode and decode the paths of the polylines and polygons.

Getting ready

It would be handy to have a quick glance at the first recipe—*Drawing shapes on the map*—of this chapter, as it covers every detail on how to draw a shape using the Google Maps JavaScript API.

How to do it...

Here are the steps you can use to view the encoded and decoded versions of your paths:

1. Add the `geometry` and `drawing` libraries to the bootstrap URL:

```
<script type="text/javascript"
    src="https://maps.googleapis.com/maps/api/js?
      libraries=drawing,geometry&sensor=false">
</script>
```

2. Organize your HTML so that you can view the original, encoded, and decoded coordinates of your shapes in a `div` element:

```
<div>
    <H3>Original, Encoded and Decoded Coordinate Pairs:<H3>
    <div id="loggingDiv"></div>
</div>
```

3. Keep a reference to the `loggingDiv` div element in your `initMap()` function:

```
loggingDiv = document.getElementById('loggingDiv');
```

4. Create a `polylinecomplete` event handler in your `initMap()` function after creating `drawingManager` and attaching it to the map instance:

```
google.maps.event.addListener(drawingManager,
        'polylinecomplete', function(polyline){
    var path = polyline.getPath();

    var coords = path.getArray();

    var text = '<b>Original Coordinates:</b> ' + coords;

    var encodedCoords =
        google.maps.geometry.encoding.encodePath(path);

    text += '<br/><b>Encoded Coordinates:</b> ' +
        encodedCoords;

    var decodedCoords =
        google.maps.geometry.encoding.decodePath
        (encodedCoords);

    text += '<br/><b>Decoded Coordinates:</b> ' +
        decodedCoords;

    loggingDiv.innerHTML = text;
});
```

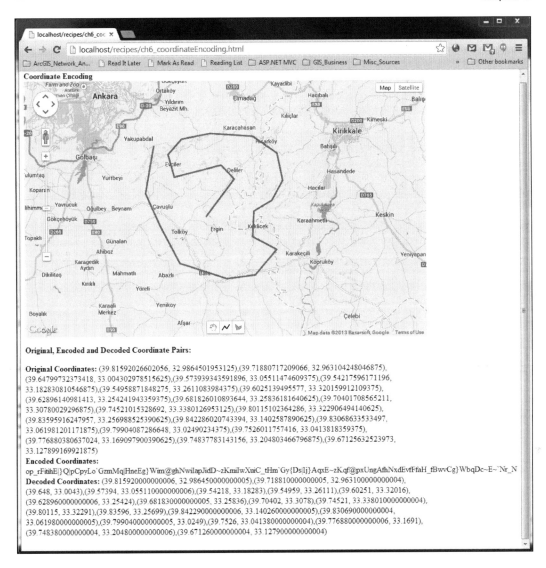

You can view the original, encoded, and decoded versions of your paths as shown in the preceding screenshot.

How it works...

The `polylinecomplete` event is fired when you finish drawing your polyline. You can get the `MVCArray` of the object of type `LatLng` that comprises your polyline in the following manner:

```
var path = polyline.getPath();
```

Having the path object at hand, you can encode it easily by using the `encodePath()` method:

```
var encodedCoords =
    google.maps.geometry.encoding.encodePath(path);
```

The `encodePath()` method takes either the `MVCArray` of the object of type `LatLng` objects or an array of `LatLng` objects. So, here in our recipe, this will also be possible:

```
var encodedCoords =
    google.maps.geometry.encoding.encodePath(coords);
```

The `encodePath()` method returns a string that is perfectly fit for saving to a DB and potentially saves a considerable amount of time that would be spent serializing and deserializing operations:

```
op_rFitihE|}Q|pCpyLo`GzmMq|HneEg}Wim@ghNwiIapJidD~zKmiIwXuiC_tHm`G
y{Ds|Ij}AqxE~zKqf@pxUngAfhNxdEvfFfaH_fBwvCg}WbqDc~E~`Nr_N
```

Without encoding, the `coords` array would look like this:

```
(39.81592026602056, 32.9864501953125),(39.71880717209066,
32.963104248046875),(39.64799732373418,
33.004302978515625),(39.573939343591896,
33.05511474609375),(39.54217596171196,
33.182830810546875),(39.54958871848275,
33.2611083984375),(39.6025139495577,
33.320159912109375),(39.62896140981413,
33.254241943359375),(39.681826010893644,
33.25836181640625),(39.70401708565211,
33.30780029296875),(39.74521015328692,
33.3380126953125),(39.80115102364286,
33.322906494140625),(39.83595916247957,
33.256988525390625),(39.842286020743394,
33.1402587890625),(39.83068633533497,
33.061981201171875),(39.79904087286648,
33.02490234375),(39.7526011757416,
33.0413818359375),(39.776880380637024,
33.169097900390625),(39.74837783143156,
33.204803466796875),(39.67125632523973, 33.127899169921875)
```

Encoding polylines and polygons is not a one-way operation. You can decode the encoded coordinate pairs as follows:

```
var decodedCoords =
    google.maps.geometry.encoding.decodePath(encodedCoords);
```

The `decodePath()` method takes encoded coordinates in the form of a string and returns an array of `LatLng` objects.

Searching for and showing nearby places

Google Maps is not only about beautiful base maps with an immense cartographic quality or regularly updated satellite images. In your daily life, not as a programmer but as an ordinary user of Google Maps, you will have no doubt used Google Maps to search for places; be it The Metropolitan Museum of Arts in New York, or a commonplace *farmacia* in Rome.

This information is in Google Maps, but how can you reach and serve this information through the Google Maps JavaScript API?

The `places` library is there exactly for this purpose, and it enables you to look for places by using certain search parameters.

You can perform nearby searches where place results would be near the location that you have provided, most commonly, the user's location. You can search within a radius, or you can just specify a search string. You can even request for additional details, such as related photos, review ratings, phone numbers, and opening hours for particular places.

This recipe will focus on nearby searches by using the `places` library of the Google Maps JavaScript API.

Getting ready

This recipe will make use of the `drawing` library, therefore, it is advised to go over the first recipe—*Drawing shapes on the map*—of this chapter and refresh your understanding on the subject matter.

How to do it...

You can draw a circle, search for places within this circle with a keyword, and get detailed information on each of the places by following the ensuing steps:

1. Add the `drawing` and `places` libraries to the bootstrap URL:

```
<script type="text/javascript"
    src="https://maps.googleapis.com/maps/api/js?
    libraries=drawing,places&sensor=false">
</script>
```

2. Add the `circles` and `markers` global variables to push and pop the respective overlays outside the `initMap()` function:

```
var circles;
var markers;
```

3. Add a popup global variable to hold the value of the `infoWindow` object:

```
var popup;
```

4. Initialize the `circles` and `markers` arrays and the `infoWindow` object in the `initMap()` function:

```
circles = new Array();
markers = new Array();
popup = new google.maps.InfoWindow();
```

5. Create a `circlecomplete` event handler in your `initMap()` function after creating the `drawingManager` object and attaching it to the map instance (items from number 6 to number 12 will be in this event handler):

```
google.maps.event.addListener(drawingManager,
'circlecomplete', function(circle){

});
```

6. Inside the `circlecomplete` event handler, set `drawingMode` to `null`:

```
drawingManager.setDrawingMode(null);
```

7. Add the latest drawn circle to the `circles` array and then reverse the order inside the array:

```
circles.push(circle);
circles.reverse();
```

8. Pop the previous circle and set its map handle to null so that only the last drawn circle is shown:

```
while(circles[1]){
    circles.pop().setMap(null);
}
```

9. Clear all previously drawn markers:

```
while(markers[0]){
    markers.pop().setMap(null);
}
```

10. Create nearby search settings, setting the location as the circle center and the radius as the circle radius. Also, add a `keyword` property to return the places containing that keyword:

```
var nearbyPlacesRequest = {
    location: circle.getCenter(),
    radius: circle.radius,
    keyword: 'pizza'
};
```

11. Get the handle for the `PlacesService` service object:

```
var placesService = new
    google.maps.places.PlacesService(map);
```

12. Send the request with a callback function:

```
placesService.nearbySearch(nearbyPlacesRequest,
    resultsCallback);
```

13. Outside the `initMap()` function, create a callback function for the `nearbySearch` request, using the following code snippet:

```
function resultsCallback(results, status) {
    if (status ==
        google.maps.places.PlacesServiceStatus.OK) {
        for (var i = 0, l=results.length; i < l; i++) {
            pinpointResult(results[i]);
        }
    }
}
```

14. Create a function to create a marker per the places result (the steps from number 15 to number 17 will be in this function):

```
function pinpointResult(result) {


}
```

15. Create the marker inside the `pinpointResult()` function:

```
var marker = new google.maps.Marker({
    map: map,
    position: result.geometry.location
});
```

16. Add a click event handler to the marker so that when it is clicked, the `infoWindow` object pops up:

```
google.maps.event.addListener(marker, 'click', function() {
    var popupContent = '<b>Name: </b> ' + result.name +
    '<br/>' + '<b>Vicinity: </b>' + result.vicinity +
    '<br/><b>Rating: </b>' + result.rating;
    popup.setContent(popupContent);
    popup.open(map, this);
});
```

17. Push the marker to the `markers` array:

```
markers.push(marker);
```

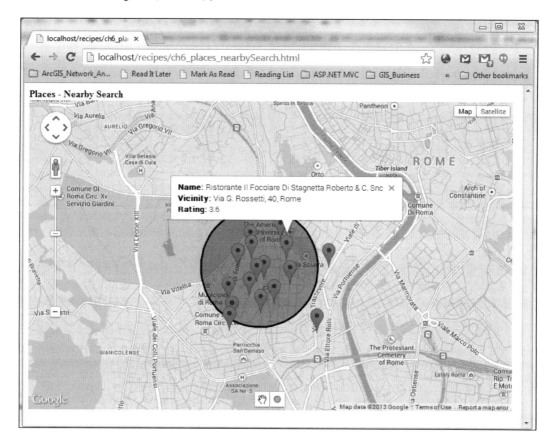

As shown in the preceding screenshot, you can draw a circle, search for places within this circle with a keyword, and get detailed information on each of the places found.

How it works...

The steps for this recipe require you to work a bit longer; however, the essence is simple. For a moment, forget about the details on the `circles` and `markers` arrays and the related logic; just concentrate on the nearby search:

```
var nearbyPlacesRequest = {
    location: circle.getCenter(),
    radius: circle.radius,
    keyword: 'pizza'
};
```

In the `circlecomplete` event handler (this is fired after we finish drawing our circle), we place a `nearbyPlacesRequest` object. This object should be of the type `google.maps.places.PlaceSearchRequest`.

The `location` property sets the `LatLng` object that should be the center of the search for the places. Usually, in nearby searches, this property is set as per the user's location. But for this recipe, we have tied it to the drawn circles' centers, as you can draw and search multiple times as per your needs.

The distance from `location` is set by the `radius` property so that the places are returned within this distance from the center of the circle. In our recipe, we have set the radius of the circle drawn.

Lastly, the `keyword` property filters the places so that the ones containing the keyword will be returned. Note that all the information not only includes the name or type of the place, but also the address and reviews, which will be matched against the keyword. So, be prepared for a place that is a cafeteria whose reviews include the keyword "pizza" in return of this request.

After preparing the request parameters, the next step is to send the request. First, we create a `PlacesService` object, taking our current map instance as a parameter:

```
var placesService = new
    google.maps.places.PlacesService(map);
```

By using the `placesService` object, we can send our request:

```
placesService.nearbySearch(nearbyPlacesRequest,
    resultsCallback);
```

The `nearbySearch` method takes two parameters, the first parameter being our old request parameters embedded in the `nearbyPlacesRequest` object and the second parameter being the callback function that returns the results. In our recipe, the second parameter is the `resultsCallback` function:

```
function resultsCallback(results, status) {
    if (status == google.maps.places.PlacesServiceStatus.OK) {
        for (var i = 0, l=results.length; i < l; i++) {
            pinpointResult(results[i]);
        }
    }
}
```

This callback function takes two arguments here (in fact, it has a third parameter, which is related to search pagination): the array of the places found in the search and the service status. In the callback function, we first check if the service status is OK or not. Then we iterate through `results`, which is an array of the `PlaceResult` class type, to create the markers and fill in the `infoWindow` objects for each returned place.

We can create an associated marker for each place, as seen in the following code snippet:

```
var marker = new google.maps.Marker({
    map: map,
    position: result.geometry.location
});
```

The `geometry` property of the `result` object embeds a `location` property, which is of the `LatLng` class type. This is perfectly fit for the `position` property of the `Marker` class.

We can reach the details of the places in our `popup` object attached in the `click` event handler for the marker:

```
google.maps.event.addListener(marker, 'click', function() {
    var popupContent = '<b>Name: </b> ' + result.name + '<br/>' +
        '<b>Vicinity: </b>' + result.vicinity + '<br/><b>Rating: </b>'
        + result.rating;

    popup.setContent(popupContent);
    popup.open(map, this);
});
```

You may have observed that we are using the `name`, `vicinity`, and `rating` properties of the place as the content for the popup. `name` represents the name of the place, `vicinity` returns a portion of the address information, and the `rating` value is the review rating of the place, 0.0 being the lowest and 5.0 being the highest.

There's more...

The details and options for searching nearby places is not limited to the options presented in this recipe. We will just dig a little more here. First comes the `nearbyPlacesRequest` object. The properties presented inside this object are: `location`, `radius`, and `keyword`.

However, the `PlaceSearchRequest` class, of which our object is a type, has much more than what we saw in this recipe. For instance, you can supply a `LatLngBounds` object instead of the location and radius:

```
var requestBounds = new google.maps.LatLngBounds(
    new google.maps.LatLng(39.85, 32.74),
    new google.maps.LatLng(40.05, 32.84)
);

var nearbyPlacesRequest = {
    bounds: requestBounds,
    keyword: 'pizza'
};
```

Please bear in mind that one option is to use `bounds`, and another option is to use the `location` and `radius` couple. Using one of them is compulsory for the `PlaceSearchRequest` class.

To filter the place results, using `keyword` is not the only solution. You can try the `name` property to directly match against the names of the places. For instance, the following code gives the places that have `Buckingham` in their name:

```
var nearbyPlacesRequest = {
    location: circle.getCenter(),
    radius: circle.radius,
    name: 'Buckingham'
};
```

If your drawn circle is in London, it will possibly bring up Buckingham Palace as well as a bunch of hotels nearby.

You can select the type of place to be returned by using the `types` property. This property takes an array of types such as:

```
var nearbyPlacesRequest = {
    location: circle.getCenter(),
    radius: circle.radius,
    types: ['stadium', 'car_rental',
        'library','university','administrative_area_level_3']
};
```

There is really an immense range of types that Google Maps has been covering. You can just insert which place type you want, from car rentals to universities, just as we have done.

Complete list of place types

You can find the complete list of place types at:

`https://developers.google.com/places/documentation/supported_types`

Other than `types`, `name`, and `bounds`, there are many more properties in the `PlaceSearchRequest` class such as `openNow`, which is a very handy property to show only the places that are open at the time of the search.

Apart from the pool of options that appear while giving the request for a nearby search, there is also another bunch of properties in returning the results; in other words, the places represented by the `PlaceResult` class.

For example, an `icon` property of the `PlaceResult` class that we can use in the following code block inside our `pinpointResult()` function:

```
var placeIcon = {
    url: result.icon,
    scaledSize: new google.maps.Size(30, 30)
};

var marker = new google.maps.Marker({
    map: map,
    position: result.geometry.location,
    icon: placeIcon
});
```

This code block will return the places together with their respective icons:

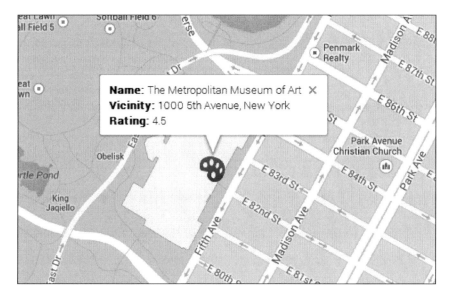

Notice the painter's palette icon in the preceding screenshot, incorporated with the returned place, which is The Metropolitan Museum of Art in New York.

You can also access the types to which the place belongs. The `types` property of the `PlaceResult` class returns the types in a string array. Therefore, the `Result.types` property returns the following parameters for The Metropolitan Museum of Art in New York:

```
["art_gallery", "museum", "establishment"]
```

You can also get information on whether a place is open or closed at the time of search if you change the click handler of the marker, as shown in the following code snippet:

```
google.maps.event.addListener(marker, 'click', function() {
    var popupContent = '<b>Name: </b> ' + result.name + '<br/>' +
    '<b>Vicinity: </b>' + result.vicinity;
    if (result.opening_hours){
        if (result.opening_hours.open_now){
            popupContent += '<br/><b>Is Open Now: </b> '
            + 'YES'
        }
        else {
            popupContent += '<br/><b>Is Open Now: </b> '
            + 'NO'
        }
    }
    popup.setContent(popupContent);
    popup.open(map, this);
});
```

Using the preceding code, you would have come up with information such as the following:

Complete list of properties for the PlaceResult class

You can find the complete list of properties of the `PlaceResult` class at:

`https://developers.google.com/maps/documentation/javascript/reference#PlaceResult`

Finding places with the autocomplete option

The Google Maps JavaScript API offers a variety of ways to search for places and additional information. You can apply nearby searches and have detailed information about places together with their geometry, as you have observed in the recipe named *Searching and showing nearby places* in this chapter.

How about having a text field control with an autocomplete feature for searching places? You can hardcode it, but there is no need to do so, as Google already has a feature exactly for this.

In this recipe, we will go over the autocomplete feature of the `places` library for the Google Maps JavaScript API.

Getting ready

This recipe will make use of the concepts related to the `places` library introduced in the *Searching and showing nearby places* recipe of this chapter. It is advised to go over this recipe to have a general understanding of places and their properties.

How to do it...

You can add the text field and search for places with the autocomplete feature by carrying out the following steps:

1. Insert an input HTML element that will be used as the autocomplete field:

    ```
    <div id="searchDiv">
    <input id="autocomplete_searchField" type="text"
        size="40"  placeholder="Search for Places">
    </div>
    ```

2. Define the markers and pop-up variables as global outside the `initMap()` function:

    ```
    var markers;
    var popup;
    ```

3. Initialize the global variables in `initMap()`:

```
markers = new Array();
popup = new google.maps.InfoWindow();
```

4. Get the `div` tag with its ID as `searchDiv` and push it as a custom control after creating the map with its `initMap()` options:

```
var searchDiv =
    document.getElementById('autocomplete_searchField');
map.controls[google.maps.ControlPosition.TOP_CENTER].push(
    searchDiv);
```

5. Get the handle for the input element:

```
var searchField =
    document.getElementById('autocomplete_searchField');
```

6. Supply the properties for the autocomplete search request:

```
var searchOptions = {
    bounds: new google.maps.LatLngBounds(
        new google.maps.LatLng(8.54, 17.33),
         new google.maps.LatLng(39.67, 43.77)
    ),
    types: new Array()
};
```

7. Get the `autocomplete` object by supplying the input HTML element to be used, namely `searchField`, and the `searchOptions`:

```
var autocompleteSearch = new
    google.maps.places.Autocomplete(searchField,
        searchOptions);
```

8. Create a `place_changed` event handler for the `autocomplete` object (steps 9 to 11 will be in this event handler):

```
google.maps.event.addListener(autocompleteSearch,
'place_changed', function() {
});
```

9. In the event handler, clear the previous markers first:

```
while(markers[0]) {
    markers.pop().setMap(null);
}
```

10. Get the `PlaceResult` object in response to the autocompleted search:

```
var place = autocompleteSearch.getPlace();
```

11. If the place has a geometry, call a function to create the associated marker:

```
if (place.geometry) {
    pinpointResult(place);
}
```

12. Create a function for creating a marker and adding a click event handler for the marker:

```
function pinpointResult(result) {
    var placeIcon = {
        url: result.icon,
        scaledSize: new google.maps.Size(30, 30)
    };

    var marker = new google.maps.Marker({
        map: map,
        position: result.geometry.location,
        icon: placeIcon
    });

    map.setCenter(result.geometry.location);
    map.setZoom(16);

    google.maps.event.addListener(marker, 'click',
    function() {
        var popupContent = '<b>Name: </b> ' + result.name +
        '<br/>' + '<b>Vicinity: </b>' + result.vicinity;

        popup.setContent(popupContent);
        popup.open(map, this);
    });
    markers.push(marker);
}
```

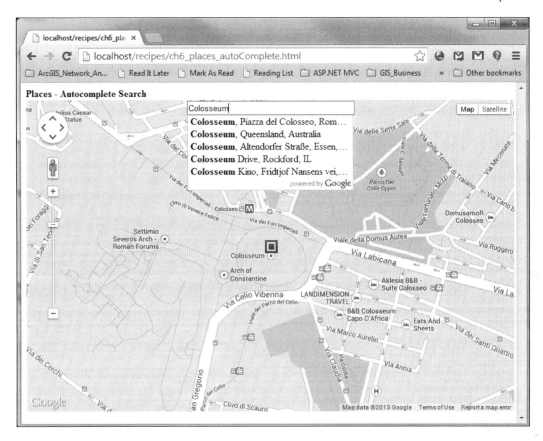

You can make use of the autocomplete search features as shown in the preceding screenshot.

How it works...

In this recipe, we first created an input element with some placeholder text (beware that this is not supported in older browsers) that will serve as our text field for searching places:

```
<input id="autocomplete_searchField" type="text"
   size="40"  placeholder="Search for Places">
</input>
```

Then, we added the `div` container tag as a custom control for the Google Maps JavaScript API to have the text field inside the Google Maps UI:

```
var searchDiv = document.getElementById('searchDiv');
map.controls[google.maps.ControlPosition.TOP_CENTER].push(
   searchDiv);
```

We set the properties for the autocomplete search in an `AutocompleteOptions` object named `searchOptions`:

```
var searchOptions = {
    bounds: new google.maps.LatLngBounds(
    new google.maps.LatLng(8.54, 17.33),
        new google.maps.LatLng(39.67, 43.77)
    ),
    types: new Array()
};
```

In the preceding code snippet, `bounds` serves to define the boundaries for the places to be found. Here, we are setting it to a large predefined boundary; you can set it to another `LatLngBounds` object of your taste.

The `types` array is empty for this recipe; actually this array is for restricting the types of places to be found, whether it be a business, city, or region. In our example, it is empty, so our searches will return every type of `PlaceResult` object.

We created our autocomplete object with two ingredients: `searchField` being the input element and `searchOptions` having the `bounds` and `types` properties:

```
var autocompleteSearch = new
    google.maps.places.Autocomplete(searchField,
        searchOptions);
```

Then, we create our `place_changed` event handler for our `Autocomplete` object, which gets fired when the user selects the `PlaceResult` provided:

```
google.maps.event.addListener(autocompleteSearch,
'place_changed', function() {
    while(markers[0]) {
        markers.pop().setMap(null);
    }

    var place = autocompleteSearch.getPlace();
    if (place) {
        if (place.geometry) {
            pinpointResult(place);
        }
    }
});
```

In the event handler, we detach the marker previously mapped on the map; then, we call the `getPlace()` method to get the `Place` object of type `PlaceResult` in this context. If the place exists and if it has geometry (meaning that, a proper `PlaceResult` instance is found), we call the `pinpoint()` function to create a marker from `PlaceResult` and attach a click event handler for the marker to popup the associated `InfoWindow` object:

There's more...

In our recipe, we set the `bounds` property in the `searchOptions` object to a predefined boundary:

```
bounds: new google.maps.LatLngBounds(
    new google.maps.LatLng(8.54, 17.33),
    new google.maps.LatLng(39.67, 43.77)
),
```

This line sets the autocomplete operation to find the searched places primarily within, but not limited to, the specific `LatLngBounds` object. Therefore, do not get surprised if you happen to give a small boundary and find results outside the boundary.

We're setting the boundary to a `LatLngBounds` object, such as boundary of the map, and you can change it afterwards:

```
autocompleteSearch.setBounds(map.getBounds());
```

But what happens if you need to set the bounds to the current viewport, which gets updated as you pan and zoom in/out the map? There is a way, as follows:

```
autocompleteSearch.bindTo('bounds', map)
```

By using this `bindTo()` function, the `bounds` property is bound to the current viewport boundary and gets updated when it changes.

Apart from the `bounds` property, there is a `types` property that we have set as an empty array, but it does not need to be empty to filter out the predictions done by our `autocompleteSearch` object:

```
types: ['(regions)']
```

This renders the `autocompleteSearch` object, searching only for administrative regions instead of all places. So when you type `colos`, the Colosseum in Rome does not come up, as only administrative regions are permitted to be displayed in the `autocompleteSearch` object; you can observe this in the following screenshot:

Complete list of entries for the types property in the google.maps. places.AutocompleteOptions class

You can find the complete list of entries for the `types` property in the `AutocompleteOptions` class at:

`https://developers.google.com/maps/documentation/ javascript/reference#AutocompleteOptions`

Adding drag zoom to the map

Google Maps has a zoom control and the JavaScript API makes use of this control to offer a variety of options for programmers. It is a very useful and easy-to-use control. But there are other ways for zooming; for instance, by drawing an area of interest by dragging a box, so that the map zooms to that area.

This functionality does not exist in the standard Google Maps JavaScript API and any of its libraries; you have to code it. Or, you can make use of the utility libraries, developed by the good guys, at the following link:

`https://code.google.com/p/google-maps-utility-library-v3/wiki/ Libraries`

One of their libraries, `KeyDragZoom`, is exactly for this zoom functionality, and we will use this library in this recipe.

Getting ready

You have to download the `keydragzoom.js` JavaScript source file from the following link (the latest release is 2.0.9 as of the time of writing this book) and place it in the same directory as our recipe source code:

`http://google-maps-utility-library-v3.googlecode.com/svn/tags/ keydragzoom/`

How to do it...

Here are the steps to perform zoom by dragging a box and zooming into the area inside the box:

1. Use a reference for the `keydragzoom.js` file:

```
<script type="text/javascript"
    src="keydragzoom.js">
</script>
```

2. Enable the functionality after setting all the map-related options in the `initMap()` function:

```
map.enableKeyDragZoom({
    visualEnabled: true,
    visualPosition: google.maps.ControlPosition.LEFT,
    visualPositionOffset: new google.maps.Size(35, 0),
    visualPositionIndex: null,
    visualSprite:
      'http://maps.gstatic.com/mapfiles/ftr/controls/
      dragzoom_btn.png',
    visualSize: new google.maps.Size(20, 20),
    visualTips: {
        off: "Turn on",
        on: "Turn off"
    }
});
```

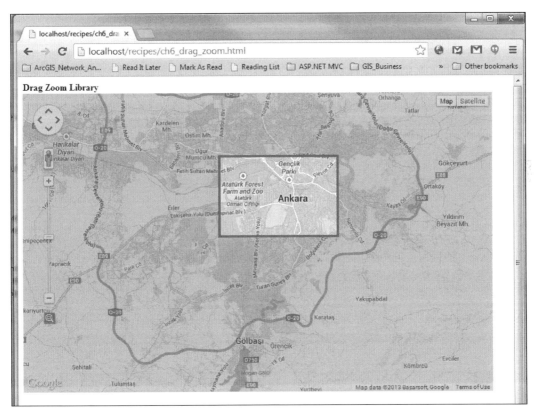

You can make use of zooming by dragging a box as shown in the preceding screenshot.

How it works...

You can perform drag zooms either by pressing the control button and drawing a box, or simpler than that, holding the *Shift* key and drawing the box to zoom into the area inside the box.

To do this, we first added the JavaScript source file of the drag zoom library in our recipe. After setting the map options and using the map instance we can enable the drag zoom functionality by using the `enableKeyDragZoom()` method of the map instance.

This extension method is not a part of the Google Maps JavaScript API and comes with the `keydragzoom` library. There are a few associated options that are embedded under the `KeyDragZoomOptions` class.

Keep in mind that, in its simplest form, you can use the key drag zoom functionality by enabling it:

```
map.enableKeyDragZoom();
```

The only difference would be that you would have to use the *Shift* key as your only way because there would be no drag zoom control button.

The properties embedded in the `KeyDragZoomOptions` class are all about the control button that is placed below the standard zoom control:

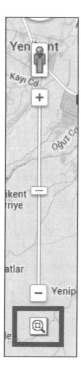

The `visualEnabled` property sets the control to be seen or not, so if this property is `false`, there is no need for other properties as well. The `visualPosition` property sets the control position; we have placed it to the left. A detailed description on control positions can be found in the *Changing the position of controls* recipe of *Chapter 4, Working with Controls*.

Complete list of properties in the KeyDragZoomOptions class

You can find the complete list of properties in the `KeyDragZoomOptions` class at the following link:

`http://google-maps-utility-library-v3.googlecode.com/svn/tags/keydragzoom/2.0.9/docs/reference.html`

See also

▶ You can review the Google Maps JavaScript API controls and their use in *Chapter 4, Working with Controls*

Creating custom popups/infoboxes

We have already created popups or infoboxes in *Chapter 3, Adding Vector Layers*. As it is stated there, almost every mapping application has the ability to display information that is related to the features shown on it. This information can be related to a marker or a map. Instead of showing all the information on the map, popups or info boxes are used only when needed.

The Google Maps JavaScript API has a `google.maps.InfoWindow` class to create a default infobox for developers. In some cases, you need custom infoboxes to show information. There are two ways to do this:

▶ The first way is to create a custom class that inherits from the `google.maps.OverlayView` class and fill the methods to show/hide infoboxes with custom CSS styles.

▶ The other, easier way is to use a library created for you. There is a project on Google Code named `google-maps-utility-library-v3` that holds the number of libraries extending the Google Maps JavaScript API. Here's the link:

`https://code.google.com/p/google-maps-utility-library-v3/wiki/Libraries`

This project has a library named `InfoBox` that makes it possible to create custom infoboxes or map labels.

In this recipe, we will use the previously mentioned library to create custom infoboxes that can be bound to a marker and a map. The same infobox shows different information according to its binding. We will also add a simple map label at a fixed place, if extra information needs to be added to the map.

Getting ready

The first recipe of *Chapter 1, Google Maps JavaScript API Basics*, will do our work. We will add to it in this recipe.

How to do it...

You can get custom infoboxes by completing the following steps:

1. First, go to the following address to get the latest InfoBox source code and save it into a file named infobox.js under the lib directory. We used the /1.1.9/src/ infobox_packed.js file under the following URL:

   ```
   http://google-maps-utility-library-v3.googlecode.com/svn/tags/
   infobox/
   ```

2. Then, we get the codes by creating a simple map recipe, and add the following code to add our library to the page:

   ```
   <script type="text/javascript"
       src='lib/infobox.js'></script>
   ```

3. The next step is to create the contents of the infobox with the help of a div element:

   ```
   //Creating the contents for info box
   var boxText = document.createElement('div');
   boxtext.className = 'infoContent';
   boxText.innerHTML = '<b>Marker Info Box</b> <br> Gives
       information about marker';
   ```

4. Now we create an object that defines the options of the infobox:

   ```
   //Creating the info box options.
   var customInfoBoxOptions = {
       content: boxText,
       pixelOffset: new google.maps.Size(-100, 0),
       boxStyle: {
           background: "url('img/tipbox2.gif') no-repeat",
           opacity: 0.75,
           width: '200px'
       },
   ```

```
        closeBoxMargin: '10px 2px 2px 2px',
        closeBoxURL: 'img/close.gif',
        pane: 'floatPane'
};
```

5. We can initialize our custom infobox in the following manner:

```
//Initializing the info box
var customInfoBox = new InfoBox(customInfoBoxOptions);
```

6. Also, we create a JSON object that defines the options of a map label:

```
//Creating the map label options.
var customMapLabelOptions = {
        content: 'Custom Map Label',
        closeBoxURL: "",
        boxStyle: {
            border: '1px solid black',
            width: '110px'
        },
        position: new google.maps.LatLng(40.0678,
                    33.1252),
        pane: 'mapPane',
        enableEventPropagation: true
};
```

7. Then, we initialize the map label and add it to the map in the following manner:

```
//Initializing the map label
var customMapLabel = new InfoBox(customMapLabelOptions);
//Showing the map label
customMapLabel.open(map);
```

8. Create a simple marker that will be bound to the infobox:

```
//Initializing the marker for showing info box
var marker = new google.maps.Marker({
        map: map,
        draggable: true,
        position: new google.maps.LatLng(39.9078,
                    32.8252),
        visible: true
});
```

9. When the map is ready, we will open the infobox attached to the marker:

```
//Opening the info box attached to marker
customInfoBox.open(map, marker);
```

10. We should create event listeners for the marker and map for their click events to show the infobox. An infobox will appear at the bottom of the marker when the marker is clicked or when the map is clicked on at some point:

```
//Listening marker to open info box again with contents
//related to marker
google.maps.event.addListener(marker, 'click', function (e)
{
    boxText.innerHTML = '<b>Marker Info Box</b> <br>
            Gives information about marker';
    customInfoBox.open(map, this);
});


//Listening map click to open info box again with
//contents related to map coordinates
google.maps.event.addListener(map,'click', function (e)
{
    boxText.innerHTML = '<b>Map Info Box</b> <br>
            Gives information about coordinates <br>
            Lat: ' + e.latLng.lat().toFixed(6) + " -
            Lng: ' + e.latLng.lng().toFixed(6);
    customInfoBox.setPosition(e.latLng);
    customInfoBox.open(map);
});
```

11. You can also listen to events of infoboxes. We will add a listener to the click event of the close button of the infobox:

```
//Listening info box for clicking close button
google.maps.event.addListener(customInfoBox,
'closeclick', function () {
        console.log('Info Box Closed!!!');
});
```

12. Go to your local URL where your HTML file is stored in your favorite browser; you will see a popup with an infobox below. If you click on the map, you will see the coordinates of the mouse click inside the infobox, or if you click on the marker, you will see the infobox with the contents related to the marker. There is also a fixed map label at the top right of the map with some content; it says **Custom Map Label**.

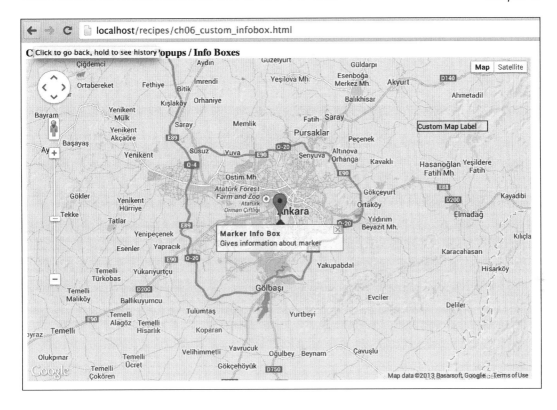

You can get your custom infobox as shown in the preceding screenshot.

How it works...

Using libraries in your web applications is common. The use of libraries saves development and debugging time for developers. Compared to your limited cases, libraries are tested in different environments for different cases.

As stated earlier, you can also write your own custom class to show custom infoboxes or map labels, but this is not a suggested way to discover America from the beginning. We used the library named `InfoBox`, which is written for this purpose. The documentation of this library is similar to the Google Maps JavaScript API documentation (found at `http://google-maps-utility-library-v3.googlecode.com/svn/tags/infobox/1.1.9/docs/reference.html`). The latest version of the library is 1.1.9 at the time this book was being written. Please update the library if there is a new version when you are using it.

The `InfoBox` library is built on the Google Maps JavaScript API base class named `google.maps.OverlayView`, which is used for adding extra layers or views to the map.

As expected, there is a need for content, which is defined in the `div` elements.

```
//Creating the contents for info box
var boxText = document.createElement('div');
boxtext.className = 'infoContent';
boxText.innerHTML = '<b>Marker Info Box</b> <br> Gives
          information about marker';
```

The `InfoBox` library can be initialized to show an infobox with its constructor, with a parameter created from the `InfoBoxOptions` class, as follows:

```
//Creating the info box options.
var customInfoBoxOptions = {
    content: boxText,
    pixelOffset: new google.maps.Size(-100, 0),
    boxStyle: {
        background: "url('img/tipbox2.gif') no-repeat",
        opacity: 0.75,
        width: '200px'
    },
    closeBoxMargin: '10px 2px 2px 2px',
    closeBoxURL: "img/close.gif",
    pane: 'floatPane'
};
```

The `InfoBox` library can be initialized to create a map label with its constructor with a parameter created from the `InfoBoxOptions` class, as follows:

```
//Creating the map label options.
var customMapLabelOptions = {
    content: 'Custom Map Label',
    closeBoxURL: '',
    boxStyle: {
        border: '1px solid black',
        width: '110px'
    },
    position: new google.maps.LatLng(40.0678, 33.1252),
    pane: 'mapPane',
    enableEventPropagation: true
};
```

The parameters for the `InfoBoxOption` class are explained in the following list:

- **content**: This can be a string or an HTML element. In our example, we used HTML `div` elements to create a beautiful decorated infobox. You can use the CSS style elements to create your custom infobox.

- **pixelOffset**: This is the offset in pixels from the top-left corner of the infobox. In this recipe, we want to center the infobox, so we used half the width of the infobox.

- **boxStyle**: This defines the CSS styles used for the infobox. The `background` style property used in this recipe shows the upper-headed arrow image. This image is a customized image to be placed in the middle of the infobox. The names of the `width` and `opacity` style properties suggest how they are used.

- **closeBoxMargin**: This is used to define where the close box will be placed in the CSS margin style value. In this recipe, we used the upper-headed arrow at the top of the infobox, so we must move the close box below the arrow image.

- **closeBoxURL**: This is the image URL of the close box. Google's standard close box image is used here. If you do not want to add a close box, set this property to empty.

- **pane**: This is the pane where the infobox will appear. If you are using it as an infobox, then use `floatPane`. If you are using it as a map label, use `mapPane`.

- **position**: This is the geographic location of the infobox or map label defined in the objects created from `google.maps.LatLng class`.

- **enableEventPropagation**: This is used to propagate the events. If you are using the `InfoBox` class for map labels, you don't need to get the events of the label. The map's events are more important in this case.

It doesn't matter whether it is an infobox or map label, you can show `InfoBox` objects with the `open()` method. If there isn't an anchor point, such as a marker, it only gets one parameter as a map; otherwise you should add the second parameter as an anchor object. Two usage examples are as follows:

```
//Showing the map label
customMapLabel.open(map);
//Opening the info box attached to marker
customInfoBox.open(map, marker);
```

If you need to change the position of the infobox like in the event handlers, you should use the `setPosition()` method of the class. This method gets objects created from the `google.maps.LatLng` class.

```
//Changing the position of info box
customInfoBox.setPosition(e.latLng);
```

The events used in this recipe were the topic of *Chapter 5, Understanding Google Maps JavaScript API Events*. We did not go into detail, but for some purposes, there are also events of the `InfoBox` class to handle. The following code block will listen to the clicking of the close button that will result in the closing of the infobox. The event handler of the listener will log only a message to the console for demonstration:

```
//Listening info box for clicking close button
google.maps.event.addListener(customInfoBox, 'closeclick',
function () {
    console.log('Info Box Closed!!!');
});
```

As you can see, in the preceding code, the Google Maps JavaScript API has a lot of potential that can be extracted with the help of extra libraries. The Google Maps JavaScript API gives you the base, and you can build whatever you want on it.

See also

▸ The *Creating a simple map in a custom DIV element* recipe in *Chapter 1, Google Maps JavaScript API Basics*

▸ The *Getting the coordinates of a mouse click* recipe in *Chapter 5, Understanding Google Maps JavaScript API Events*

7
Working with Services

In this chapter, we will cover:

- ▶ Finding coordinates for an address
- ▶ Finding addresses on a map with a click
- ▶ Getting elevations on a map with a click
- ▶ Creating a distance matrix for the given locations
- ▶ Getting directions for the given locations
- ▶ Adding Street View to your maps

Introduction

This chapter focuses on the various services offered by the Google Maps JavaScript API. These services add significant functionality that largely differentiates Google Maps from its competitors. The reliability and the quality of the underlying data makes these services even more appreciated, as this allows applications making use of Google Maps to provide added functionalities.

These services generally follow an asynchronous pattern in which a request is sent to an external server and a callback method is provided to process the responses.

 These services are not available all over the world; there are restrictions or quotas—even if it is available—to prevent the abuse of these services. Detailed information will be given on these services in related recipes.

The good part of these services is, as they are part of the Google Maps JavaScript API, they are fully compatible with the classes and objects of the API.

For instance, you can find directions between two addresses using the Google Maps API Directions Service. Firstly, you make the request supplying the necessary parameters. Then, by using your callback function, you will get the directions if everything goes on track. But, for a time lapse, you may have to think of ways to overlay these directions on the base maps. Luckily, the API provides the infrastructure for this so that with one line of additional code, you can observe your requested directions on top of your base maps.

This chapter will describe each of the service types in detail, including geocoding, directions, elevation, distance matrix, and Street View, with each recipe consisting of a related scenario.

Finding coordinates for an address

Locating an address or place on the map has always been a tedious task, and the Google Maps JavaScript API eases this task with the geocoding service. Geocoding, in its simplest definition, is to associate geographic coordinates with the address information, be it only a street name, the detailed building number and zip code, or only a locality name.

By having the coordinates of your respective addresses, you can easily overlay them in your map applications.

In this recipe, you will succeed in entering your holiday places and addresses and then map them as markers on top of your base maps in your application.

Getting ready

This recipe will make use of the concepts related to adding vector layers, particularly markers, introduced in the *Adding markers to maps* recipe in *Chapter 3, Adding Vector Layers*. It is advised to go through this recipe to have a general understanding of vector layers and their properties.

How to do it...

You can locate your addresses by following the given steps:

1. Create HTML markup so that you can enter your addresses and search for them:

    ```
    <input id="addressField" type="text" size="30"
      placeholder="Enter your Address" />
    <input type="button" id="listAddressBtn" value="Pin Address
      On Map" />
    <p id="placesText"></p>
    <ul id="addressList" class="addressList"></ul>
    ```

2. Define the global `geocoder` object:

```
var geocoder;
```

3. Initialize the `geocoder` object in your `initMap()` function:

```
geocoder = new google.maps.Geocoder();
```

4. Get the `listAddressBtn` button element and add a `click` event listener:

```
var listAddressBtn =
document.getElementById('listAdressBtn');
listAddressBtn.addEventListener('click', function(){
    listAddresses();
});
```

5. Create a function for listing addresses on the `addressList` element and send the geocoding request:

```
function listAddresses() {
    //get text input handler
    var addressField =
    document.getElementById('addressField');
    //get addressList <ul> element handle
    var addressList =
    document.getElementById('addressList');
    if (addressList.children.length === 0) {
        var placesText =
        document.getElementById('placesText');
        placesText.innerHTML = 'Places You Have Visited
        (Click on the place name to see on map):';
    }
    //create a list item
    var listItem = document.createElement('li');
    //get the text in the input element and make it a
    //list item
    listItem.innerHTML = addressField.value;
    listItem.addEventListener('click', function() {
        geocodeAddress (listItem.innerHTML);
    });
    //append it to the <ul> element
    addressList.appendChild(listItem);
    //call the geocoding function
    geocodeAddress(addressField.value);
}
```

6. Create a function for geocoding the addresses entered:

```
function geocodeAddress(addressText) {
    //real essence, send the geocoding request
    geocoder.geocode( {'address': addressText},
    function(results, status) {
        //if the service is working properly...
        if (status == google.maps.GeocoderStatus.OK) {
            //show the first result on map
            pinpointResult(results[0]);
        } else {
            alert('Cannot geocode because: ' + status);
        }
    });
}
```

7. Place a marker on the map and attach an `InfoWindow` object to display its details:

```
function pinpointResult(result) {
    var marker = new google.maps.Marker({
        map: map,
        position: result.geometry.location
    });

    map.setCenter(result.geometry.location);
    map.setZoom(16);

    //infowindow stuff
    google.maps.event.addListener(
    marker, 'click', function() {
        var popupContent = '<b>Address: </b> ' +
        result.formatted_address;
        popup.setContent(popupContent);
        popup.open(map, this);
    });
}
```

8. You will have your addresses pinned on your map as shown in the following screenshot:

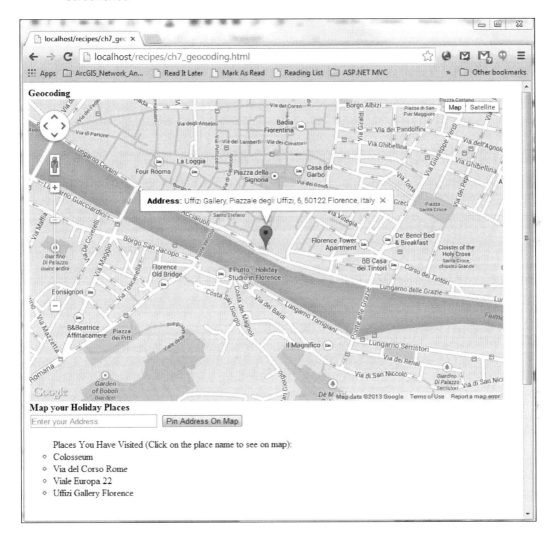

How it works...

Making a geocoding request is in fact quite simple. Firstly, you create a `Geocoder` object:

```
geocoder = new google.maps.Geocoder();
```

Then, you call the `geocode()` method from the `geocoder` object, supplying its address parameter with an address, place, or locality name:

```
geocoder.geocode( {'address': addressText},
    function(results, status) {…});
```

This method takes the address, sends it to the Google servers to be geocoded, and by a callback function, gets back the results in the form of the `GeocoderResult` object array.

The responses come in an array in order of the most relevant matches. For instance, when you search for `Colosseum`, the `formatted_address` property of the first `GeocoderResult` object is:

```
Colosseum, Piazza del Colosseo, 1, 00184 Rome, Italy
```

The second is:

```
Colosseum, Enschede, The Netherlands
```

You can quickly grasp that the ancient and highly touristic Colosseum in Rome is more popular than the second result. You can, of course, bias results through the restriction of map boundaries and country codes (we will review this in detail in the upcoming sections). However, without any intervention, you will see the geocoded results of high popularity at the top through various countries and continents.

The `GeocoderResult` object has its `geometry` property so that you can view it via a marker overlay on top of base maps. In our recipe, the `pinpointResult()` function makes use of this, where it takes the `GeocoderResult` object named `result` as its only parameter:

```
function pinpointResult(result) {
    var marker = new google.maps.Marker({
        map: map,
        position: result.geometry.location
    });
    ...
}
```

There's more...

The geocoding service request and response has an extensive set of options and properties. Let's start with the request first. In addition to the `address` parameter, which is the primary and required parameter of the `GeocodeRequest` object (supplied as the first parameter for the `geocode()` method of the `Geocoder` object), there is a `bounds` property that you can use to specify the returning geocoded results, as shown in the following code:

```
geocoder.geocode({
    'address': addressText,
    'bounds': new google.maps.LatLngBounds(
    new google.maps.LatLng(
    25.952910068468075, -15.93734749374994),
    new google.maps.LatLng(57.607047845370246,
    54.37515250625006)
    )
    },
    function(results, status) {...}
);
```

When you supply the bounds property, such as the one used in the preceding code covering Europe, and then when you search for Sun Street, the first result is the UK. This is because the bounds property biases the geocoding results present inside the LatLngBounds object supplied. When you delete the bounds property, the first result from the same search comes from the USA.

In addition, you can bias the results by using the region parameter, in which an IANA language region subtag is accepted.

> The complete listing for IANA language region subtags can be found at http://www.iana.org/assignments/language-subtag-registry/language-subtag-registry.
>
> Detailed information on the GeocodeRequest object can be found at https://developers.google.com/maps/documentation/javascript/reference#GeocoderRequest.

For instance, supplying the region parameter with 've' for Venezuela as shown in the following code and searching for 'Valencia' returns the city of 'Valencia' in Venezuela in the first place:

```
geocoder.geocode({
    'address': addressText,
    'region':'ve'},
    function(results, status) {...}
);
```

Without the region parameter, this would return the city of 'Valencia' in Spain in the first place.

Passing the returned results and their properties to the GeocoderResult object, this object carries an accuracy indicator since certain geocoding processes are about interpolation and matching and not about one-to-one equality.

The value of the result is stored in the `geometry` property of the `GeocoderResult` object, which contains the `location_type` property. These values are in the order of their highest to lowest accuracies:

- `google.maps.GeocoderLocationType.ROOFTOP`
- `google.maps.GeocoderLocationType.RANGE_INTERPOLATED`
- `google.maps.GeocoderLocationType.GEOMETRIC CENTER`
- `google.maps.GeocoderLocationType.APPROXIMATE`

In the preceding code, the `ROOFTOP` value represents the exact address, `RANGE_INTERPOLATED` represents that there is an interpolation between certain sections of the road, `GEOMETRIC_CENTER` represents the geometric center of the road or region, and finally `APPROXIMATE` tells us that the returned result's location is an approximation.

For instance, when we search for `'William Village'`, the first result's `formatted_address` is:

```
"Bremerton, WA, USA"
```

The `location_type` property of the geometry of the result is `APPROXIMATE`. This generally happens when there is no direct linkage between the search phrase and the returned result, as it is in our case.

Apart from the accuracy of the geocoding process, we can get the type of the `GeocoderResult` object through its `types` property. The `types` property is an array that is of the category to which the returned result belongs.

For instance, for the Colosseum in Rome, the `types` property is:

```
["point_of_interest", "establishment"]
```

While for Via del Corso, Rome, it is:

```
["route"]
```

For Uffizi Gallery, Florence, it is:

```
["museum", "point_of_interest", "establishment"]
```

> The complete listing for the possible values of the `types` property of the `GeocoderResult` object can be found at `https://developers.google.com/maps/documentation/javascript/geocoding#GeocodingAddressTypes`.

It is important to note that the callback function through which we get our results of the geocoding request requires another parameter, which is about the status of the request. The most prominent possible values for this parameter are:

- `google.maps.GeocoderStatus.OK`

- `google.maps.GeocoderStatus.ZERO_RESULTS`

- `google.maps.GeocoderStatus.OVER_QUERY_LIMIT`

- `google.maps.GeocoderStatus.REQUEST_DENIED`

- `google.maps.GeocoderStatus.INVALID_REQUEST`

The values except `GeocoderStatus.OK` point to a problem. Among all, `GeocoderStatus.OVER_QUERY_LIMIT` requires special attention. In the introduction of this chapter, we have mentioned that all of these Google Maps services are subject to limited use in terms of geography and request rates. And, this status code is fired when you go beyond the limit of the usage of the geocoding services.

A detailed explanation of the `OVER_QUERY_LIMIT` status code can be found at `https://developers.google.com/maps/documentation/business/articles/usage_limits#limitexceeded`.

The complete listing for the possible values of the `GeocoderStatus` object can be found at `https://developers.google.com/maps/documentation/javascript/geocoding#GeocodingStatusCodes`.

See also

- The *Adding markers to maps* recipe in *Chapter 3, Adding Vector Layers*

Finding addresses on a map with a click

In the previous recipe, we had the address in our hand and our aim was to find the map location; in other terms, the coordinates of the address on earth. But, what happens if we have the exact coordinates and try to find the address that matches these exact coordinates?

This process is known as reverse geocoding, and it is the process of converting coordinates to human-readable addresses.

In this recipe, we will make use of the reverse geocoding capabilities of the Google Maps JavaScript API. When the user clicks on the map, we will find the address where the user clicked and imminently display it to him/her.

Getting ready

Reviewing the recipe *Drawing shapes on the map* in *Chapter 6, Google Maps JavaScript Libraries*, will ease your work because greater detail on drawing shapes and their background is required for this recipe.

How to do it...

Here are the steps to allow your user to click on the map and find the address of the place that he/she clicked on:

1. Define the geocoder object as global:

    ```
    var geocoder;
    ```

2. Define the popup object as global:

    ```
    var popup;
    ```

3. Initialize the geocoder and popup objects, inside the initMap() function:

    ```
    geocoder = new google.maps.Geocoder();
    popup = new google.maps.InfoWindow();
    ```

4. Create the drawingManager object inside initMap():

    ```
    var drawingManager = new
      google.maps.drawing.DrawingManager(
    {
        //initial drawing tool to be enabled, we want to be in
        //no drawing mode at start
        drawingMode:null,
        //enable the drawingControl to be seen in the UI
        drawingControl:true,
        //select which drawing modes to be seen in the
        //drawingControl and position the drawingControl itself
        drawingControlOptions: {
            //select a control position in the UI
            position: google.maps.ControlPosition.TOP_CENTER,
            //selected drawing modes to be seen in the control
            drawingModes:[
            google.maps.drawing.OverlayType.MARKER
            ]
        }
    });
    ```

5. Enable the drawing functionality:

```
drawingManager.setMap(map);
```

6. Add an event listener for the completion of the user-drawn marker, perform the reverse geocoding task, and find the address:

```
google.maps.event.addListener(drawingManager,
'markercomplete', function(marker) {
    //get the LatLng object of the marker, it is necessary
    //for the geocoder
    var markerPosition = marker.getPosition();
    //reverse geocode the LatLng object to return the
    //addresses
    geocoder.geocode({'latLng': markerPosition},
    function(results, status) {
        //if the service is working properly...
        if (status == google.maps.GeocoderStatus.OK) {
            //Array of results will return if everything
            //is OK
            if (results) {
                //infowindow stuff
                showAddressOfResult(results[0],marker);
            }
        }
        //if the service is not working, deal with it
        else {
            alert('Reverse Geocoding failed because: ' +
                status);
        }
    });
});
```

7. Create a function for displaying the address on the `InfoWindow` object of the marker drawn:

```
function showAddressOfResult(result, marker) {
    //set the center of the map the marker position
    map.setCenter(marker.getPosition());
    map.setZoom(13);

    //create the InfoWindow content
    var popupContent = '<b>Address: </b> ' +
    result.formatted_address;

    //set the InfoWindow content and open it
    popup.setContent(popupContent);
    popup.open(map, marker);
}
```

8. You can now click on and get the address information in the info window as shown in the following screenshot:

How it works...

If you have looked at the *Finding coordinates for an address* recipe in this chapter, you may have realized that we are again using the same `geocoder` object as shown:

```
geocoder = new google.maps.Geocoder();
```

However, this time we are supplying the coordinate pairs in the form of the `LatLng` object instead of the address text for the familiar `geocode()` method of the `geocoder` object:

```
geocoder.geocode({'latLng': markerPosition},
function(results, status) {
...
});
```

In fact, there was another property that the `geocode()` method has which we have not discussed in the previous recipe; that is, the `latlng` property that accepts the `LatLng` object.

Therefore, the `geocode()` method of the `geocoder` object can be used bi-directionally, both for geocoding and reverse geocoding. For geocoding, we must use the `address` property to fill in the address for which we want to have the location. For reverse geocoding, we must use the `latlng` property to fill in the `LatLng` object for which we want the address information.

We get the `LatLng` object of the marker that the user draws by using the `getPosition()` method of the marker:

```
var markerPosition = marker.getPosition();
```

In our callback function, which we have to supply for our reverse geocoding request, we have two parameters that get their values when we get the replies of our request:

```
function(results, status) {
    ...
}
```

The first parameter is an array of the `GeocoderResult` objects, and the second one is an array of the `GeocoderStatus` object.

 You can review the available for the `GeocoderStatus` object as a well-detailed breakdown on the `GeocoderResult` object in the *Finding coordinates for an address* recipe of this chapter.

After testing the service status, we can work with our array of the `GeocoderResult` objects if everything is OK:

```
if (status == google.maps.GeocoderStatus.OK) {
    //Array of results will return if everything //is //OK
    if (results) {
        //infowindow stuff
        showAddressOfResult(results[0], marker);
    }
}
```

We have picked the first object because it is the most precise one. For instance, for the marker position in our recipe, the complete array of address information is:

```
results[0].formatted_address: "764-768 5th Avenue, New York,
    NY 10019, USA"
results[1].formatted_address: "5 Av/West 60 - 59 St, New York,
    NY 10019, USA"
```

```
results[2].formatted_address: "New York, NY 10153, USA"
results[3].formatted_address: "5 Av/59 St, New York, NY 10022,
   USA"
results[4].formatted_address: "New York, NY 10019, USA"
results[5].formatted_address: "Midtown, New York, NY, USA"
results[6].formatted_address: "Manhattan, New York, NY, USA"
results[7].formatted_address: "New York, NY, USA"
results[8].formatted_address: "New York, NY, USA"
...
results[10].formatted_address: "New York, USA"
results[11].formatted_address: "United States"
```

You can observe that iterating from the start of the array to the end, we end up in `"United States"`, the least precise address information for our reverse geocoding request.

See also

▶ The *Finding coordinates for an address* recipe in this chapter

▶ The *Drawing shapes on the map* recipe in *Chapter 6, Google Maps JavaScript Libraries*

Getting elevations on a map with a click

The Google Maps JavaScript API provides information on elevation data, returning positive values on the terrain relative to the sea surface. It also gives information on the depth of ocean floors in negative values.

Using the `ElevationService` object, we can get elevation information on individual locations as well as paths.

In this recipe, firstly we will show how to get an elevation data from a single point that the user selects, and then we will go over the same scenario with the paths.

Getting ready

It is a good idea to have a quick glance at the *Drawing shapes on the map* recipe in *Chapter 6, Google Maps JavaScript Libraries*, as the recipe covers every detail on how to draw a shape using the Google Maps JavaScript API.

How to do it...

You can view the elevation data of a location of your choice if you follow the given steps:

1. Define the `elevator` object as global:

    ```
    var elevator;
    ```

2. Define the `popup` object as global:

    ```
    var popup;
    ```

3. Initialize the `elevator` and `popup` objects, inside the `initMap()` function:

    ```
    elevator = new google.maps.ElevationService();
    popup = new google.maps.InfoWindow();
    ```

4. Create the `drawingManager` object inside `initMap()`:

    ```
    var drawingManager = new google.maps.drawing.DrawingManager(
    {
        //initial drawing tool to be enabled, we want to be in
        //no drawing mode at start
        drawingMode:null,
        //enable the drawingControl to be seen in the UI
        drawingControl:true,
        //select which drawing modes to be seen in the
        //drawingControl and position the drawingControl itself
        drawingControlOptions: {
            //select a control position in the UI
            position: google.maps.ControlPosition.TOP_CENTER,
            //selected drawing modes to be seen in the control
            drawingModes: [
            google.maps.drawing.OverlayType.MARKER
            ]
        }
    });
    ```

5. Enable the drawing functionality:

    ```
    drawingManager.setMap(map);
    ```

6. Add an event listener for the completion of the user-drawn marker, send the request using the `elevator` object, and find the elevation data for the location of the marker:

```
google.maps.event.addListener(drawingManager,
   'markercomplete', function(marker) {
      //get the LatLng object of the marker, it is necessary
      //for the geocoder
      var markerPosition = marker.getPosition();
      //embed the marker position in an array
      var markerPositions = [markerPosition];
      //send the elevation request and get the results in the
      //callback function
      elevator.getElevationForLocations({'locations':
      markerPositions}, function(results, status) {
         //if the service is working properly...
         if (status == google.maps.ElevationStatus.OK) {
            //Array of results will return if everything
            //is OK
            if (results) {
               //infowindow stuff
               showElevationOfResult(results[0], marker);
            }
         }
         //if the service is not working, deal with it
         else {
            alert('Elevation request failed because: ' +
               status);
         }
      });
});
```

7. Create a function for displaying the elevation data on the `InfoWindow` object of the marker drawn:

```
function showElevationOfResult(result, marker) {
   //set the center of the map the marker position
   map.setCenter(marker.getPosition());
   map.setZoom(13);

   //create the InfoWindow content
   var popupContent = '<b>Elevation: </b> ' +
   result.elevation;

   //set the InfoWindow content and open it
   popup.setContent(popupContent);
   popup.open(map, marker);
}
```

8. You will now get the elevation of the point that you have clicked on, as shown in the following screenshot:

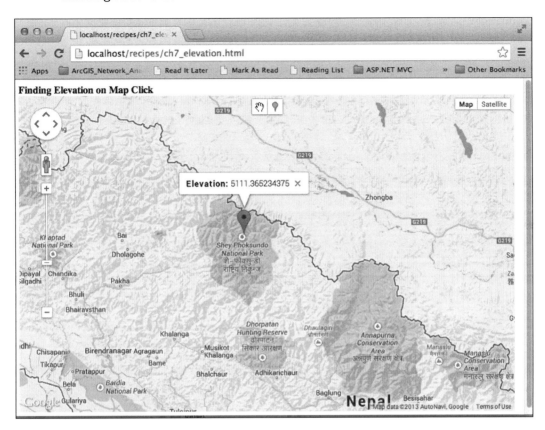

How it works...

We get the elevation data using the `ElevationService` object:

```
elevator = new google.maps.ElevationService();
```

The `elevator` object has the `getElevationForLocations()` method that takes an array of `LatLng` objects to return the elevation data for each position that the specific `LatLng` object is standing for. In other words, if you allocate three `LatLng` objects in your array, you get three `ElevationResult` objects as an array in your callback function:

```
elevator.getElevationForLocations({'locations':
markerPositions}, function(results, status) {
...});
```

However, bear in mind that the accuracy of the elevation is lowered when the number of the `LatLng` objects are embedded in the array. Therefore, if you want to have high accuracy, you must opt for the `LatLng` array containing a single element, as seen in our case.

The `LatLng` object array is given for the locations property of the `getElevationForLocations()` method. However, we have one `marker` object in hand to handle the `markercomplete` event when it is fired upon the drawing of the marker by the user:

```
google.maps.event.addListener(drawingManager,
'markercomplete',    function(marker)
{...});
```

Therefore, we are converting the single marker position to an array containing only one element:

```
var markerPosition = marker.getPosition();
var markerPositions = [markerPosition];
```

In the callback function, we get the status of the service together with the `ElevationResult` object array:

```
function(results, status) {
    //if the service is working properly...
    if (status == google.maps.ElevationStatus.OK) {
        //Array of results will return if everything //is OK
        if (results) {
            //infowindow stuff
            showElevationOfResult(results[0],marker);
        }
    }
    //if the service is not working, deal with it
    else {
        alert('Elevation request failed because: ' + status);
    }
}
```

The `status` parameter is of the type `ElevationStatus`, and it is very similar to the `GeocoderStatus` object in terms of its constants, which are listed as follows:

▶ `google.maps.ElevationStatus.OK`

▶ `google.maps.ElevationStatus.UNKNOWN_ERROR`

▶ `google.maps.ElevationStatus.OVER_QUERY_LIMIT`

▶ `google.maps.ElevationStatus.REQUEST_DENIED`

▶ `google.maps.ElevationStatus.INVALID_REQUEST`

Apart from `ElevationStatus.OK`, all the status values point to a problem. Other values are self-explanatory within their names.

 The complete listing and details for the possible values of the `ElevationStatus` object can be found at `https://developers.google.com/maps/documentation/javascript/reference#ElevationStatus`.

The `results` parameter is of the type `ElevationResult`. The `ElevationResult` object has three properties called `elevation`, `location`, and `resolution`. We are making use of the `elevation` property in our `showElevationOfResult()` function:

```
var popupContent = '<b>Elevation: </b> ' + result.elevation;
```

The elevation data is the positive number for the terrain and the negative number for the ocean floor.

The location property is the `LatLng` object of `ElevationResult`, and the resolution property is the distance in meters between the sample points that is used to generate/interpolate this elevation data. The higher the resolution, the less accurate the elevation data.

See also

▶ The *Drawing shapes on the map* recipe in *Chapter 6*, *Google Maps JavaScript Libraries*

Creating a distance matrix for the given locations

The Google Maps JavaScript API carries some interesting and particularly helpful properties, one of them being the Distance Matrix Service. Using this service, you can compute the travel time and distance between multiple origins and destination locations.

This is especially useful when you want to have a one-to-one report of your travel nodes, be it a delivery business or only a summertime holiday. This service gives you the travel time and distances within your choice of travel mode (driving, walking, and cycling); you can see the results oriented for each origin and destination.

It is worth noting that the output of this service cannot be mapped onto the base maps; you can have the information about the travel time and duration, but for the directions, you have to use the Directions service, explained in detail in the *Getting a direction for the given locations* recipe later in this chapter.

In this recipe, we will locate the origin and destination locations and get the distance matrix result for our locations.

Getting ready

This recipe will make use of the drawing library; therefore, it is advisable to go through the *Drawing shapes on the map* recipe in *Chapter 6, Google Maps JavaScript Libraries,* and gain some understanding on the subject matter.

How to do it...

You can draw your origin and destination points and then request for a distance matrix by clicking on the button. You can see how to do this by following the given steps:

1. Add the HTML `input` element of the `button` type to kick off the distance matrix request:

   ```
   <input type="button" id ="generateDistanceMatrix"
     value="Generate Distance Matrix" />
   ```

2. Define the global variables:

   ```
   //define an array that includes all origin LatLng objects
   var originLatLngs;
   //define an array that includes all destination LatLng objects
   var destinationLatLngs;
   //define a global DistanceMatrixService object
   var distanceMatrixService;
   //define a global markerCount variable
   var markerCount;
   //define a global matrixResultDiv variable
   var matrixResultDiv;
   ```

3. Initialize the global variables in the `initMap()` function:

   ```
   //initialize originLatLngs array
   originLatLngs = [];
   //initialize destinationLatLngs array
   destinationLatLngs = [];
   //initialize markerCount - the count of markers to be drawn
   markerCount = 0;
   //assign matrixResultDiv to the specific div element
   matrixResultDiv =
   document.getElementById('matrixResultDiv');
   ```

4. Get the `button` element and add a `click` event handler:

   ```
   var generateDistanceMatrixBtn = document.getElementById('generateD
   istanceMatrix');
   generateDistanceMatrixBtn.addEventListener('click', function(){
       makeDistanceMatrixRequest();
   });
   ```

5. Initialize the `distanceMatrixService` object in the `initMap()` function:

```
distanceMatrixService = new
google.maps.DistanceMatrixService();
```

6. Create the `drawingManager` object inside `initMap()`:

```
var drawingManager = new google.maps.drawing.DrawingManager(
{
    //initial drawing tool to be enabled, we want to be in
    //no drawing mode at start
    drawingMode: null,
    //enable the drawingControl to be seen in the UI
    drawingControl: true,
    //select which drawing modes to be seen in the
    //drawingControl and position the drawingControl itself
    drawingControlOptions: {
        //select a control position in the UI
        position: google.maps.ControlPosition.TOP_CENTER,
        //selected drawing modes to be seen in the control
        drawingModes: [
        google.maps.drawing.OverlayType.MARKER
        ]
    }
});
```

7. Enable the drawing functionality:

```
drawingManager.setMap(map);
```

8. Add an event listener for the completion of the user-drawn marker, set the marker icons based upon the positions they are pointing towards, whether origin or destination, and limit the total number of markers:

```
google.maps.event.addListener(drawingManager, 'markercomplete',
function(marker) {
    //count the number of markers drawn
    markerCount++;

    //limit the number of markers to 10
    if (markerCount > 10) {
        alert('No more origins or destinations allowed');
        drawingManager.setMap(null);
        marker.setMap(null);
        return;
    }
```

```
    //distinguish the markers, make the blue ones be
    //destinations and red ones origins
    if (markerCount % 2 === 0) {
        destinationLatLngs.push(marker.getPosition());
        marker.setIcon('icons/b' +
          destinationLatLngs.length + '.png');
    }
    else {
        originLatLngs.push(marker.getPosition());
        marker.setIcon('icons/r' + originLatLngs.length +
          '.png');
    }
});
```

9. Create a function for preparing the request properties and sending the request for the distanceMatrixService object by using the getDistanceMatrix() method:

```
function makeDistanceMatrixRequest() {
    distanceMatrixService.getDistanceMatrix(
        {
            origins: originLatLngs,
            destinations: destinationLatLngs,
            travelMode: google.maps.TravelMode.DRIVING,
        },
        getDistanceMatrixResult
    );
}
```

10. Create a callback function named getDistanceMatrixResult for the getDistanceMatrix() method call of the distanceMatrixService object:

```
function getDistanceMatrixResult(result, status) {
    //clear the div contents where matrix results will be
    //written
    matrixResultDiv.innerHTML = '';

    //if everything is OK
    if (status == google.maps.DistanceMatrixStatus.OK) {
        //get the array of originAddresses
        var originAddresses = result.originAddresses;
        //get the array of destinationAddresses
        var destinationAddresses =
        result.destinationAddresses;
```

```
//there are two loops, the outer is for origins,
//the inner will be for destinations,
//their intersection will be the element object
//itself
for (var i = 0, l= originAddresses.length; i < l;
i++) {
    //get the elements array
    var elements = result.rows[i].elements;
    for (var j = 0, m= elements.length;  j < m;
    j++) {
        var originAddress = originAddresses[i];
        var destinationAddress =
        destinationAddresses[j];
        //get the element object
        var element = elements[j];

        //get distance and duration properties for
        //the element object
        var distance =  element.distance.text;
        var duration = element.duration.text;
        //write the results to the div for each
        //element object

        writeDistanceMatrixResultOnDiv(
        originAddress, destinationAddress,
        distance, duration, i, j);
    }
  }
 }
else {
    alert('Cannot find distance matrix because: ' +
    status);
  }
}
```

11. Create a function to be called by the callback function listed earlier to write the results to the `matrixResultDiv` object:

```
function writeDistanceMatrixResultOnDiv(originAddress,
destinationAddress, distance, duration,
originAddressCount, destinationAddressCount) {
    //get the existing content
    var existingContent = matrixResultDiv.innerHTML;
```

```
        var newContent;
        //write the Origin Address and Destination Address
        //together with travel distance and duration
        newContent = '<b>Origin ' +
        letterForCount(originAddressCount) + ' :</b><br />';
        newContent += originAddress + '<br />';
        newContent += '<b>Destination ' +
        letterForCount(destinationAddressCount) + ' :</b>
        <br />';
        newContent += destinationAddress + '<br />';
        newContent += '<b>Distance: </b> ' + distance +
        '<br />';
        newContent += '<b>Duration: </b> ' + duration +
        '<br />';
        newContent += '<br />';

        //add the newContent to the existingContent of the
        //matrixResultDiv
        matrixResultDiv.innerHTML = existingContent +
        newContent;
    }
```

12. Create a function for converting counts to letters; the aim is to match the counts with the marker icons:

```
function letterForCount(count)
{
    switch (count)
    {
        case 0:
        return 'A';
        case 1:
        return 'B';
        case 2:
        return 'C';
        case 3:
        return 'D';
        case 4:
        return 'E';
        default:
        return null;
    }
}
```

13. You will now have the distance matrix between the points of your selection, as shown in the following screenshot:

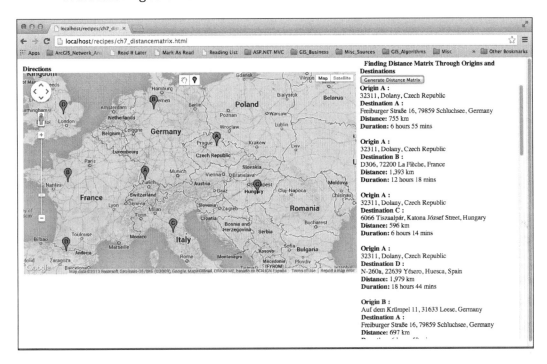

How it works...

In our recipe, we are allowing the users to point the markers downward at the location of their choice. However, we are just following a scheme such that the first marker will point to the first origin, the second will point to the first destination, the third will point to the second origin, the fourth will point to the second destination location, and so on. In addition, we are limiting the number of markers that have to be drawn to 10.

This was about drawing markers. Then, we will prepare the origin and destination locations to be supplied to the `distanceMatrixService` object. The object is initialized as shown in the following code:

```
distanceMatrixService = new
google.maps.DistanceMatrixService();
```

The user pressed the input button element and we fire the request via the `getDistanceMatrix()` method:

```
function makeDistanceMatrixRequest() {
    distanceMatrixService.getDistanceMatrix(
    {
```

```
        origins: originLatLngs,
        destinations: destinationLatLngs,
        travelMode: google.maps.TravelMode.DRIVING,
    },
    getDistanceMatrixResult
);
}
```

Here, we supply `originLatLngs` to the `origins` property, where `originLatLngs` is an array of the `LatLng` objects collected out of user-drawn markers—the odd-numbered ones—in the `markercomplete` event listener for the `drawingManager` object:

```
if (markerCount % 2 === 0) {
    destinationLatLngs.push(marker.getPosition());

}
else {
    originLatLngs.push(marker.getPosition());

}
```

The `destinations` property is set for the `destimationLatLngs` array in the same logic.

As a quick reminder, the `destinations` and `origins` properties can take an array of address strings as well as an array of `LatLng` objects, as in our case.

The third property that we have used in our request is the `travelMode` property, which is used to set the mode of travel. The options other than `TravelMode.DRIVING` available for this property are:

- ▶ `TravelMode.WALKING`
- ▶ `TravelMode.BICYCLING`

In addition to the `DistanceMatrixRequest` object carrying the `origins`, `destinations`, and `travelMode` properties, we are supplying a callback function named `getDistanceMatrixResult` for the `getDistanceMatrix()` method call. The `getDistanceMatrixResult` function has two parameters: one is for the response of the service and the other one is for the status of the service. It is shown in the following code:

```
function getDistanceMatrixResult(result, status)
{...}
```

In this function, firstly we check whether the service is working properly:

```
if (status == google.maps.DistanceMatrixStatus.OK)
{...}
```

The complete listing and details for the possible values of the `DistanceMatrixStatus` object can be found at `https://developers.google.com/maps/documentation/javascript/reference# DistanceMatrixStatus`.

Then, we process the results of the type `DistanceMatrixResponse` object, which carries the `originAddresses` and `destinationAddresses` arrays of strings and a `DistanceMatrixResponseRow` array called `rows`. Firstly, we get the `originAddresses` and `destinationAddresses` arrays:

```
var originAddresses = result.originAddresses;
var destinationAddresses = result.destinationAddresses;
```

The `rows` array consists of another array called `elements`, in which its children are of the type `DistanceMatrixResponseElement`. Therefore, we have to have two loops to iterate through the `DistanceMatrixResponseElement` objects:

```
for (var i = 0, l=originAddresses.length; i < l; i++) {
    //get the elements array
    var elements = result.rows[i].elements;
    for (var j = 0, m=elements.length;j < m; j++) {
        ...
        var element = elements[j];
                ...
    }
}
```

The `DistanceMatrixResponseElement` object has two prominent properties that we have used in our recipe: one is distance and the other is duration. They are elaborated in the following code:

```
var distance =  element.distance.text;
var duration = element.duration.text;
```

By using these properties, we reach the particular distance and duration properties of the corresponding origin address and destination address.

See also

▶ The *Drawing shapes on the map* recipe in *Chapter 6, Google Maps JavaScript Libraries*

Getting directions for the given locations

Having directions between two or more locations has always been a favorite among users, car drivers, tourists, and so on. The need for navigation products either for driving, walking, or any other transit options is qualified by the sales of these products.

A good Directions service would need comprehensive road data with several attributes filled in such as the direction of traffic flow, turn restrictions, bridges, and underground tunnels. Hopefully, Google Maps has this data in the background; therefore, it is very natural for Google to include this functionality in Google Maps.

In Google Maps, directions is perhaps one of the most used features. It is also included in the Google Maps JavaScript API, giving developers the ability to generate directions programmatically between locations of their choice with a broad range of options.

In this recipe, firstly we will have the user enter an address or any location of a place, map them using the Geocoder service, and then provide the directions between them in the order of their entrance.

Getting ready

This recipe will make use of concepts related to the Geocoder service introduced in the *Finding coordinates for an address* recipe at the beginning of this chapter. It is highly advisable to go through this recipe to have a general understanding of Geocoder and its usage.

How to do it...

You can enter your addresses and get directions between them by executing the following steps:

1. Insert a `ContainerDiv` element of HTML that will be placed on the right-hand side of the `div` element of the map:

```
<div id="DirectionsContainerDiv">
    <div id="PlacesContainerDiv">
        <b>Get Directions Between your Places</b></br>
        <input id="addressField" type="text" size="30"
          placeholder="Enter your Address" />
        <input type="button" id ="pinAddressOnMapBtn"
          value="Pin Address On Map"
          onclick="listAddresses()" />
        <input type="button" id = "getDirectionsBtn"
          disabled value="Get Directions"
          onclick="getDirections()" />
```

```
        <p id="placesText"></p>
        <ul id="addressList" class="addressList">
        </ul>
    </div>
    <div id="DirectionsListContainerDiv">
        <div id="DirectionsListDiv">
        </div>
    </div>
</div>
```

2. Define the global variables:

```
//define global marker popup variable
var popup;
//define global geocoder object
var geocoder;
//define global markers array
var markers;
//define global DirectionsService object
var directionsService;
//define global DirectionsRenderer object
var directionsRenderer;
```

3. Initialize the global variables in the `initMap()` function:

```
//initialize geocoder object
geocoder = new google.maps.Geocoder();
//initialize markers array
markers = [];
//initialize directionsService object
directionsService = new google.maps.DirectionsService();
//initialize directionsRenderer object
directionsRenderer = new google.maps.DirectionsRenderer();
```

4. Give the instructions on `directionsRenderer` so that it will draw the directions on the map and will list the directions on the right-hand side of the map:

```
//directionsRenderer will draw the directions on current
//map
directionsRenderer.setMap(map);
//directionsRenderer will list the textual description of
//the directions
//on directionsDiv HTML element
directionsRenderer.setPanel(document.getElementById(
'DirectionsListDiv'));
```

5. Create a function for listing the addresses the user has entered and calling the function that does the geocoding:

```
function listAddresses() {
    //get text input handler
    var addressField =
    document.getElementById('addressField');
    //get addressList <ul> element handle
    var addressList =
    document.getElementById('addressList');
    if (addressList.children.length == 0) {
        var placesText =
        document.getElementById('placesText');
        placesText.innerHTML = 'Places You Have Visited
        (Click on the place name to see on map):';
    }
    //create a list item
    var listItem = document.createElement('li');
    //get the text in the input element and make it a list
    //item
    listItem.innerHTML = addressField.value;
    listItem.addEventListener('click', function() {
        pinAddressOnMap(listItem.innerHTML);
    });
    //append it to the <ul> element
    addressList.appendChild(listItem);
    //call the geocoding function
    pinAddressOnMap(addressField.value);
    if (addressList.children.length > 1) {
        //get getDirectionsBtn button handler
        var getDirectionsBtn =
        document.getElementById('getDirectionsBtn');
        //enable the getDirectionsBtn
        getDirectionsBtn.disabled = false;
    }
    addressField.value = '';
}
```

6. Create a function that does the real geocoding task:

```
function pinAddressOnMap(addressText) {
    //real essence, send the geocoding request
    geocoder.geocode({'address': addressText},
    function(results, status) {
        //if the service is working properly...
```

```
            if (status == google.maps.GeocoderStatus.OK) {
                //show the first result on map
                pinpointResult(results[0]);
            } else {
                alert('Cannot geocode because: ' + status);
            }
        });
    }
```

7. Create a function for placing a marker for the geocoding result of the user-entered address information and attaching an `InfoWindow` object to display its details:

```
function pinpointResult(result) {
    var marker = new google.maps.Marker({
        map: map,
        position: result.geometry.location,
        zIndex: -10
    });

    map.setCenter(result.geometry.location);
    map.setZoom(16);

    //infowindow stuff
    google.maps.event.addListener(marker, 'click',
    function() {
        var popupContent = '<b>Address: </b> ' +
        result.formatted_address;
        popup.setContent(popupContent);
        popup.open(map, this);
    });
    markers.push(marker);
}
```

8. At last, the real directions can be called upon by using the `getDirectionsBtn` button handler. Create a function for sending the request to the `directionsService` object, ensuring that the results are drawn and listed on the map:

```
function getDirections() {
    //define an array that will hold all the waypoints
    var waypnts = [];
    //define a directionsRequest object
    var directionRequest;
```

```
    //if there are stops other than the origin and the
    //final destination
    if (markers.length > 2) {
        for (i=1;i<=markers.length-2;i++) {
            //add them to the waypnts array
            waypnts.push({
                location: markers[i].getPosition(),
                stopover: true
            });
        }

        //prepare the directionsRequest by including
        //the waypoints property
        directionRequest = {
            origin:markers[0].getPosition(),
            destination: markers[
             markers.length-1].getPosition(),
          waypoints: waypnts,
           travelMode: google.maps.TravelMode.DRIVING
        };
    }
    else {
        //this time, do not include the waypoints property as
        //there are no waypoints
        directionRequest = {
            origin:markers[0].getPosition(),
            destination:markers[
            markers.length-1].getPosition(),
            travelMode: google.maps.TravelMode.DRIVING
        };
    }

    //send the request to the directionsService
    directionsService.route(directionRequest,
      function(result, status) {
        if (status == google.maps.DirectionsStatus.OK) {
            directionsRenderer.setDirections(result);
        }
        else
        {
            alert('Cannot find directions because: ' +
              status);
        }
    });
}
```

9. You will now have the directions mapped between the points of your selection, as shown in the following screenshot:

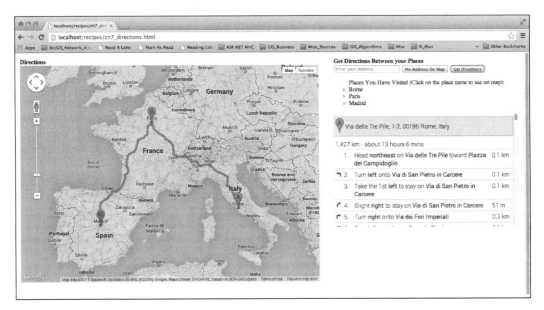

How it works...

In this recipe, we are making use of both `GeocoderService` and `DirectionsService`. However, in order to avoid redundancy (it is strongly recommended to go through the *Finding coordinates for an address* recipe of this chapter), we will mostly concentrate on `DirectionsService`, preparing the request properties, sending and getting back the results to draw on the map, and also its step-by-step textual descriptions.

At first, we are waiting for the user to enter addresses to be geocoded and shown on the map. These are the places that we will generate directions for. We are collecting all the markers that are the results of the user's geocoding requests so that we can use them for directions:

```
function pinpointResult(result) {
    ...
    markers.push(marker);
}
```

As soon as the numbers of the geocoded addresses are more than 1, the button labeled **Get Directions** gets enabled so that users can request for directions between their geocoded addresses:

```
function listAddresses()
{
    ...
```

```
        if (addressList.children.length > 1) {
            //get getDirectionsBtn button handler
            var getDirectionsBtn =
            document.getElementById('getDirectionsBtn');
            //enable the getDirectionsBtn
            getDirectionsBtn.disabled = false;
        }
        ...
    }
```

After this, everything is ready for generating directions provided that we have prepared the infrastructure, so use the following code:

```
directionsService = new google.maps.DirectionsService();
directionsRenderer = new google.maps.DirectionsRenderer();
```

The `DirectionsService` object is responsible for sending the `DirectionsRequest` object to the service servers at Google, while the `DirectionsRenderer` object, as its name implies, renders the `DirectionsResult` object onto the map and its textual description.

An origin and a destination are compulsory for `DirectionsRequest` logically; however, there may be waypoints in between the origin and the destination. If the user geocodes two addresses and presses the **Get Directions** button, there is no place for waypoints, and the first address becomes the origin, while the second becomes the destination.

If there are more than two addresses on the list of the geocoded addresses, the first will be the origin and the last will be the destination again. In addition to this, the waypoints will be present in between the addresses. We are preparing the `DirectionsRequest` parameters considering these factors, as shown in the following code:

```
function getDirections() {
    ...
    //if there are stops other than the origin and the
    //final destination
    if (markers.length > 2)
    {
        for (var i=1, markers.length;i<=l-2;i++)
        {
            //add them to the waypnts array
            waypnts.push({
                location: markers[i].getPosition(),
                stopover: true
            });
        }
```

```
        //prepare the directionsRequest by including
        //the waypoints property
        directionRequest = {
            origin:markers[0].getPosition(),
            destination:markers[
              markers.length-1].getPosition(),
            waypoints: waypnts,
            travelMode: google.maps.TravelMode.DRIVING
        };
    }
    else
    {
        //this time, do not include the waypoints property as
        //there are no waypoints
        directionRequest = {
            origin:markers[0].getPosition(),
            destination:markers[
            markers.length-1].getPosition(),
            travelMode: google.maps.TravelMode.DRIVING
        };
    }
    ...
}
```

You may have realized that we are supplying the `LatLng` objects for the `origin` and `destination` properties of the `directionsRequest` object. This does not have to be the case: you can also provide addresses as strings for the `origin` and `destination` properties, as well as the `location` property of the `DirectionsWaypoint` object that we are adding to our `waypnts` array. Also, there is a `stopover` property for the `DirectionsWaypoint` object. It specifies that the waypoint is actually a stop and splits the route. Another property for the `DirectionsRequest` object is `travelMode,` where we have opted for `DRIVING`.

> The complete listing and details for the possible values of the `TravelMode` object can be found at `https://developers.google.com/maps/documentation/javascript/reference#TravelMode`.

We have included a few properties that are mostly required; however, the `DirectionsRequest` object has a lot more.

The complete listing of the properties of the `DirectionsRequest` object can be found at `https://developers.google.com/maps/documentation/javascript/reference#DirectionsRequest`.

After preparing our `directionsRequest` object, we can send the request using our `directionsService` object through its `route()` method:

```
function getDirections() {
    ...
    //send the request to the directionsService
    directionsService.route(directionRequest, function(
    result, status) {
        if (status == google.maps.DirectionsStatus.OK) {
            directionsRenderer.setDirections(result);
        }
        else
        {
            alert('Cannot find directions because: ' +
                status);
        }
    });
}
```

The `route()` method takes two parameters: one is the `DirectionsRequest` object and the other is the callback function that has the `DirectionsResult` and `DirectionsStatus` objects as parameters in return.

We test whether everything is on track using our `status` object, which is of the type `DirectionsStatus`.

 The complete listing of constants of the DirectionsStatus object can be found at `https://developers.google.com/maps/documentation/javascript/reference#DirectionsStatus`.

Then, we map the results and have textual descriptions on a `div` element using our old `directionsRenderer` object:

```
directionsRenderer.setDirections(result);
```

But how did the `directionsRenderer` object know where to map the results, or which `div` to write the step-by-step instructions to? Hopefully, we have given the instructions earlier to the `DirectionsRenderer` object in our `initMap()` function:

```
directionsRenderer.setMap(map);
directionsRenderer.setPanel(document.getElementById(
'DirectionsListDiv'));
```

The `setMap()` method of the `DirectionsRenderer` object maps the `DirectionsResult` object to the selected map object. And, similarly, the `setPanel()` method is used for selecting an HTML `div` element to have the step-by-step instructions written on it. This is so that we can have both our directions mapped in our map instance. The map imminently gets zoomed out to show the entire route, and we can see the order of our journey with the help of additional markers with letters on each.

See also

▶ The *Finding coordinates for an address* recipe in this chapter

Adding Street View to your maps

Google Maps already has good map data updated continuously with the ultimate cartographic quality. In addition, there comes the up-to-date satellite imagery. Although these were sufficient for Google Maps to be so popular and successful, there is another view that takes much interest—Street View.

Street View is the 360-degree panorama view from the roads that are covered under this service.

> The complete listing of countries and cities where Street View is available can be found at `http://maps.google.com/intl/ALL/maps/about/behind-the-scenes/streetview/`.

In this recipe, we will go over how to add Street View panoramas to the current view, switch between the map view and Street View, and set the panorama properties.

Getting ready

In this recipe, we will make use of the concepts related to the geocoding service introduced in the *Finding coordinates for an address* recipe in this chapter. It is highly advisable to read this recipe to have a general understanding of Geocoder and its usage.

How to do it...

The following steps will enable your geocoded addresses to be seen on Street View:

1. Firstly, use the HTML markup:

```
<div id="addressDiv">
    <b>Map your Holiday Places</b><br />
    <input id="addressField" type="text" size="30"
      placeholder="Enter your Address" />
    <input type="button" id="pinAddress" value="Pin Address
      On Map" onclick="listAddresses()">
    <input type="button" value="Show Map"
      onclick="showMap()">
    <input type="button" value="Show StreetView"
      onclick="showStreetView()">
    <p id="placesText"></p>
    <ul id="addressList" class="addressList">
    </ul>
</div>
```

2. Define the global objects:

```
var geocoder;
var streetView;
```

3. Initialize the global objects in the `initMap()` function:

```
geocoder = new google.maps.Geocoder();
//initialize streetView object of type StreetViewPanorama
streetView = map.getStreetView();
```

4. Create a function for listing addresses on the `addressList` element and for calling the geocoding function:

```
function listAddresses() {
    //get text input handler
    var addressField =
    document.getElementById('addressField');
    //get addressList <ul> element handle
    var addressList =
    document.getElementById('addressList');
    if (addressList.children.length == 0) {
        var placesText =
        document.getElementById('placesText');
        placesText.innerHTML = 'Places You Have Visited
        (Click on the place name to see on map):';
    }
```

```
            //create a list item
            var listItem = document.createElement('li');
            //get the text in the input element and make it
            // a list item
            listItem.innerHTML = addressField.value;
            listItem.addEventListener('click', function() {
                pinAddressOnMapOrStreetView(listItem.innerHTML);
            });
            //append it to the <ul> element
            addressList.appendChild(listItem);
            //call the geocoding function
            pinAddressOnMapOrStreetView(addressField.value);
        }
```

5. Create a function for geocoding the addresses:

```
        function pinAddressOnMapOrStreetView(addressText) {
            //send the geocoding request
            geocoder.geocode({'address': addressText},
            function(results, status) {
                //if the service is working properly...
                if (status == google.maps.GeocoderStatus.OK) {
                    //show the first result on map, either on
                    showAddressMarkerOnMapOrStreetView(results[0]);
                    if (streetView.getVisible())
                    {
                        //set the streetView properties, its
                        //location and "Point Of View"
                        setStreetViewOptions(
                        results[0].geometry.location);
                    }
                } else {
                    alert('Cannot geocode because: ' + status);
                }
            });
        }
```

6. Create a function for placing the marker in the map for the geocoded addresses:

```
        function showAddressMarkerOnMapOrStreetView(result) {
            var marker = new google.maps.Marker({
                map:map,
                position: result.geometry.location
            });
            map.setCenter(result.geometry.location);
            map.setZoom(16);
        }
```

7. Create a function for setting the Street View panorama properties:

```
function setStreetViewOptions(location)
{
    //set the location of the streetView object
    streetView.setPosition(location);
    //set the "Point Of View" of streetView object
    streetView.setPov({
        heading: 0,
        pitch: 10
    });
}
```

8. Create a function for displaying the familiar map view, which is called by the HTML click button labeled **Show Map**:

```
function showMap()
{
    var pinAddressBtn =
    document.getElementById('pinAddress');
    pinAddressBtn.value = 'Pin Address On Map';
    streetView.setVisible(false);
}
```

9. Create a function for displaying the Street View panorama taking the location as the map's center location, which is called by the HTML click button labeled **Show StreetView**:

```
function showStreetView() {
    var pinAddressBtn =
    document.getElementById('pinAddress');
    pinAddressBtn.value = 'Pin Address On StreetView';
    setStreetViewOptions(map.getCenter());
    streetView.setVisible(true);
}
```

10. You will now have the geocoded addresses with Street View, as shown in the following screenshot:

How it works...

In our recipe, our aim is to perform the ordinary task of geocoding addresses, in addition to providing the availability of the Street View feature of the Google Maps JavaScript API in the same map's `div` element. To do this, we need the `StreetViewPanorama` object available:

```
streetView = map.getStreetView();
```

This object enables us to display the Street View either within our map's `div` element or within a separate `div` element of our will.

 The complete description of properties and methods of the `StreetViewPanorama` class can be found at `https://developers.google.com/maps/documentation/javascript/reference#StreetViewPanorama`.

Then, we can display the Street View when the button labeled **Show Street View** is clicked, providing the `map` object's center location as the `LatLng` object:

```
setStreetViewOptions(map.getCenter());
```

Then, we set the properties of the `StreetViewPanorama` object by specifying the position and setting the point of view of the `streetView` object:

```
function setStreetViewOptions(location) {
    //set the location of the streetView object
    streetView.setPosition(location);
    //set the "Point Of View" of streetView object
    streetView.setPov({
        heading: 0,
        pitch: 10
    });
}
```

The `setPosition()` method takes the `LatLng` object as its parameter, and we are providing either the map center or the geocoded address' location. By using the `setPov()` method, we are arranging the camera view of the Street View. To have a camera view, the object must have an angle towards both true north and the street view origin—the street vehicle mostly.

The `heading` property of the `StreetViewPov` object is for the angle in reference to true north, where 0 degrees is true north, 90 degrees is east, 180 degrees is south, and 270 degrees is west. In our recipe, we have set the `heading` property to 0 degrees.

The `pitch` property is for the angle in reference to the Street View vehicle. This means that 90 degrees is totally upwards, viewing the sky or clouds, whereas -90 degrees is totally downwards, viewing the road ground in most cases.

8
Mastering the Google Maps JavaScript API through Advanced Recipes

In this chapter, we will cover:

- ▶ Adding WMS layers to maps
- ▶ Adding Fusion Tables layers to maps
- ▶ Adding CartoDB layers to maps
- ▶ Accessing ArcGIS Server with the Google Maps JavaScript API
- ▶ Accessing GeoServer with the Google Maps JavaScript API

Introduction

The Google Maps JavaScript API may seem like a simple library that only shows basic geo-related features, but there are a lot of capabilities that could be explored. The Google Maps JavaScript API gives developers many foundation classes to build complex solutions for different cases, especially for **Geographical Information Systems** (**GIS**).

The Google Maps JavaScript API has a lot of potential with GIS services and tools. Most of the GIS solutions need base maps and services to support the tool itself and the Google Maps JavaScript API is the best solution with its base maps and services.

There are different GIS solutions from proprietary software and services to open source ones, such as Google Fusion Tables, CartoDB, ArcGIS Server, or GeoServer. In this chapter, we will integrate these servers or services with the Google Maps JavaScript API. Some of the GIS service creation processes are skipped due to space constraints. If you need more information, please check other books by *Packt Publishing* to dive into details.

Adding WMS layers to maps

Web Map Service (**WMS**) is an **Open Geospatial Consortium** (**OGC**) standard for publishing georeferenced map images over the Internet that are generated by a map server using data from various geospatial sources such as shapefiles or geospatial databases. There are various versions used in WMS services but the most used ones are 1.1.1 or 1.3.0. WMS has two required request types: GetCapabilities and GetMap.

This recipe shows how to add a WMS layer to the Google Maps JavaScript API by extending the google.maps.OverlayView class.

Getting ready

By now, you should already know how to create a map, so only additional code lines are explained in this recipe.

You can find the source code at Chapter 8/ch08_wms_map.html.

How to do it...

Adding WMS layers to the map is quite easy if you perform the following steps:

1. First, create a wms.js file to include in the HTML later. This JavaScript file has a WMSUntiled class that is written as follows:

    ```
    function WMSUntiled (map, wmsUntiledOptions) {
      this.map_ = map;
      this.options = wmsUntiledOptions;
      this.div_ = null;
      this.image_ = null;
      this.setMap(map);
    }
    ```

2. Then, extend our base class by inheriting the google.maps.OverlayView class:

    ```
    WMSUntiled.prototype = new google.maps.OverlayView();
    ```

3. The next step is to implement three methods of the OverlayView class.

    ```
    WMSUntiled.prototype.draw = function() {
      var overlayProjection = this.getProjection();
    ```

```
    var sw = overlayProjection.fromLatLngToDivPixel
      (this.map_.getBounds ().getSouthWest());
    var ne = overlayProjection.fromLatLngToDivPixel
      (this.map_.getBounds().getNorthEast());
    var div = this.div_;
    if (this.image_ != null)
      div.removeChild(this.image_);


    // Create an IMG element and attach it to the DIV.
    var img = document.createElement('img');
    img.src = this.prepareWMSUrl();
    img.style.width = '100%';
    img.style.height = '100%';
    img.style.position = 'absolute';
    img.style.opacity = 0.6;
    this.image_ = img;
    div.appendChild(this.image_);

    div.style.left = sw.x + 'px';
    div.style.top = ne.y + 'px';
    div.style.width = (ne.x - sw.x) + 'px';
    div.style.height = (sw.y - ne.y) + 'px';
};

WMSUntiled.prototype.onAdd = function() {
  var that = this;
  var div = document.createElement('div');
  div.style.borderStyle = 'none';
  div.style.borderWidth = '0px';
  div.style.position = 'absolute';

  this.div_ = div;
  this.getPanes().floatPane.appendChild(this.div_);

  google.maps.event.addListener(this.map_, 'dragend',
    function() {
      that.draw();
  });
};

WMSUntiled.prototype.onRemove = function() {
  this.menuDiv.parentNode.removeChild(this.div_);
  this.div_ = null;
};
```

4. Finally, add the following methods to finish the `WMSUntiled` class:

```javascript
WMSUntiled.prototype.prepareWMSUrl = function() {
  var baseUrl = this.options.baseUrl;
  baseUrl += 'Service=WMS&request=GetMap&CRS=EPSG:3857&';
  baseUrl += 'version=' + this.options.version;
  baseUrl += '&layers=' + this.options.layers;
  baseUrl += '&styles=' + this.options.styles;
  baseUrl += '&format=' + this.options.format;

  var bounds = this.map_.getBounds();
  var sw = this.toMercator(bounds.getSouthWest());
  var ne = this.toMercator(bounds.getNorthEast());

  var mapDiv = this.map_.getDiv();
  baseUrl += '&BBOX=' + sw.x + ',' + sw.y + ',' + ne.x
    + ',' + ne.y;
  baseUrl += '&width=' + mapDiv.clientWidth +
    '&height=' + mapDiv.clientHeight;
  return baseUrl;
};

WMSUntiled.prototype.toMercator = function(coord) {
  var lat = coord.lat();
  var lng = coord.lng();
  if ((Math.abs(lng) > 180 || Math.abs(lat) > 90))
    return;

  var num = lng * 0.017453292519943295;
  var x = 6378137.0 * num;
  var a = lat * 0.017453292519943295;

  var merc_lon = x;
  var merc_lat = 3189068.5 * Math.log((1.0 + Math.sin(a)) /
    (1.0 - Math.sin(a)));

  return { x: merc_lon, y: merc_lat };
};

WMSUntiled.prototype.changeOpacity = function(opacity) {
  if (opacity >= 0 && opacity <= 1){
    this.image_.style.opacity = opacity;
  }
};
```

5. Now this JavaScript class file must be added to the HTML after adding the Google Maps JavaScript API:

```
<script type="text/javascript" src="lib/wms.js">
</script>
```

6. After initializing the map, we create our WMS options as follows:

```
var wmsOptions = {
  baseUrl:
    'http://demo.cubewerx.com/cubewerx/cubeserv.cgi?',
  layers: 'Foundation.gtopo30',
  version: '1.1.1',
  styles: 'default',
  format: 'image/png'
};
```

7. At the end, we initialize the WMS layer with the WMS options created in steps 1 to 4:

```
var wmsLayer = new WMSUntiled(map, wmsOptions);
```

8. Go to your local URL where your HTML file is stored in your favorite browser and see the result. The following topological map coming from WMS is shown on the satellite base map of Google Maps:

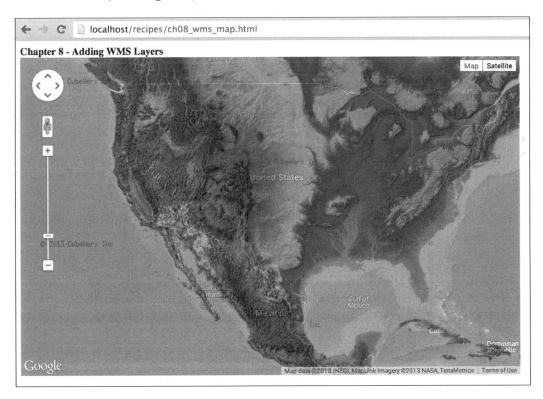

As you can see in the preceding screenshot, we added a WMS layer to our map.

How it works...

WMS is a standard for serving georeferenced images. The main idea behind WMS is serving the image according to the width/height and bounding box of the map with additional parameters such as projection type, layer names, and return format.

Most of the WMS classes for the Google Maps JavaScript API around the Web are based on a tiled structure, which is the base for most mapping APIs. This tiled structure gets the bounding box of each tile and sends it to the server. This can be a good usage for user interactivity wherein users only get missing tiles when dragging the map, but there is a problem with map servers. Getting lots of tiles instead of a single image causes a big load on map servers if there isn't a caching mechanism with a high volume of usage.

In this recipe, we used the untiled structure to get WMS images from the server. This approach is getting one image from the server on each user interaction that can be useful in some cases. There isn't much information about this approach, so we encourage you to read and implement both approaches for your geo-web applications.

The JavaScript class named `WMSUntiled` is created in a different file in order to make the HTML file readable. This class is created with functional style and methods are added to the prototype of the constructor function:

```
function WMSUntiled (map, wmsUntiledOptions) {
    this.map_ = map;
    this.options = wmsUntiledOptions;
    this.div_ = null;
    this.image_ = null;
    this.setMap(map);
};
```

The Google Maps JavaScript API has a base class to extend in these cases named as `google.maps.OverlayView`. The `WMSUntiled` class extends this class to create a WMS overlay on top of the map:

```
WMSUntiled.prototype = new google.maps.OverlayView();
```

The `OverlayView` class has three methods to implement in order to show the overlays as `draw()`, `onAdd()`, and `onRemove()`. The `onAdd()` and `onRemove()` methods are called during initialization and removal respectively. The `div` element is created and added to the map with the help of the `appendChild` function in the `onAdd()` method. Also, the `drag` event of the map is started to listen and draw the WMS layer on each user drag in this method. The `onRemove()` method removes the `div` element created earlier:

```
WMSUntiled.prototype.onAdd = function() {
    var that = this;
```

```
    var div = document.createElement('div');
    div.style.borderStyle = 'none';
    div.style.borderWidth = '0px';
    div.style.position = 'absolute';

    this.div_ = div;
    this.getPanes().floatPane.appendChild(this.div_);

    google.maps.event.addListener(this.map_, 'dragend', function() {
      that.draw();
    });
  };

  WMSUntiled.prototype.onRemove = function() {
    this.menuDiv.parentNode.removeChild(this.div_);
    this.div_ = null;
  };
```

The most important part of the class is the `draw()` method. This method creates an `img` element and attaches this element to the created `div` element in the `onAdd()` method. If there is an `img` element created before, it is removed from the `div` element. The `img` source is obtained from another method of the class named `prepareWMSUrl()`:

```
    var div = this.div_;
    if (this.image_ != null)
      div.removeChild(this.image_);
    var img = document.createElement('img');
    img.src = this.prepareWMSUrl();
    img.style.width = '100%';
    img.style.height = '100%';
    img.style.position = 'absolute';
    img.style.opacity = 0.6;
    this.image_ = img;
    div.appendChild(this.image_);
```

We need pixel coordinates to place the `div` element. We get a projection of the layers in order to locate the `div` and `img` elements in the right place on the map. The `fromLatLngToDivPixel()` method converts the `LatLng` coordinates to screen pixels, which are used for placing the `div` element in the correct place:

```
    var overlayProjection = this.getProjection();
    var sw = overlayProjection.fromLatLngToDivPixel
      (this.map_.getBounds().getSouthWest());
    var ne = overlayProjection.fromLatLngToDivPixel
      (this.map_.getBounds().getNorthEast());
```

WMS has a bounding box parameter (BBOX) that defines the boundaries of a georeferenced image. The BBOX parameter must be in the same unit defined in the CRS parameter. Google Maps is based on the Web Mercator projection, which is defined as EPSG:900913 or EPSG:3857. The Google Maps JavaScript API used Web Mercator as a base projection, but gives us the LatLng objects in geographic projection defined as EPSG:4326. In order to get the right WMS image on Google Maps, there is a need for transformation of coordinates from EPSG:4326 to EPSG:3857. This transformation can be done via the toMercator() method of the class.

The prepareWMSUrl() method gets most of the parameters from the wmsoptions object and creates a WMS URL to get the georeferenced image. The BBOX and width/height parameters are gathered from the map functions:

```
WMSUntiled.prototype.prepareWMSUrl = function() {
   var baseUrl = this.options.baseUrl;
   baseUrl += 'Service=WMS&request=GetMap&CRS=EPSG:3857&';
   baseUrl += 'version=' + this.options.version;
   baseUrl += '&layers=' + this.options.layers;
   baseUrl += '&styles=' + this.options.styles;
   baseUrl += '&format=' + this.options.format;

   var bounds = this.map_.getBounds();
   var sw = this.toMercator(bounds.getSouthWest());
   var ne = this.toMercator(bounds.getNorthEast());

   var mapDiv = this.map_.getDiv();
   baseUrl += '&BBOX=' + sw.x + ',' + sw.y + ',' + ne.x +
     ',' + ne.y;
   baseUrl += '&width=' + mapDiv.clientWidth + '&height=' +
     mapDiv.clientHeight;
   return baseUrl;
};
```

The WMSUntiled class handles almost everything. In order to add WMS layers to the Google Maps JavaScript API, you need to define the parameters of WMS layers and create an object from the WMSUntiled class. Since we give map as a parameter, there is no need to add the WMS layer to the map object:

```
var wmsOptions = {
   baseUrl: 'http://demo.cubewerx.com/cubewerx/cubeserv.cgi?',
   layers: 'Foundation.gtopo30',
   version: '1.1.1',
   styles: 'default',
   format: 'image/png'
};
var wmsLayer = new WMSUntiled(map, wmsOptions);
```

There are lots of parameters to get WMS from the server, but that is out of the scope of this book. The sample WMS server used in this example cannot be available when you want to use it, so please use your own WMS servers in order to be sure of the availability of the services.

There's more...

As stated at the beginning of the recipe, we create an overlay class to add WMS layers to the Google Maps JavaScript API without using the tiled structure. This is just a use case for developers. You should check for both tiled and untiled structures for your cases. There is an example use of the tiled structure in the *Accessing GeoServer with the Google Maps JavaScript API* recipe in this chapter.

See also

- ▸ The *Creating a simple map in a custom DIV element* recipe in *Chapter 1, Google Maps JavaScript API Basics*
- ▸ The *Accessing GeoServer with the Google Maps JavaScript API* recipe

Adding Fusion Tables layers to maps

Fusion Tables (`http://tables.googlelabs.com/`) is an experimental tool provided by Google to store different types of tabular data. Fusion Tables is important for geo developers because it supports feature types such as points, polylines, and polygons. There is also support for geocoding of the address, place names, or countries that make Fusion Tables a powerful database for your features. Fusion Tables also has an API so that developers can connect it to different applications. There are some limitations in Fusion Tables but these limitations are enough for most developers.

The OpenStreetMap POI database can be downloaded via different sources. We downloaded the restaurant POI database of Switzerland in the KML format and imported it into Fusion Tables. There are 7967 points in this table. In this recipe, we will use this table as a sample to help us visualize.

The map view of the Switzerland POI database of restaurants can be seen using Fusion Tables as shown in the following screenshot:

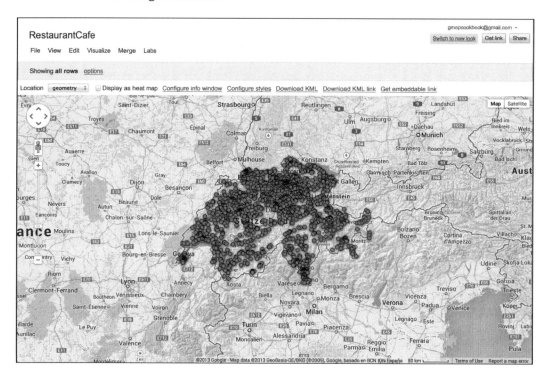

This is how we achieve adding a Fusion Tables layer to the map that shows thousands of points without a problem.

Getting ready

We assume that you already know how to create a simple map. We will only cover the code that is needed for adding a Fusion Tables layer.

You can find the source code at `Chapter 8/ch08_fusion_tables.html`.

How to do it...

If you want to add Fusion Tables layers to the map, you should perform the following steps:

1. First, add the following line for jQuery to simplify our work after the Google Maps JavaScript API is added:

    ```
    <script src="http://code.jquery.com/jquery-
      1.10.1.min.js"></script>
    ```

2. Then, add the following HTML code before the map's DIV element for interactivity with the Fusion Tables layer:

```
<input type="checkbox" id="status"/>HeatMap Enabled
  <input type="text" id="query"/>
  <input type="button" id="search" value="Search"/><br/>
```

3. Now, create the Fusion Tables layers and add it to the map after the initialization of the `map` object as follows:

```
var layer = new google.maps.FusionTablesLayer({
  query: {
    select: 'geometry',
    from: '1_1TjGKCfamzW46TfqEBS7rXppOejpa6NK-FsXOg'
  },
  heatmap: {
    enabled: false
  }
});
layer.setMap(map);
```

4. The next step is to listen to the `click` event of the checkbox to switch between the normal view and the heat map view:

```
$('#status').click(function() {
  if (this.checked) {
    layer.setOptions({
      heatmap: { enabled: true } });
  }
  else {
    layer.setOptions({
      heatmap: { enabled: false } });
  }
});
```

5. Add the following lines to listen to the `click` event of the **Search** button to filter the Fusion Tables layer according to the value entered in the textbox:

```
$('#search').click(function() {
  var txtValue = $('#query').val();
  layer.setOptions({query: {
    select: 'geometry',
    from:
    '1_1TjGKCfamzW46TfqEBS7rXppOejpa6NK-FsXOg',
    where: 'name contains "' + txtValue + '"' } });
});
```

6. Go to your local URL where your HTML is stored in your favorite browser and click on the map to see the result. If you click on the heat map checkbox, the Fusion Tables layer will change into a heat map. You can also search for the names of restaurants with the **Search** button:

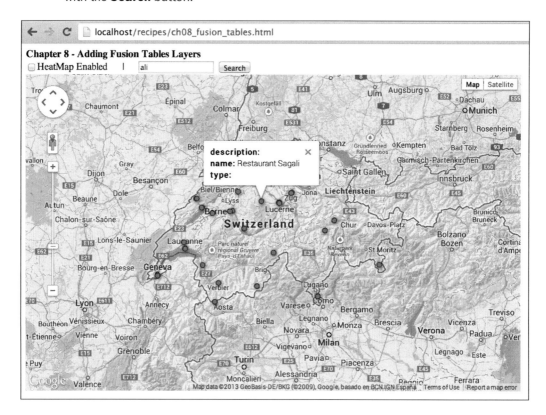

The preceding screenshot is also showing a filtered Fusion Tables layers added to a map.

How it works...

As stated earlier, Fusion Tables is an experimental tool to use and classes related to Fusion Tables that are under the Google Maps JavaScript API are also experimental according to the documentation. As far as we have used them, both Fusion Tables and classes under Google Maps JavaScript API are stable and can be ready for production environments, but it is at your own risk to use them in your geo-web application.

By the way, please make sure that your tables do not pass 100,000 rows in order to use them properly, because there is a limitation written in the API.

Fusion Tables supports the importing of various data types such as CSV, TSV, TXT, or KML with coordinates of geometries. Fusion Tables geometry columns can be in different formats, such as a geometry column in the KML format, address column, or latitude/longitude coordinates in single column or two separate columns. If you have addresses or city names, these columns can also be geocoded in order to be used in your applications. We uploaded a KML file to Fusion Tables gathered from OpenStreetMap that is full of restaurant points with names.

There is also a REST API for Fusion Tables to access and manipulate the data within tables with/without OAuth regardless of the Google Maps JavaScript API.

There is a `google.maps.FusionTablesLayer` class in the Google Maps JavaScript API to access and visualize the data from Fusion Tables. We need the table ID and name of the geometry column to access the Fusion Tables layer in the Google Maps JavaScript API. Remember that your table must be shared as public or unlisted in order to be accessible from the Google Maps JavaScript API. Developers can get the table ID by navigating to **File | About** in the Fusion Tables web interface. The following code block is needed to add Fusion Tables to the Google Maps JavaScript API:

```
var layer = new google.maps.FusionTablesLayer({
  query: {
    select: 'geometry',
    from: '1_1TjGKCfamzW46TfqEBS7rXppOejpa6NK-FsXOg'
  },
  heatmap: {
    enabled: false
  }
});
layer.setMap(map);
```

If you want to enable the heat map option at the beginning of the API, you should set the enabled option to `true` under the `heatmap` parameter. We will switch these parameters with the `checkbox` options in our recipe as follows:

```
$('#status').click(function(){
  if (this.checked) {
    layer.setOptions({heatmap: { enabled: true } });
  }
  else {
    layer.setOptions({heatmap: { enabled: false } });
  }
});
```

Using heat maps is a good way to summarize the data you have and show where most of the points are gathered. Heat maps are mostly used in various fields in order to show the important places such as most dense crime spots in crime mapping. If users enable the heat map, you will see the following results in the application. The following map shows in red where the restaurant population is crowded:

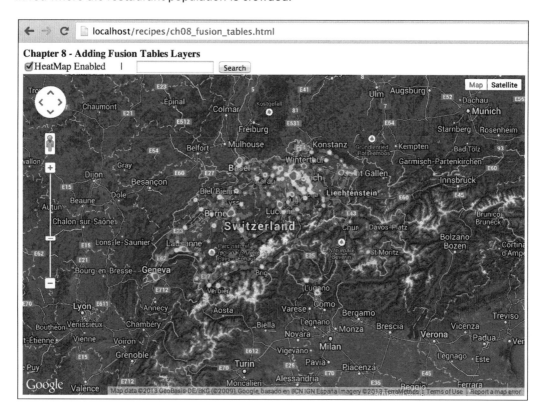

Fusion Tables also supports filtering rows with SQL-like queries. SQL queries can be added to the `query` parameter with the `where` field. This can be a starting value or added later to filter the visualized data. In this recipe, we filter our data according to the value entered in the textbox. The following code listens to the **Search** button and when a click occurs, it gets the value of the textbox and set the options of the Fusion Tables layer according to the textbox value. The filtered data is immediately shown on the map:

```
$('#search').click(function() {
  var txtValue = $('#query').val();
  layer.setOptions({
  query: {
    select: 'geometry',
    from: '1_1TjGKCfamzW46TfqEBS7rXppOejpa6NK-FsXOg',
      where: 'name contains "' + txtValue + '"' } });
});
```

The `google.maps.FusionTablesLayer` class also has the ability to change the style of the map according to filters. You can change the marker type of points, line color of polylines, or fill color of polygons consistent with the values of columns.

Fusion Tables can be a good candidate to store, analyze, and visualize your data if developers know the limitations. Also, developers do not forget that Fusion Tables are still in the experimental stage, so Google can change something in Fusion Tables in the future that can cause your application to stop.

>
> **More about data**
>
> The data used in this application can be downloaded from `http://poi-osm.tucristal.es/`, which uses OpenStreetMap as a source. The data used in this recipe is available with the code. The data is also available from Fusion Tables as a public share.

See also

▸ The *Creating a simple map in a custom DIV element* recipe in *Chapter 1, Google Maps JavaScript API Basics*

▸ The *Creating a heat map* recipe in *Chapter 2, Adding Raster Layers*

Adding CartoDB layers to maps

CartoDB is a geospatial database on the cloud that allows for the storage and visualization of data on the Web. Using CartoDB will allow you to quickly create map-based visualizations. According to the CartoDB website (`www.cartodb.com`), you can use CartoDB in the following ways:

▸ Upload, visualize, and manage your data using the CartoDB dashboard

▸ Quickly create and customize maps that you can embed or share via public URL using the map-embedding tool

▸ Analyze and integrate data you store on CartoDB into your applications using the SQL API

▸ For more advanced integrations of CartoDB maps on your website or application, use `CartoDB.js`

CartoDB is an open source project for which you can fork the code from GitHub and start your own CartoDB instance on your own hardware, but the power of CartoDB is the cloud backend. CartoDB is based on PostgreSQL, PostGIS, and Mapnik, which are the most popular and powerful open source geo tools nowadays.

There is a free tier for developers to explore the power of CartoDB, which has a limit of up to 5 MB storage and five tables.

In this recipe, the simplified version of world borders is imported from the CartoDB dashboard to play with. The following screenshots show both the tabular and map view of the world borders. This data will be published on the Google Maps JavaScript API with the help of the `CartoDB.js` library:

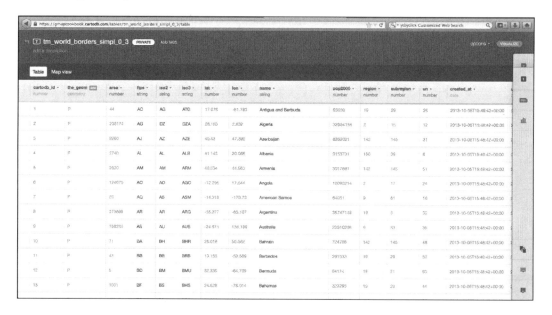

And now the map view of the world border is shown in the following screenshot:

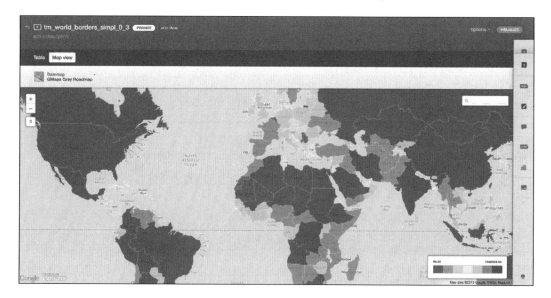

Getting ready

In this recipe, we assume you already know how to create a simple map. So, we will only show the extra code lines to add CartoDB layers on top of the Google Maps base maps.

You can find the source code at `Chapter 8/ch08_cartodb_layer.html`.

How to do it...

If you perform the following steps, you can add CartoDB layers to the map:

1. First, CartoDB-related files are added to the HTML document:

```
<link rel="stylesheet"
  href="http://libs.cartocdn.com/
  cartodb.js/v3/themes/css/cartodb.css" />
<!--[if lte IE 8]>
<link rel="stylesheet"
  href="http://libs.cartocdn.com/
  cartodb.js/v3/themes/css/cartodb.ie.css" />
<![endif]-->
<script
  src="http://libs.cartocdn.com/
  cartodb.js/v3/cartodb.js"></script>
```

2. Then, the jQuery file is added after CartoDB files:

```
<script src="http://code.jquery.com/jquery-
  1.10.1.min.js"></script>
```

3. The next step is to add a global variable to access from everywhere after the `map` variable:

```
var cartoLayer;
```

4. After initialization of the map, the following lines are added to define the cartography of the layers. This can be single line string, but it is separated into multiple lines in order to improve readability:

```
var cartoStyle = '#world_borders { ' +
  'polygon-fill: #1a9850; ' +
  'polygon-opacity:0.7; ' +
  '} ' +
  '#world_borders [pop2005 > 10000000] { ' +
  'polygon-fill: #8cce8a ' +
  '} ' +
```

```
  '#world_borders [pop2005 > 40000000] { ' +
  'polygon-fill: #fed6b0 ' +
  '} ' +
  '#world_borders [pop2005 > 70000000] { ' +
  'polygon-fill: #d73027 ' +
'} ';
```

5. The important part of the code is the initialization of the CartoDB layer as follows:

```
//Creating CartoDB layer and add it to map.
cartodb.createLayer(map, {
  user_name: 'gmapcookbook',
  type: 'cartodb',
  sublayers: [{
    sql: 'SELECT * FROM world_borders',
    cartocss: cartoStyle,
    interactivity: 'cartodb_id, name, pop2005, area',
  }]
})
.addTo(map)
.done(function(layer) {
  cartoLayer = layer;

  //Enabling popup info window
  cartodb.vis.Vis.addInfowindow(map, layer.getSubLayer(0),
    ['name', 'pop2005', 'area']);

  //Enabling UTFGrid layer to add interactivity.
  layer.setInteraction(true);
  layer.on('featureOver', function(e, latlng, pos, data) {
    $('#infoDiv').html('<b>Info : </b>' + data.name +
      ' (Population : ' + data.pop2005 + ')');
  });
});
```

6. Now, add the following part to listen to the `click` event of the **Search** button in order to update the map contents according to the textbox value:

```
//Listening click event of the search button to filter the
//data of map
$('#search').click(function() {
  var txtValue = $('#query').val();
  cartoLayer.setQuery('SELECT * FROM world_borders WHERE
    name LIKE \'%' + txtValue + '%\'');
  if (txtValue == '') {
    cartoLayer.setCartoCSS(cartoStyle);
  }
```

```
    else {
      cartoLayer.setCartoCSS('#world_borders {
        polygon-fill: #00000d; polygon-opacity:0.7; }');
    }
});
```

7. Do not forget to add the following lines before and after the map's `div` element:

```
<input type="text" id="query"/> <input type="button"
  id="search" value="Search"/><br/>
<div id="mapDiv"></div>
<div id="infoDiv">--</div>
```

8. Go to your local URL where your HTML is stored in your favorite browser and take a look at the CartoDB layer on top of the Google Maps base map. When you move on the map, the bottom line of the map changes according to where your mouse is placed. When you click on the map, you will also see an info window about that country as shown in the following screenshot:

As a result of this recipe, we can add CartoDB layers to the map, which gets live data from your data source.

How it works...

As mentioned earlier, CartoDB is based on PostGIS and Mapnik technologies, so you can use CartoCSS as a styling language of the layer. CartoCSS is much like CSS with some additional tags to define the cartography. In this recipe, we will define a choropleth cartography according to population values. Using population values seems to be simple for cartography but this is the most easiest way to understand CartoCSS:

```
var cartoStyle = '#world_borders { ' +
    'polygon-fill: #1a9850; ' +
    'polygon-opacity:0.7; ' +
    '} ' +
  '#world_borders [pop2005 > 10000000] { ' +
    'polygon-fill: #8cce8a ' +
    '} ' +
  '#world_borders [pop2005 > 40000000] { ' +
    'polygon-fill: #fed6b0 ' +
    '} ' +
  '#world_borders [pop2005 > 70000000] { ' +
    'polygon-fill: #d73027 ' +
  '} ';
```

The #world_borders layer is the name of the layer defined in the CartoDB dashboard. The first brackets include all the features in the layer with a polygon-fill and a polygon-opacity. The second brackets target the features with a population of more than 10 million with a different color. The third brackets and fourth brackets target the features with a population of more than 40 and 70 million respectively with different colors. So, we have four different categories defined in this CartoCSS tag according to the population of countries. Each CartoCSS rule overwrites the one written before.

Now that we have the cartography of the layer, it is time to create the layer and add it to the map:

```
cartodb.createLayer(map, {
  user_name: 'gmapcookbook',
  type: 'cartodb',
  sublayers: [{
    sql: 'SELECT * FROM world_borders',
    cartocss: cartoStyle,
    interactivity: 'cartodb_id, name, pop2005, area'
  }]
})
.addTo(map)
```

We have used chaining methods to create the layer and add it to the map. The following part is explained later. There is a `user_name` field to define your CartoDB account. The important part to define the layer is the `sublayers` field. You can define more than one layer but we will add only one layer at this time. The JavaScript object within the `sublayers` field is very important. The `sql` field defines, which features to be shown on the map. You can even write very complex SQL queries here like your own PostGIS database. The `cartocss` field is the part where you define the cartography of your layer. This is defined before, so just pass that variable to this field.

The next field is the `interactivity` field. This is important due to the technology behind it called **UTFGrid**. UTFGrid is a specification for rasterized interaction data. According to MapBox, who introduced this standard, UTFGrid's solution to this problem is to rasterize polygons and points in JSON as a grid of text characters. Each feature is referenced by a distinct character and associated to JSON data by its character code. The result is a cheap, fast lookup that even Internet Explorer 7 can do instantly.

With UTFGrid, you can load some attribute data to the client with the loading of layer tile images and you can show this attribute data while your mouse is moving without sending any requests to the server. This is the quickest way to interact with users and remove the load from servers. You can still get detailed information from the server when it is really needed. Most of the time, users are very happy with this fast data interaction and there is no need to get more information from the server.

More about UTFGrid

If you are interested in more technical details of UTFGrid, the following web addresses are suggested for further reference:

- `https://github.com/mapbox/utfgrid-spec`
- `https://www.mapbox.com/developers/utfgrid/`

As we have previously covered, there is a field named `interactivity`. This should be filled with the column names that will be used for interactivity; it is important to make sure that interactivity is quick for users. So, adding complex text columns to show on interactivity is not advised in order to increase the loading of UTFGrids. Then we add this layer to the map with the chaining method.

We added the CartoDB layer to the map but there are still missing pieces to activate the interactivity. We add another chaining method to add the necessary functionality as follows:

```
.done(function(layer) {
  cartoLayer = layer;
  //Enabling popup info window
  cartodb.vis.Vis.addInfowindow(map, layer.getSubLayer(0),
    ['name', 'pop2005', 'area']);
});
```

This done() method is called when the layer is created and added to the map. First, we assign the local variable layer to the global variable cartoLayer to manipulate the SQL query of the layer variable later. Then, we activate the info window with the cartodb.vis.Vis.addInfoWindow() method. But there are still required code parts for activating UTFGrid, which are given as follows:

```
layer.setInteraction(true);
layer.on('featureOver', function(e, latlng, pos, data) {
  $('#infoDiv').html('<b>Info : </b>' + data.name +
    ' (Population : ' + data.pop2005 + ')');
});
```

The first line activated the UTFGrid interaction, but we still need to know where and when to show the data. With the featureOver event of the layer, we catch each mouse move, get the related data from UTFGrid, and show it on the div element defined. We only show the name and pop2005 fields of the layer on each mouse move.

The final part of the recipe is to search for the countries by typing their names. This part is like writing the SQL query. On each click event of the **Search** button, we get the value of the textbox and assign it to a local variable named txtValue:

```
$('#search').click(function() {
  var txtValue = $('#query').val();
});
```

When we have the txtValue variable, we set the query of the CartoDB layer by using the setQuery() method:

```
cartoLayer.setQuery('SELECT * FROM world_borders WHERE
  name LIKE \'%' + txtValue + '%\'');
```

If the txtValue variable is empty, we recover the defined cartography; otherwise, we change the cartography of the layers to a black color to see which countries are selected by using the setCartoCSS() method:

```
if (txtValue == '') {
  cartoLayer.setCartoCSS(cartoStyle);
}
else {
  cartoLayer.setCartoCSS('#world_borders {
    polygon-fill: #00000d; polygon-opacity:0.7; }');
}
```

The following screenshot is taken after searching countries whose names include `Turk`:

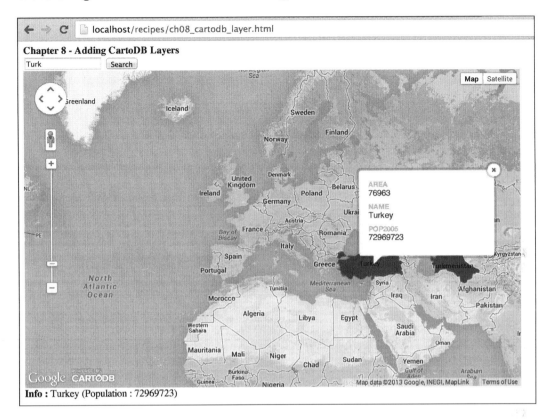

As we have seen in this recipe, CartoDB is a complete solution for everyone, from basic map visualization to complex GIS analysis. You can use the complete power of PostGIS behind your geo-web applications.

See also

▶ The *Creating a simple map in a custom DIV element* recipe in *Chapter 1, Google Maps JavaScript API Basics*

Accessing ArcGIS Server with the Google Maps JavaScript API

ArcGIS Server is the mapping and spatial server developed by ESRI. It is a proprietary software, but the capabilities and integration with desktop software make ArcGIS Server better than other spatial server products. ArcGIS Server is a complete spatial server solution for enterprise corporations or institutions. ArcGIS Server is used for creating and managing GIS web services, applications, and data. ArcGIS Server is typically deployed on-premises within the organization's **Service-oriented Architecture** (**SOA**) or off-premises in a cloud computing environment.

ESRI releases APIs for the ArcGIS Server to use in multiple platforms, but ESRI does not support the Google Maps JavaScript API v3. There was an extension for the Google Maps JavaScript API v2, but it does not work with the new API. There is an open source library to extend the Google Maps JavaScript API v3 to work with ArcGIS Server.

In this recipe, we will use the open source library to work with ArcGIS Server. We will add both a tiled and dynamic layer to the Google Maps JavaScript API. We also identify the dynamic layer with mouse clicks and show the underlying information.

More about the open source ArcGIS Server library

ArcGIS Server link for the Google Maps JavaScript API v3 is an open source library and can be found the following web address. It is advised to download and check the library at `https://google-maps-utility-library-v3.googlecode.com/svn/trunk/arcgislink/docs/reference.html`.

Getting ready

This recipe is still using the same map creation process defined in *Chapter 1*, *Google Maps JavaScript API Basics*, but there are some additional code blocks to add ArcGIS tiled/dynamic layers and listen for mouse clicks to identify the dynamic layer.

You can find the source code at `Chapter 8/ch08_arcgis_layer.html`.

How to do it...

The following are the steps we need to access ArcGIS Server with the Google Maps JavaScript API:

1. First, download the ArcGIS Server link for the Google Maps JavaScript API v3 from the following address: `https://google-maps-utility-library-v3.googlecode.com/svn/trunk/arcgislink/docs/reference.html`.

2. The next step is to add the downloaded library to your HTML file:

    ```
    <script src="lib/arcgis.js"></script>
    ```

3. The jQuery library is also needed in this recipe:

    ```
    <script src="http://code.jquery.com/jquery1.10.1.min.js">
      </script>
    ```

4. We also need some global variables as follows:

    ```
    var overlays = [];
    var infowindow = null;
    ```

5. Now, create a tiled map layer named `tiledMap` with an opacity of `0.6`:

    ```
    //Creating a tiled map layer
    var topoMapURL =
      'http://server.arcgisonline.com/ArcGIS/
      rest/services/World_Topo_Map/MapServer';
    var tiledMap = new gmaps.ags.MapType(topoMapURL, {
      name: 'TopoMap',
      opacity: 0.6
    });
    ```

6. Then, create a dynamic map layer named `dynamicMap` with an opacity of `0.8`.
    Also, a copyright control is added to the map:

    ```
    //Creating a dynamic map layer
    var dynamicMapURL =
      'http://sampleserver1.arcgisonline.com/ArcGIS/rest/
      services/Demographics/ESRI_Census_USA/MapServer';
    var copyrightControl = new gmaps.ags.CopyrightControl(map);
    var dynamicMap = new gmaps.ags.MapOverlay(dynamicMapURL, {
      opacity: 0.8
    });
    ```

7. We also need a map service for identifying with the same URL used in the dynamic
    map layer:

    ```
    //Creating a map service layer
    var mapService = new gmaps.ags.MapService(dynamicMapURL);
    ```

8. Now, start listening to the `map` object for each mouse click event:

    ```
    //Listening map click event for identifying
    google.maps.event.addListener(map, 'click', identify);
    ```

9. Let's create the function that is called on each mouse click event:

    ```
    //Function that is called on each mouse click
    function identify(evt) {
    ```

```
      mapService.identify({
        'geometry': evt.latLng,
        'tolerance': 3,
        'layerIds': [5],
        'layerOption': 'all',
        'bounds': map.getBounds(),
        'width': map.getDiv().offsetWidth,
        'height': map.getDiv().offsetHeight
      }, function(results, err) {
        if (err) {
          alert(err.message + err.details.join('\n'));
        } else {
          showResult(results.results, evt.latLng);
        }
      });
    }
```

10. Afterward, we will show the results in an info window:

```
    //Function that is showing the result of identify
    function showResult(results, position) {
      if (infowindow != null) {
        infowindow.close();
      }

      var info = '<b>State Name : </b>' +
        results[0].feature.attributes.STATE_NAME +
        '<br><b>2007 Population : </b>' +
        results[0].feature.attributes.POP2007;
      infowindow = new google.maps.InfoWindow({
        content: info,
        position: position
      });

      infowindow.open(map);

      removePolygons();

      for (var j=0; j < results[0].geometry.rings.length; j++){
        addPolygon(results[0].geometry.rings[j]);
      }
    }
```

11. Next, we add the function used for showing polygons. This function is used in the previous recipes:

```
//Function that is used for adding polygons to map.
function addPolygon(areaCoordinates) {
  //First we iterate over the coordinates array to create
  // new array which includes objects of LatLng class.
  var pointCount = areaCoordinates.length;

  var areaPath = [];
  for (var i=0; i < pointCount; i++) {
    var tempLatLng = new
      google.maps.LatLng(areaCoordinates[i][1],
      areaCoordinates[i][0]);
    areaPath.push(tempLatLng);
  }
  //Polygon properties are defined below
  var polygonOptions = {
    paths: areaPath,
    strokeColor: '#FF0000',
    strokeOpacity: 0.9,
    strokeWeight: 3,
    fillColor: '#FFFF00',
    fillOpacity: 0.25
  };

  var polygon = new google.maps.Polygon(polygonOptions);

  //Polygon is set to current map.
  polygon.setMap(map);

  overlays.push(polygon);
}
```

12. Now, add the following function for removing all the polygons:

```
//Function that is used for removing all polygons
function removePolygons() {
  if (overlays) {
    for (var i = 0; i < overlays.length; i++) {
      overlays[i].setMap(null);
    }
    overlays.length = 0;
  }
}
```

13. The following code block listens to the checkboxes and switches the visibility of both tiled and dynamic layers:

```
//Start listening for click event to add/remove tiled map layer
$('#statusTile').click(function(){
  if (this.checked) {
    map.overlayMapTypes.insertAt(0, tiledMap);
  }
  else {
    map.overlayMapTypes.removeAt(0);
  }
});

//Start listening for click event to add/remove dynamic map layer
$('#statusDynamic').click(function(){
  if (this.checked) {
    dynamicMap.setMap(map);
  }
  else {
    dynamicMap.setMap(null);
  }
});
```

14. The last step is to add the necessary HTML tags for checkboxes:

```
<input type="checkbox" id="statusTile"/>
  Add Topo Map Overlay <br/>
<input type="checkbox" id="statusDynamic"/>
  Add Dynamic Map <br/>
```

15. Go to your local URL where the HTML is stored in your favorite browser and enable **Add Topo Map Overlay** by clicking on the checkbox nearby. The following topological map is shown on the satellite base map:

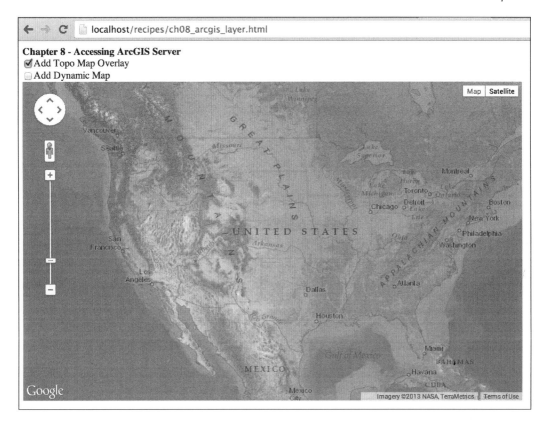

Thus, we have successfully created a map that accesses the ArcGIS Server layers with the Google Maps JavaScript API.

How it works...

ArcGIS Server has different capabilities to use with the Google Maps JavaScript API. The library used to access ArcGIS Server in this recipe has almost every method for the REST API of the ArcGIS Server. The library is created on the Google Maps JavaScript API base classes, so using it is not as difficult as expected.

The service URLs used in this recipe are serving by ESRI, so you can use them for developing purposes without any problems. If you want to use them in a production environment, please contact ESRI to get valid licenses.

In the first step, we will add a tiled map showing the topology of the world on the satellite base map. With the help of the `gmaps.ags.MapType` class, you can easily create a tiled map with a URL to the map service:

```
var topoMapURL =
  'http://server.arcgisonline.com/ArcGIS/rest/services/
  World_Topo_Map/MapServer';
var tiledMap = new gmaps.ags.MapType(topoMapURL, {
  name: 'TopoMap',
  opacity: 0.6
});
```

Adding and removing the tiled map is done in the the same way as we did in *Chapter 2, Adding Raster Layers*. Please get the index of the layer. This index is used when removing the layer from map:

```
// Adding layer to the map.
map.overlayMapTypes.insertAt(0, tiledMap);
// Removing layer from the map
map.overlayMapTypes.removeAt(0);
```

Creating a dynamic layer is also very easy thanks to the library. The library handles all the code for drawing the dynamic layer. The sample dynamic layer used in this recipe is the CENSUS data layer, which has the demographic information about states, counties, or census blocks of the U.S.:

```
var dynamicMapURL = 'http://sampleserver1.arcgisonline.com/ArcGIS
  /rest/services/Demographics/ESRI_Census_USA/MapServer';
var dynamicMap = new gmaps.ags.MapOverlay(dynamicMapURL, {
  opacity: 0.8
});
```

The following is the screenshot of the CENSUS layer:

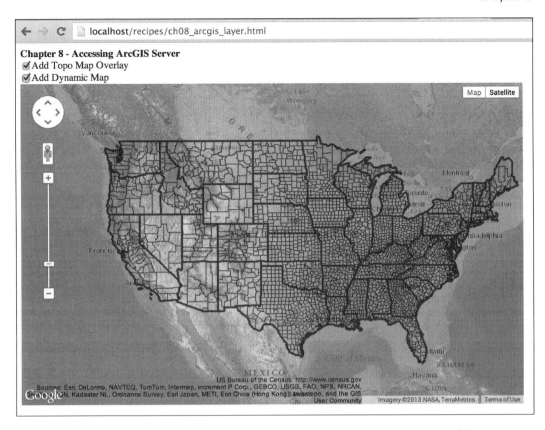

Adding and removing the dynamic layer are the same as overlays because the `gmaps.ags.MapOverlay` class is extended from the `google.maps.OverlayView` base class:

```
// Adding layer to the map.
dynamicMap.setMap(map);
// Removing layer from the map
dynamicMap.setMap(null);
```

Identifying a map layer is a very important task for most geo-web applications. This gives information to users about the layer at known points. To achieve this, we need to define a map service as follows. The `gmaps.ags.MapService` class only gets the URL parameters, which are defined for the dynamic layer before:

```
var mapService = new gmaps.ags.MapService(dynamicMapURL);
```

When a map `click` event occurs, we need to handle it with a function named `identify`. This function gets the `latLng` object and trigger the `identify` method of the `gmaps.ags.MapService` class:

```
function identify(evt) {
  mapService.identify({
    'geometry': evt.latLng,
    'tolerance': 3,
    'layerIds': [5],
    'layerOption': 'all',
    'bounds': map.getBounds(),
    'width': map.getDiv().offsetWidth,
    'height': map.getDiv().offsetHeight
  }, function(results, err) {
    if (err) {
        alert(err.message + err.details.join('\n'));
    } else {
        showResult(results.results, evt.latLng);
    }
  });
}
```

The `identify` method gets some parameters as follows:

▶ `geometry`: This gets `LatLng`, `Polyline`, or `Polygon` objects.

▶ `tolerance`: This is the distance in screen pixels where the mouse is clicked.

▶ `layerIds`: This array contains layer IDs. The value 5 in this recipe defines the state's layer.

▶ `layerOption`: These options can be `top`, `visible`, or `all`.

▶ `bounds`: This gets an object created from the `LatLngBounds` class. This defines the current bounds of the map.

▶ `width`: This is the width of the map `div` element.

▶ `height`: This is the height of the map `div` element.

The return of the function contains an array of features that contains both the attribute and geometry data. The result function can iterate over this array and show the attribute data in an info window. The geometry of each feature can also be shown on the map. The result of the `identify` operation is shown in the following screenshot:

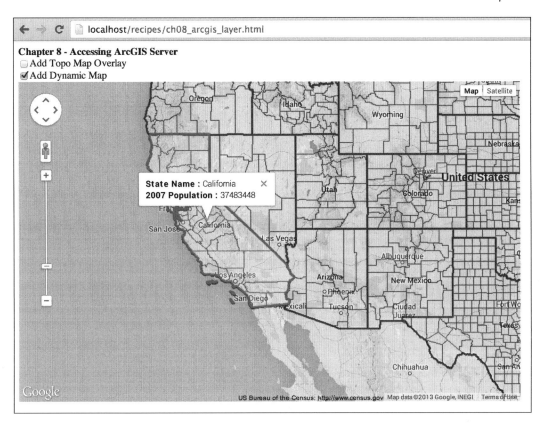

ArcGIS Server is a powerful tool to use with the Google Maps JavaScript API if you have the license. There are also other GIS functionalities such as geoprocessing, geocoding, or geometry service, which are not included in this recipe due to the scope, but their usage is no different from the `identify` operation.

The Google Maps JavaScript API is a perfect mapping tool and is powerful with this kind of service and libraries.

There's more...

In this recipe, we focused on the ArcGIS Server, but ESRI also has an alternative cloud solution named ArcGIS Online (`www.arcgis.com`). It is the cloud version of the ArcGIS Server and the usage of its services are almost the same as ArcGIS Server's services.

See also

▸ The *Creating a simple map in a custom DIV element* recipe in *Chapter 1, Google Maps JavaScript API Basics*

▸ The *Adding popups to markers or maps* recipe in *Chapter 3, Adding Vector Layers*

▸ The *Adding polygons to maps* recipe in *Chapter 3, Adding Vector Layers*

▸ The *Getting coordinates of a mouse click* recipe in *Chapter 5, Understanding Google Maps JavaScript API Events*

Accessing GeoServer with the Google Maps JavaScript API

GeoServer is an open source map server written in Java that allows users to share and edit geospatial data. It is one of the popular open source map servers that can publish OGC compliant services such as WMS and WFS. **Web Map Service** (**WMS**) is used for publishing georeferenced images and simple querying. On the other side, **Web Feature Service** (**WFS**) is used for publishing vector data to any kind of GIS clients. WFS is mostly used for data sharing purposes.

In this recipe, we will use one of GeoServer's standard published service named `topp:states` in WMS format. As stated in the *Adding WMS layers to maps* recipe of this chapter, WMS has different request types such as `GetMap` or `GetCapabilities`. We will also use a `GetFeatureInfo` addition to the `GetMap` request. This new request gets the information of the point on the map. Also, we used a tiled structure in this recipe to get WMS images in order to make a comparison between the untiled structure in the *Adding WMS layers to maps* recipe and the tiled structure in this recipe.

Getting ready

In this recipe, we will use the first recipe defined in *Chapter 1, Google Maps JavaScript API Basics*, as a template in order to skip the map creation.

You can find the source code at `Chapter 8/ch08_geoserver.html`.

How to do it...

You can easily access GeoServer with the Google Maps JavaScript API after performing the following steps:

1. First, we create a `wms-tiled.js` file to include in the HTML later. This JavaScript file has the `WMSTiled` and `WMSFeatureInfo` classes. Let's add the `WMSTiled` class as follows:

```javascript
function WMSTiled(wmsTiledOptions) {

    var options = {
      getTileUrl: function(coord, zoom) {
        var proj = map.getProjection();
        var zfactor = Math.pow(2, zoom);

        // get Long Lat coordinates
        var top = proj.fromPointToLatLng(new
          google.maps.Point(coord.x * 256 / zfactor,
          coord.y * 256 / zfactor));
        var bot = proj.fromPointToLatLng(new
          google.maps.Point((coord.x + 1) * 256 / zfactor,
          (coord.y + 1) * 256 / zfactor));

        //create the Bounding box string
        var ne = toMercator(top);
        var sw = toMercator(bot);
        var bbox = ne.x + ',' + sw.y + ',' + sw.x + ','
            + ne.y;

        //base WMS URL
        var url = wmsTiledOptions.url;
        url += '&version=' + wmsTiledOptions.version;
        url += '&request=GetMap';
        url += '&layers=' + wmsTiledOptions.layers;
        url += '&styles=' + wmsTiledOptions.styles;
        url += '&TRANSPARENT=TRUE';
        url += '&SRS=EPSG:3857';
        url += '&BBOX='+ bbox;
        url += '&WIDTH=256';
        url += '&HEIGHT=256';
        url += '&FORMAT=image/png';
        return url;
      },
      tileSize: new google.maps.Size(256, 256),
      isPng: true
    };

    return new google.maps.ImageMapType (options);
}
```

2. Then, create the `WMSFeatureInfo` class and its `getUrl` method:

```javascript
function WMSFeatureInfo(mapObj, options) {
    this.map = mapObj;
```

```
    this.url = options.url;
    this.version = options.version;
    this.layers = options.layers;
    this.callback = options.callback;
    this.fixedParams = 'REQUEST=GetFeatureInfo&EXCEPTIONS=
      application%2Fvnd.ogc.se_xml&SERVICE=
      WMS&FEATURE_COUNT=50&styles=&srs=
      EPSG:3857&INFO_FORMAT=text/javascript&format=
      image%2Fpng';

    this.overlay = new google.maps.OverlayView();
    this.overlay.draw = function() {};
    this.overlay.setMap(this.map);
}


WMSFeatureInfo.prototype.getUrl = function(coord) {
  var pnt = this.overlay.getProjection().
    fromLatLngToContainerPixel (coord);
  var mapBounds = this.map.getBounds();
  var ne = mapBounds.getNorthEast();
  var sw = mapBounds.getSouthWest();

  var neMerc = toMercator(ne);
  var swMerc = toMercator(sw);
  var bbox = swMerc.x + ',' + swMerc.y + ',' +
    neMerc.x + ',' + neMerc.y;

  var rUrl = this.url + this.fixedParams;
  rUrl += '&version=' + this.version;
  rUrl += '&QUERY_LAYERS=' + this.layers + '&Layers='
    + this.layers;
  rUrl += '&BBOX=' + bbox;
  rUrl += '&WIDTH=' + this.map.getDiv().clientWidth +
    '&HEIGHT=' + this.map.getDiv().clientHeight;
  rUrl += '&x=' + Math.round(pnt.x) + '&y=' +
    Math.round(pnt.y);
  rUrl += '&format_options=callback:' + this.callback;
  return rUrl;
};
```

3. The last step in the `wms-tiled.js` file is to add the `toMercator()` method:

```
function toMercator(coord) {
  var lat = coord.lat();
  var lng = coord.lng();
  if ((Math.abs(lng) > 180 || Math.abs(lat) > 90))
    return;

  var num = lng * 0.017453292519943295;
  var x = 6378137.0 * num;
  var a = lat * 0.017453292519943295;

  var merc_lon = x;
  var merc_lat = 3189068.5 * Math.log((1.0 + Math.sin(a))
    / (1.0 - Math.sin(a)));

  return { x: merc_lon, y: merc_lat };
}
```

4. Now, we have our JavaScript class file; add the following line after adding the Google Maps JavaScript API:

```
<script src="lib/wms-tiled.js"></script>
```

5. We also need to add a jQuery library to the HTML file:

```
<script src="http://code.jquery.com/jquery-1.10.1.min.js">
  </script>
```

6. Now, create a tiled WMS from the class written in the `wms-tiled.js` file:

```
//Creating a tiled WMS Service and adding it to the map
var tiledWMS = new WMSTiled({
  url:
    'http://localhost:8080/geoserver/topp/wms?service=WMS',
  version: '1.1.1',
  layers: 'topp:states',
  styles: ''
});
map.overlayMapTypes.push(tiledWMS);
```

7. The next step is to create an object from the `WMSFeatureInfo` class to be used later in the event listener:

```
//Creating a WMSFeatureInfo class to get info from map.
var WMSInfoObj = new WMSFeatureInfo(map, {
  url: 'http://localhost:8080/geoserver/topp/wms?',
  version: '1.1.1',
  layers: 'topp:states',
  callback: 'getLayerFeatures'
});
```

8. The last step is to listen to the `click` event of the map to get information from the map:

```
google.maps.event.addListener(map, 'click', function(e){
  //WMS Feature Info URL is prepared by the help of
  //getUrl method of WMSFeatureInfo object created before
  var url = WMSInfoObj.getUrl(e.latLng);
  $.ajax({
    url: url,
    dataType: 'jsonp',
    jsonp: false,
    jsonpCallback: 'getLayerFeatures'
  }).done(function(data)  {
    if (infowindow != null) {
      infowindow.close();
    }

    var info = '<b>State Name : </b>' +
      data.features[0].properties.STATE_NAME +
      '<br><b>Population : </b>' +
      data.features[0].properties.SAMP_POP;
    infowindow = new google.maps.InfoWindow({
      content: info,
      position: e.latLng
    });

    infowindow.open(map);
  });
});
```

9. Go to your local URL where the HTML is stored in your favorite browser and try to click on the map where you want to get info.

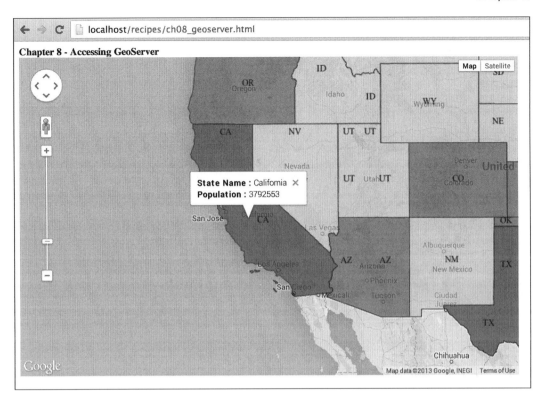

The previous screenshot is the result of the recipe that shows WMS layers created by GeoServer on the Google Maps JavaScript API.

How it works...

Accessing GeoServer is not much different from accessing a WMS server because they share the same standards. With GeoServer, you can publish your data on your own servers with your security standards.

In this recipe, we installed a fresh GeoServer to our Mac OS X and its sample data is ready for serving WMS and WFS. We used the sample states data of the U.S. on WMS to show the interaction.

In our case, we are serving HTML files from `localhost` on port 80, but GeoServer is working from `localhost` on port 8080. This is a problem for our case, because we cannot access GeoServer when getting information due to the cross-site scripting security limitation of HTML. The solution is using a JSONP format to pass over the limitation. GeoServer can give the JSONP format, but you should activate it from the options.

In the *Adding WMS layers to maps* recipe of this chapter, we used the untiled structure to get WMS images, but this time, we are using the tiled structure to get WMS images. The difference can be seen in the screenshot of untiled and tiled usage of WMS that the abbreviation of states' names occurring more than once on tiled WMS because the geometry of the same state can be seen in different images of tiled WMS. As said, the choice is yours whether it is tiled or untiled according to your geo-web application's needs.

Creating a tiled structure in WMS is done in exactly the same way as we did in the *Adding tile overlays to maps* recipe in *Chapter 2, Adding Raster Layers*. The important part here is to create the URL for each tile. The BBOX parameter for each tile is calculated as follows:

```
var proj = map.getProjection();
var zfactor = Math.pow(2, zoom);
// get Long Lat coordinates
var top = proj.fromPointToLatLng(new google.maps.Point(coord.x
   * 256 / zfactor, coord.y * 256 / zfactor) );
var bot = proj.fromPointToLatLng(new google.maps.Point(
   (coord.x + 1) * 256 / zfactor, (coord.y + 1) * 256 / zfactor));
//create the Bounding box string
var ne = toMercator(top);
var sw = toMercator(bot);
var bbox = ne.x + ',' + sw.y + ',' + sw.x + ',' + ne.y;
```

There is a need for projection transformation to get tiles that will fit exactly on the Google Maps' base map. Google Maps has a Web Mercator projection so the overlays need to be in this projection.

One of the other parameters needed for URL is the WMS standard parameter, but be sure about the difference of parameters according to the WMS versions.

The SRS parameter used in this recipe is EPSG:3857, which is the equivalent of EPSG:900913, ESRI:102113, or ESRI:102100. All SRS parameters mentioned here define the Web Mercator projection systems.

The WMSFeatureInfo class is written for creating WMS get info requests. The parameters of the URL are important, which are as follows:

- x: This is the x coordinate of the mouse in pixels.
- y: This is the y coordinate of the mouse in pixels.
- width: This is the width of the map div element.
- height: This is the height of the map div element.
- info_format: This is a string that describes the return format of information. In this case, Text/JavaScript is used for getting info in the format of JSONP.
- query_layers: This is the comma-separated list of layers to be queried.

- `layers`: This is the comma- separated list of layers to be shown (coming from the `GetMap` request).

- `bbox`: This is the bounding box of the map shown.

- `format_options`: This is required for JSONP to define the name of the `callback` function. The `callback` function's name must be the same as in the jQuery AJAX request to get information without any errors.

The `getUrl` method gets the `LatLng` object as an input, but there is a need for screen coordinates in the `GetFeatureInfo` request. We came up with a trick in order to convert `LatLng` to screen coordinates in the `getUrl` method. In the constructor, we create an overlay with the `google.maps.OverlayView` class and use its functions to convert `LatLng` to screen coordinates:

```
var pnt = this.overlay.getProjection ().
  fromLatLngToContainerPixel (coord);
rUrl += '&x=' + Math.round(pnt.x) + '&y=' + Math.round(pnt.y);
```

The `google.maps.Projection` class has a method named `fromLatLngToPoint ()` to convert the `LatLng` object to screen coordinates but this does not work as it is expected to. This converts the `LatLng` coordinates to screen coordinates in world scale, but we need to get the screen coordinates in the map's `div` reference. To achieve this, we use the `google.maps.MapCanvasProjection` class method named `fromLatLngToContainerPixel ()`.

We didn't go into detail with listening to the map `click` event and showing popups. Also, we used the `ajax` method of jQuery to get a JSONP request, which is also out of the scope of this book. If you want to get details of these topics, please refer to previous recipes of related chapters.

See also

- The *Creating a simple map in a custom DIV element* recipe in *Chapter 1, Google Maps JavaScript API Basics*

- The *Adding popups to markers or maps* recipe in *Chapter 3, Adding Vector Layers*

- The *Getting coordinates of a mouse click* recipe in *Chapter 5, Understanding Google Maps JavaScript API Events*

- The *Adding WMS layers to maps* recipe

Index

A

addIconMarker() function 71
address
  coordinates, finding for 212-216
  finding, on map with click 219-224
addStandardMarker() function 71
animated lines
  adding, to maps 88-93
ArcGIS 164
ArcGIS Desktop 124
ArcGIS Online
  URL 285
ArcGIS Server
  about 254, 276
  accessing, with Google Maps JavaScript API
      276-285
area
  calculating, of polygons 175-180
  calculating, of polylines 175-180
AutoCAD 164
autocomplete option
  places, finding with 194-198

B

base maps
  about 21
  modifying 21-24
  tile sources, using as 33-39
BBEdit 6
bicycling layer
  adding 60, 61
Bing Maps 5
bounding box (BBOX) 70
bounds_changed event 139

C

CartoDB 254, 267
CartoDB layers
  adding, to maps 267-275
center_changed event 139
circles
  adding, to maps 83-88
context menu
  about 144
  creating, on maps 145-150
controls
  about 111
  adding 112-114
  creating, for coordinates display in
      real time 155-158
  logo, adding as 132, 133
  position, modifying 117-119
  removing 112-114
coordinates
  encoding 181-184
  finding, for address 212-216
  obtaining, of mouse click 141-144
custom DIV element
  map, creating in 6-10
custom infoboxes
  creating 204-208

D

decodePath() method 184
directions
  obtaining, for locations 238-247
distance matrix
  creating, for locations 229-237

dragend event 139
drag event 139
dragstart event 139
drag zoom
  adding, to map 200-202
drawingControl property 167
drawing library 164
DrawingManager object 166
DrawingManager options 167-174
DrawingManagerOptions class 166
drawingMode property 170
drawingModes property 169

E

elevations, on map
  obtaining, with click 224-229
enableKeyDragZoom() method 202
encodePath() method 184
events
  about 135, 158
  creating 158-160

F

fullscreen map
  creating 11-13
Fusion Tables 261
Fusion Tables layers
  adding, to maps 261-267

G

GDAL2Tiles
  URL 44
geocode() method 216
geocoding 212
geocoding service request
  options 216-219
geocoding service response
  options 216-219
geographical coordinates 155
Geographical Information Systems. *See* GIS
GeoJSON
  about 70
  adding, to Google Maps JavaScript API 98,
    99-103
geolocation control

adding 120-124
  creating 120-124
GeoLocationControl class 121
Geomedia 124
geometry library 175
GeoRSS 94
GeoRSS files
  adding, to map 94-97
GeoServer
  about 254, 286
  accessing, with Google Maps JavaScript API
    286-293
GIS 25, 253
Google 5
Google base maps
  about 26
  styling 26-32
Google Fusion Tables 254
Google Maps
  about 151, 200
  traffic information, displaying on 56, 57
Google Maps default UI 112
google.maps.event namespace 136
google.maps.InfoWindow class 203
Google Maps JavaScript API
  about 69, 111-116, 132, 163
  ArcGIS Server, accessing with 276-285
  GeoJSON, adding to 98-103
  GeoServer, accessing with 286,-293
  WKT, adding to 104-109
google.maps.LatLng class
  used, for adding maps, to markers 70-73
Google Maps map interface
  transit layers, adding to 58, 59
google.maps.MapTypeStyleElementType
    object 30
google.maps.Marker class
  used, for adding maps, to markers 70-73
google.maps.MVCArray 42
google.maps.OverlayView class
  about 203
  draw() method 149
  hide() method 149
  onAdd() method 148
  onRemove() method 149
  show(coord) method 149
Google Maps UI 120

H

heat map
about 50
creating 51-55
Here Maps 5

I

image overlays
adding, to maps 44-48
InfoBoxOption class
parameters 209
initMap() function 132

J

JavaScript
about 148
prototype-based inheritance 150

K

Keyhole Markup Language (KML) 94
KML files
adding, to map 94-97

L

layers
table of contents (ToC) control, creating for 124-132
Leaflet 5
length
calculating, of polygons 175-180
calculating, of polylines 175-180
lines
adding, to maps 77-80
locations
about 5
directions, obtaining for 238-247
distance matrix, creating for 229-237
logo
adding, as control 132, 133

M

map extent
restricting 151-155
Mapinfo 124
mapOptions object 114
map properties
modifying, programmatically 16-20
MapQuest 5
maps
about 70, 136
animated lines. adding to 88-93
CartoDB layers, adding to 267-275
circles, adding to 83-88
context menu, creating on 145-150
creating, for mobile devices 14-16
creating, in custom DIV element 6-10
drag zoom, adding to 200-202
Fusion Tables layers, adding to 261-267
GeoRSS files, adding to 94-97
image overlays, adding to 44-48
KML files, adding to 94-97
lines, adding to 77-80
markers, adding to 70-73
polygons, adding to 80, 82
popups, adding to 74-76
rectangles, adding to 83-88
shapes, drawing on 164-174
Street View, adding to 247-252
tile overlays, adding to 40-44
WMS layers, adding to 254-261
MapTiler
URL 44
markers
about 70
adding, to maps 70-73
popups, adding to 74-76
methods, OverlayView class
draw() 258
onAdd() 258
onRemove() 258
mobile devices
about 13
map, creating for 14-16
mouse click
coordinates, obtaining for 141-144

N

nearby places
   searching for 185-193
   showing 185-193
Notepad++ 6

O

Open Geospatial Consortium (OGC) 104, 254
OpenLayers 5
OpenStreetMap
   about 35
   URL 35
OpenStreetMaps 124
overlays
   about 69
   transparency, modifying 48, 49
OverlayView class
   methods 258

P

Panoramio
   about 65
   URL, for info 65
Panoramio layer
   adding 65-67
parameters, InfoBoxOption class
   boxStyle 209
   closeBoxMargin 209
   closeBoxURL 209
   content 209
   enableEventPropagation 209
   pane 209
   pixelOffset 209
   position 209
pinpointResult() function 192
places
   finding, with autocomplete option 194-198
places library 185
Point Of Interests (POI) 69
polygons
   adding, to maps 80, 82
   area, calculating of 175-180
   length, calculating of 175-180

polyline encoding algorithm 181
polylines
   area, calculating of 175-180
   length, calculating of 175-180
popups
   adding, to maps 74-76
   adding, to markers 74-76
position
   modifying, of controls 117-119
prepareWMSUrl() method 260
prototype-based inheritance, JavaScript 150

R

raster 25
raster layers 25, 69
rectangles
   adding, to maps 83-88
RotateControl control 115

S

Scalable Vector Graphics. *See* **SVG**
Service-oriented Architecture (SOA) 276
shapes
   drawing, on map 164-174
startButtonEvents() function 71
Street View
   adding, to maps 247-252
Styled Maps Wizard
   URL 33
Sublime Text 6
SVG 93
SVG path notation 91
synced maps
   creating, side by side 136-140

T

table of contents (ToC) control
   about 111, 124
   creating, for layers 124-132
TextWrangler 6
Tile Map Services. *See* **TMS**
tile overlays
   adding, to maps 40-44

tile sources
  using, as base maps 33-39
TMS 26
traffic information
  displaying, on Google Maps 56, 57
transit layers
  adding, to Google Maps map interface 58, 59
transparency
  modifying, of overlays 48, 49

U

U.S. Geological Survey (USGS) 94
UTFGrid 273

V

vector layers 69
visualEnabled property 203

W

WeatherLayerOptions 64
weather-related information
  displaying, on base maps 62-64
Web Feature Service. *See* **WFS**
Web Map Service. *See* **WMS**
WebStorm 6
Well-known Text. *See* **WKT**
WFS 286
WKT
  about 70, 104
  adding, to Google Maps JavaScript
      API 104-109
WMS 254
WMS layers
  adding, to maps 254-261

X

XML 98

Z

zoom_changed event 139

Thank you for buying
Google Maps JavaScript API Cookbook

About Packt Publishing

Packt, pronounced 'packed', published its first book "*Mastering phpMyAdmin for Effective MySQL Management*" in April 2004 and subsequently continued to specialize in publishing highly focused books on specific technologies and solutions.

Our books and publications share the experiences of your fellow IT professionals in adapting and customizing today's systems, applications, and frameworks. Our solution based books give you the knowledge and power to customize the software and technologies you're using to get the job done. Packt books are more specific and less general than the IT books you have seen in the past. Our unique business model allows us to bring you more focused information, giving you more of what you need to know, and less of what you don't.

Packt is a modern, yet unique publishing company, which focuses on producing quality, cutting-edge books for communities of developers, administrators, and newbies alike. For more information, please visit our website: `www.packtpub.com`.

Writing for Packt

We welcome all inquiries from people who are interested in authoring. Book proposals should be sent to `author@packtpub.com`. If your book idea is still at an early stage and you would like to discuss it first before writing a formal book proposal, contact us; one of our commissioning editors will get in touch with you.

We're not just looking for published authors; if you have strong technical skills but no writing experience, our experienced editors can help you develop a writing career, or simply get some additional reward for your expertise.

Google Visualization API Essentials

ISBN: 978-1-84969-436-0   Paperback: 252 pages

Make sense of your data: make it visual with the Google Visualization API

1. Wrangle all sorts of data into a visual format, without being an expert programmer

2. Visualize new or existing spreadsheet data through charts, graphs, and maps

3. Full of diagrams, core concept explanations, best practice tips, and links to working book examples

Instant Google Map Maker Starter

ISBN: 978-1-84969-528-2   Paperback: 50 pages

Learn what you can do with Google Map Maker and get started with building your first map

1. Learn something new in an Instant! A short, fast, focused guide delivering immediate results

2. Understand the basics of Google Map Maker

3. Add places of interest such as your hotels, cinemas, schools, and more

4. Edit and update details for existing places

Please check **www.PacktPub.com** for information on our titles

Printed in Great Britain
by Amazon.co.uk, Ltd.,
Marston Gate.